Advance Praise for
A Candle Against the Dark

A Candle Against the Dark brings into the light the courageous story of the Reformed Presbyterian Church's fight against slavery. This is a book that is both informative and insightful.

—Ronald C. White, author of *Lincoln in Private*

The Reformed Presbyterian Church in America, whose members are also known as Scottish Covenanters, embraced some of the most controversial political ideas of any denomination. Firm supporters of the War for American Independence, they opposed the US Constitution because it did not explicitly recognize God's sovereignty over the nation and so refused to vote or otherwise participate in national politics. But they were also among the earliest and most committed opponents of slavery in America. *A Candle Against the Dark* provides an excellent overview of this interesting group of Calvinists. Highly recommended.

—Mark David Hall, professor of political science, George Fox University, author of *Proclaim Liberty Throughout All the Land*

This is a fascinating and valuable study of a Protestant denomination that, while small in numbers, was strong in its commitment and its influence toward the abolition of slavery and recognition that all humans are of one blood.

—Steven E. Woodworth, professor of history, Texas Christian University

If you've ever wondered why a picture of John Brown the abolitionist hangs in Geneva College's Macartney Library, read this book. Copeland and Wilcox present a study that is historical as well as theological in connecting the lineage of the Reformed Presbyterian Church to the abolitionist cause. Students of American religious history and religious liberty in particular will find great value in this intriguing book.

—Greg Jones, instructor of history, University of Northwestern (St. Paul)

Copeland and Wilcox display in vivid colors the brave and brilliant resolve of Reformed Presbyterians to oppose the great sin of American slavery, to risk their own lives to emancipate slaves, and—most importantly—to shine against the dark the light of the gospel. As John Knox wrote long ago, "In the hope of the life to come, God hath made all equal." Read and weep. Then read and rejoice.

—Byron Curtis, professor of biblical studies, Geneva College

A Candle Against the Dark tells the story of a resolute people who, against strong countervailing winds, helped prod the nation toward clearer vision and truer belief. This account reminds us of a crucial truth: There is nothing more foresighted than standing on principle.

—Eric Miller, professor of history, Geneva College

A Candle against the Dark lays out the long fight of the Reformed Presbyterian Church against American slavery and racism. The earliest denomination in the USA to take this position, its Christian and biblical reasons, clearly and concisely laid out in chapter 6, give the lie to Confederate and modern neo-Confederate tales that Abolitionism was all infidel, anti-biblical, Enlightenment, and Unitarian nonsense. Extensively noted and with a large bibliography, this volume is a must-read in our time of renewed racial sensitivities.

—Phil Pockras, RPCNA minister in Belle Center, Ohio

A Candle Against the Dark

A Candle Against the Dark

*Reformed Presbyterians and the Struggle
Against Slavery in the
United States*

Robert M. Copeland
and
D. Ray Wilcox

Crown &
Covenant
PUBLICATIONS

© 2022 Robert M. Copeland
Crown & Covenant Publications
7408 Penn Avenue
Pittsburgh, PA 15208
crownandcovenant.com

ISBN: 978-1-943017-49-2
eBook: 978-1-943017-50-8
Library of Congress Control Number: 2022933976

Printed in the United States of America

Text font is ITC Galliard Pro set in 11/13 point. Chapter titles are Adobe Open Caslon.

*It is better to light
a single candle
than to curse the darkness.*

—*proverb*

Contents

Illustrations

Preface

This study originated more than seventy years ago, when D. Ray Wilcox submitted the core of it as his thesis for the M.A. in History at the University of Northern Colorado, Greeley. It was quickly recognized as an outstanding work of scholarship. Frequently urged by colleagues, friends, and family to prepare it for publication, he always demurred, urging the need for revision; but with a family of five children and the demands of being a pastor and professor, he was unable to return to it during his lifetime.

Dr. Wilcox had been born in Mount Carmel, Illinois, in 1906 and grew up in Princeton, Indiana. Although reared in another denomination, he was attracted to the Reformed Presbyterians because of their commitment to social justice. A 1928 graduate of Geneva College, he graduated in 1931 from the Reformed Presbyterian Theological Seminary. Before being called in 1950 to teach at Geneva College, he served as pastor of Reformed Presbyterian congregations in Utica, Ohio; Olathe, Kansas; Almonte, Ontario; and Oakdale, Illinois. In addition to a stint as dean of the college, he taught at various times in the departments of History, Greek, and Bible. Wilcox was deeply respected for his intellectual acumen and for his kind and modest ways. He retired in 1973 and died in 1986, following several years of declining health. Throughout his life, he never lost his concern for a Christian faith that revealed itself in care for the poor and powerless. He never waned in his love for the denomination he served and for its record of social consciousness and robust activism.

Both during and after the research for his thesis, Wilcox corresponded with many people in the denomination whose close family had participated in the events covered. He visited many of the congregations that had been active in the antislavery cause. In short, he collected and preserved a heritage that would otherwise have been lost. This material, however, was available only to those with access to a rare carbon copy or photocopy of the thesis.

Several years after his passing, Dr. Wilcox's widow, Elizabeth Edgar Wilcox, asked me if I would be willing to undertake the revisions necessary to prepare this study for publication. Since I was already very familiar with the history of the Reformed Presbyterian Church and had discussed the subject with Dr. Wilcox many times, I readily agreed. Her children—David, Mary, Sara, John, and Ted—have graciously given me access to his materials and their blessing for this project. My wife, Louise, the niece of Elizabeth Wilcox, has been a constant and long-suffering source of encouragement.

In addition to the expected challenges of editing another scholar's work, the revision of his thesis has been complicated by the lapse of time since 1948. In addition to materials Dr. Wilcox had accumulated after 1948, new sources have come to light and several generations of historians have reexamined and reinterpreted the Abolition Movement. The internet has made sources infinitely easier, faster, and cheaper to access than ever before. Incorporating such material fulfills the wish Dr. Wilcox expressed. I have endeavored to write from a twenty-first century perspective while remaining true to the vision and passion of Dr. Wilcox. Many of the notes make clear the extent of this book's indebtedness to him. I am grateful that his children have graciously invited me to be listed as the co-author.

The book includes perhaps more lengthy quotations from primary sources than would otherwise be expected in a historical monograph. This is done because in many cases these primary sources are not readily available, yet their statements are essential to preserving and understanding their times and perspectives.

As this book was in progress, a new source appeared with additional information about the Underground Railroad in Bloomington, Indiana: Cheryl Molin's *Bloomington Reformed Presbyterian Church: two hundred years of God's grace* (Bloomington, 2021), chapter 4. Unfortunately, this was received too late to incorporate here but adds greatly to our knowledge of the activities of Reformed Presbyterians in that important congregation.

In his original preface, Dr. Wilcox paid tribute to his professors at Greeley: Arthur F. Zimmerman (his advisor), Ora B. Peake, and Harold Christensen. Roy M. Carson of Oakdale, Illinois, gave encouragement and help, as did Elizabeth Faris and Finley Faris of Greeley, Colorado, and attorney James R. Thompson of Newburgh, New York. For my part, this monograph is deeply indebted to John Mitchell of the Reformed Presbyterian Archives in Pittsburgh, to Thomas Reid, then librarian of the Reformed Presbyterian Theological Seminary, and to the reference staff of McCartney Library at Geneva College. Geneva's Faculty Development Fund provided a research grant and sabbatical to make concentrated work possible. Dean David Guthrie provided helpful encouragement from the beginning. Sean G. Donaldson did invaluable work solving my computer problems. Lynne Gordon and Natalie Hacker of Crown & Covenant Publications have been helpful in myriad ways and have been delightful collaborators. I am also grateful to colleagues who have read and commented on the manuscript: Jeffrey Cole and Maureen Vanterpool of Geneva College, Donald McBurney of the University of Pittsburgh, and Robert Wuthnow of Princeton University. Errors and infelicities that remain are, of course, my own.

—Robert M. Copeland

1

Introduction

Who are these people and where did they come from?

We needed a servant. A Kentucky "gentleman," full six feet three, with broad shoulders and heavy black whiskers, came to say: "I have a woman I can let you have! A good cook, good washer and ironer, first rate housekeeper! I'll let you have her for two hundred dollars a year. But I'll tell you honestly, you'll have to horsewhip her yourself about twice a week; that wife of yours could never do anything with her."

While he talked I looked. His suit was of the finest black broadcloth, satin vest, a pompous display of chain, seals, studs and rings, his beaver [hat] on the back of his head, his thumbs in the arms of his vest, and feet spread like the Colossus of Rhodes.

This new use for Pennsylvania muscle seemed to strike my husband as infinitely amusing, for he burst out laughing, and informed the "gentleman" that he did not follow the profession of whipping women, and must decline his offer. But I wanted to be back on free soil, out of an atmosphere which killed all manhood, and furnished women-whippers as a substitute for men.[1]

The author of this anecdote was reared in the Reformed Presbyterian Church, a tiny denomination deeply rooted in the Covenanting Movement in sixteenth- and seventeenth-century Scotland and strongly devoted to its principles and beliefs about freedom and equality. Because of their background and convictions, Reformed Presbyterians held an outsized role in the crusade against American slavery. This small group occupied a singular position in the great national struggle toward freedom and equality for all people. The role they played in the decades-long history of the American antislavery movement is noteworthy because:

- they were among the earliest denominations in English-speaking North America to oppose slavery officially and may have been the first to enforce an absolute prohibition against slaveholders in the church;

- they were among the founders and leaders of various antislavery organizations during the prewar period;

- their communities and congregations were centers of activity for the Underground Railroad;

- they were the first Presbyterian body to establish a mission for education and charitable relief for the freedmen;

- their theological seminary had a racially integrated student body in the 1840s, well before most other educational institutions; and

- their only college, Geneva College, was a hotbed of Underground Railroad activity, produced many volunteers for the Union cause, and was one of the early leaders in providing post-secondary education to former slaves.

How did a tiny church, well outside the mainstream of American political life, come to have a disproportionate role in the movement that destroyed a system so deeply entrenched in American society and government? Why were they so tenaciously unwilling to yield? In the past half century, Mark A. Noll, James Davison Hunter, Joseph S. Moore, and others have examined the role played by churches and their theologies in shaping slavery and antislavery thought before and during the Civil War. This study is a small part of that ongoing discussion. It is focused on the actions of members of the Reformed Presbyterian Church of North America and the political and social milieu in which they operated.

The Center and the Periphery

Cultural change, as James Davison Hunter points out, is always a result, not of a single "great person" or even "idea," but of "networks of similarly oriented people and similarly aligned institutions."[2] The individuals and institutions that combined to destroy the culture of chattel slavery in the United States were from both the center and the periphery of national life, and their merger after the mid-nineteenth century facilitated the desired change toward a culture in which all people "are created free and equal."

The "center," or the arbiters of culture, in antebellum America consisted of the founding fathers and their heirs and in the writers and thinkers associated with the centers of education and thought, notably Harvard (and Boston more generally), Yale, and the major theological seminaries. In this center, antislavery views were frequently expressed. The "periphery" of the culture and of the antislavery movement consisted of individuals and groups with more populist and activist proclivities but who did not set the agenda for the broader culture.

Among the peripheral structures in the antislavery movement were some of the Christian churches, particularly some of the smaller denominations. The leaders of these churches were seldom from the elites, although because of widespread societal respect for the institutional church, ministers (with their greater formal education) were often granted quasi-elite status. This attributed status enabled them to work effectively with the power elites and thereby strengthen the web that led to change. They also made effective use of the communications technology of the age: peripatetic lecturers and comparatively inexpensive newspapers and magazines. By the time of the Civil War, the movement toward abolition was broad, but always far from universal.

"Ascetic" and "Mystical" Religion

Many years after the American antislavery movement culminated in the Civil War and emancipation, Max Weber made some observations that help to explain why some Christian churches were deeply involved in the movement and why others were neutral or opposed. His insights provide context for the Reformed Presbyterians' heavy involvement in what must have seemed an endless struggle.

Some religions, Weber says, have no concept of salvation; others define it in various ways. Some face the conundrum of an imperfect world created by a perfect God.[3] Weber identified the characteristics of soteriological religions (those that believe in salvation as the end and goal of human life), falling into either "ascetic" or "mystical" types.

Among ascetic religions, he develops at some length what he calls "inner-worldly asceticism," by which he means religions whose members sense an obligation to transform the world in accordance with a vision of God's will.[4] Such persons do not seek to flee from the world, but to triumph over its temptations.

In contrast, some religions are mystical—that is, they focus on achieving rest in God and Him alone. One of the major tools of mystical religions is "world-fleeing contemplation," which encourages and enables its practitioners to focus exclusively on their own salvation. "The usual result," he says, "is the acceptance of the secular social structure which happens to be at hand....In any case, the typical mystic is never a man of conspicuous social activity."[5]

More recently, Marissa D. King and Heather A. Haveman have refined Weber's categories to identify Protestant denominations of both types in pre-Civil War America. Among the major inner-worldly ascetics, they include the Congregational, Episcopal, and Presbyterian churches and the Quakers. They count among the principal mystical or other-worldly churches the Baptists, Mennonites, Methodists, and Moravians.[6]

These are, of course, generalizations, as a number of denominations have managed to incorporate members with disparate views. Baptists, for example, are congregational in structure and their congregations differ greatly among themselves. Presbyterians have divided into a bewildering number of mini- and micro-denominations, some of which are more mystical than the traditionally ascetic Calvinism that their names suggest. Members of most churches, except the Mennonites and Quakers (pacifists), could be found supporting both the Union and the Confederacy during the Civil War.

A Small Organization with a Nimble Footprint

From its origins, the group now known as Reformed Presbyterians has been decidedly "world-rejecting ascetics," in Weber's terms. Members believed strongly in their obligation to work to transform the society around them to conform to God's will. In the sixteenth and seventeenth centuries, this meant primarily attempting to influence the government of Scotland to acknowledge that church and state are independent of each other and are equally obligated to obey biblical principles of truth and justice. In nineteenth-century America, this obligation involved them in such social action as the National Reform Association, the antislavery and temperance movements, and programs for the well-being of the poor, the sick, and the freed slaves.

This was true to a greater extent than in most other Presbyterian denominations, who, for a variety of reasons, failed or refused to take strong positions on such issues. Larger denominations were often afraid to offend half of the country to satisfy the other half and, therefore, refused to take a position or even permit discussion. For example, in the 1850s, the Associate Reformed Presbyterian Church ruled that slavery was an exclusively civil matter and therefore beyond the purview of the church. Even in the twenty-first century, at least one small Presbyterian body refuses to take a stand on public issues beyond advising its members about personal righteousness.[7] Because of the size of the Reformed Presbyterian Church and their determination to maintain their cohesion as a minority within a larger society, they found it easier to take decisive positions than did larger, more inclusive and thus more cumbersome, denominations.

In order to assess the Reformed Presbyterian Church of North America and the role it played in the network that was the antislavery movement, it is necessary to situate this group in its historical background and formative experiences in Scotland and America, an essential prelude to their efforts against slavery. In order to show what the antislavery forces were actually opposing, we next explore the historical development of slavery in the United States and its complicated nature. The early decades of the nineteenth century saw the slow growth of the antislavery movement and Reformed Presbyterians' involvement, looking more closely at the activities of three of its leading ministers. Members of the denomination were often involved in the antislavery associations founded in the 1830s and 1840s while insisting that, as a church, "we have always been an abolition society," favoring immediate rather than gradual emancipation of all slaves.[8]

We shall also deal with the theoretical and theological underpinnings of Reformed Presbyterian antislavery action. Not only did the church define slaveholding as sin from at least 1800, but roundly condemned racism as sin as well. It was not enough to emancipate the slaves; they must be treated with dignity as human beings and as Christian brothers and sisters. Again, their past explains the readiness of Reformed Presbyterians to engage actively in civil disobedience by refusing to cooperate with the Fugitive Slave Laws. Just as they had refused to obey what they regarded as sinful requirements of the Scottish kings, they had no hesitation in disobeying sinful requirements of Congress or the States. Wherever their congregations were located, the so-called Underground Railroad was active. While it is essential to remember that the actual heroes of the Underground Railroad were the escaping slaves themselves, it is also true that anyone, white or Black, who helped them in their flight also risked imprisonment, fines, and occasionally death.

In the two decades preceding the war, tensions escalated and the positions of both parts of the country hardened. The "Slave Power" (which refers to the congressional and electoral advantage given slave states by the "three-fifths clause" in the Constitution, Article I, Section 2 [3]) dominated national politics and bent every effort to protect and expand slave territory. Meanwhile the abolitionists worked to limit slavery geographically and to weaken it where it existed. Both sections responded with armed violence, and some Reformed Presbyterians found themselves caught in the crossfire.

Finally, we will examine the Civil War itself, the role of Reformed Presbyterians in the conflict, and their efforts to reach out to the newly freed slaves.

In order to provide some basis to understand the size of the denomination in the antebellum years, an appendix lists all of the Reformed Presbyterian congregations in North America that functioned from 1800 to 1865. It is not a long list, which demonstrates that though these people were not numerous, they made a lot of noise and were a perceptible link in the societal network that triumphed in 1865.

2

My Kith and Kin Had Died at the Stake

The Reformed Presbyterians and Freedom

Ye are God's creatures, created and formed to his image and similitude....In the hope of the life to come, he hath made all equal....

While these words resonate with the Declaration of Independence, they were penned more than two centuries before that by John Knox, one of the most influential men of the Scottish Reformation. They became a cornerstone of Presbyterian and Reformed social action and policy wherever that faith took root—including in the United States. Knox's words laid the cornerstone for a historic struggle, as those who believed them were opposed to a system that thought, in George Orwell's famous phrase, "some are more equal than others." The Reformed Presbyterians were a tiny minority always operating at the margins of society, even when the American population was small. However, they spoke eloquently into the struggle for freedom and equality and laid their lives on the line to help point the United States toward genuine equality.

This book is not a general history of the antislavery cause or of the Civil War. The goal is to examine the movement as it involved the Reformed Presbyterians, often known as Covenanters, to help both them and the historical reader to see the remarkable role this tiny group played in the great national struggle for freedom and equality for all. Both in Scotland and in Ulster, they had a public influence far out of proportion to their numbers.[1] The same can be said of their influence in the United States.

Before and during the Civil War, opinion in the North was sharply divided. To many, and perhaps most, the principal issue initially was rebellion or revolution, not slavery. As George M. Frederickson has observed, "sermons on the sin of rebellion or revolution outnumbered those on the sin of slavery. Everywhere in the North 'unconditional loyalty' to the state was preached as a Christian imperative."[2]

To Northern historians of the postbellum period, the war had been a conflict between righteousness and sin (however defined). The radical abolitionists, mostly the Boston Unitarians such as William Lloyd Garrison and Wendell Phillips, were the heroes. Later, Charles A. Beard swept away the antislavery explanation of the war by attributing it to economic conflict: the great planters of the South versus the industrialists of the North, both vying for control of the federal government as a means of controlling the nation's wealth.[3] Another generation of historians reexamined the role of fanaticism (on all sides) in causing what they believed to be an unnecessary war, and in the words of Timothy L. Smith, "the abolitionists became important again, simply because they were numbered among the screwballs."[4]

Smith himself did much to restore balance to the study of the Abolitionist Movement and to investigate the relationships between the Unitarian radicals and the evangelical moderates in building a consensus in the Northern states against human slavery. He pointed out that "religious radicals of both Unitarian and evangelical persuasions cooperated to kindle the first blaze of antislavery feeling which swept over the nation."[5]

Smith focuses largely on evangelical leaders of the Wesleyan and Perfectionist persuasions, such as Charles G. Finney and Orange Scott. In the 1830s and 1840s, Garrison and the transcendentalist utopians attacked the churches, the Bible, and the ancient creeds, also isolating and thrusting out evangelical preachers from the antislavery movement—Methodist, Baptist, Congregationalist, and others.[6] In contrast to Garrison and many others, the Covenanters always maintained the theology of the *Westminster Confession* and saw their antislavery efforts as an outworking of its standards.

Abolitionist ministers, in general, met with no more success in their own denominational judicatories. Many parts of the Methodist, Baptist, and Episcopal churches in the early nineteenth century supported the cause of slavery—or, to be more charitable, refused to oppose it—at least in part from a desire to preserve denominational unity. From 1838, the Presbyterian Church was divided by doctrinal issues into Old School and New School, but both general assemblies refused to condemn slavery and instead condemned any manifestation of antislavery sentiment.[7] James G. Birney, who documented the decisions in these denominations, also noted that

> We take pleasure in assuring [the reader] that there are considerable portions of the Methodist, Baptist, and Presbyterian churches, as well as the entirety of some of the smaller religious bodies in America, that maintain a commendable testimony against slavery and its abominations.[8]

Those smaller religious bodies, caught between competing social forces and largely ignored in the national scene, nevertheless had an impact on the social consciousness of the United States and helped to shape the consensus demanding the abolition of slavery. The Covenanters in particular maintained both a strict theological confessionalism and progressive social action.[9]

The Struggle in Scotland

The Reformed Presbyterians originated in Scotland in the seventeenth century. Their movement began as the struggle of all of Scotland, then the struggle of all Presbyterians, then the struggle of the Covenanters, and finally the struggle of a small remnant of Covenanters who refused to accept defeat.

Earlier, the most influential leader of the Scottish Reformation in the sixteenth century was John Knox. In a remarkable proclamation, *To his Beloved Brethren, the Commonalty of Scotland*, Knox articulated a position that has been fundamental to Reformed and Presbyterian social action ever since: the equality of all people because all are created in God's image. Urging the common people to take responsibility for reforming the church, he said:

> ...I desire, that ye, concurring with your nobility, would compel your bishops and clergy to cease their tyranny....Beloved brethren, ye are God's creatures, created and formed to his image and similitude, for whose redemption was shed the most precious blood of the Only Beloved SON of GOD....*In the hope of the life to come, he hath made all equal....*It will not excuse you, dear brethren, in the presence of God, neither yet will it avail you in the day of his visitation, to say, 'We were but simple subjects, we could not redress the faults and crimes of our rulers, bishops and clergy.'[10]

Knox intended the people not only to understand the equality of all persons before God, but also to be ready to fight for it. When Queen Mary summoned Knox to answer for his rash words, she asked him, "Think you...that subjects having power, may resist their princes?"

He replied, "If princes do exceed their bounds...madam, and do against that wherefore they should be obeyed, there is no doubt but they may be resisted, even by power [force]...but my travail is, that both princes and subjects obey God."[11]

At the General Assembly of the church in 1561, the right of free assembly was argued and won by Knox. Secretary of State William Maitland of Lethington objected that the queen had not given permission to assemble, but the assembly continued anyway. They invited the queen to send observers to their meetings but proceeded to act as they believed best.

The characteristic feature of the Scottish Reformation is the "bond" or "covenant" by which the people bound themselves together. For many years, the Scots used covenants as the basis for ordinary confederations in which the parties promised to assist each other in the work proposed and to defend each other from the consequences. The covenant was drawn up in legal style and sworn to before public notaries.[12] This Scottish custom was given a new and spiritual meaning as those who covenanted now made public promise to God to be faithful to His Word. These religious covenants began around 1546 and were renewed and enlarged time after time during the next century and more.[13] At their coronations, the latter Stuart monarchs swore to honor and abide by these covenants, a vow that each broke as soon as it was convenient.

Beginning in 1584, the Stuarts pressed the Scots to overturn the reforming acts of the past quarter century. Pressed beyond what they saw as the tipping point, the nation at length adopted what was known as the National Covenant in 1638. Historian Allan I. Macinnes has argued that the National Covenant was, in effect, the Constitution of Scotland from 1638 to 1651, establishing important limitations on the king's prerogative in both state and church and consolidating the nation's political and ecclesiastical revolt against absentee monarchy.[14]

A war ensued that lasted intermittently for fifty years (1638–88), a struggle between the divine right of kings and the God-given rights of man. By means of the Solemn League and Covenant in 1643, the Scots were drawn into the English Civil War on the side of Parliament, but both Cromwell and the king proved broken reeds. When Cromwell became Lord Protector in 1653, he was not particularly sympathetic to the Covenanters, and when Charles II was restored to the throne in 1660, full-throated persecution began in earnest. As time wore on, many fell out and would have permitted the Stuart kings to have their way, at least by compromise. However, others would not give in and were driven to the hills. An estimated 18,000 people suffered under the royal persecution, suffering that long remained in the memories of the Covenanters.[15]

During the Killing Time, the strictest group of Covenanters met secretly for prayer and the preaching of the gospel. They formed praying societies or society meetings, to maintain their identity. Beginning in 1662, shortly after the Restoration of Charles II and the outlawing of Presbyterian pastors and preaching, they held conventicles in the fields, caves, or mountains for larger gatherings when the Lord's Supper was dispensed. Faithful to the words of Paul in Romans 9:4-5, 11:1-2, and 17-22, they continued to pray for the "old, off-casten Israel" (i.e., the Jews),[16] the "pagans," and others throughout the world. They had a warm, evangelical faith, as demonstrated in their sermons and writings. They searched the Scriptures for words of comfort and assurance. Privately, they met in small groups called societies.[17]

They were also politically astute and adopted a position that other branches of the nation had never reached. The draft of a document known as the Queensferry Paper, which was with just cause considered treasonous, stated:

> We do declare, that we shall set up over ourselves, and over what God shall give us power of, government and governors according to the Word of God,...That we shall no more commit the government of ourselves, and the making of laws for us, to any one single person, or lineal successor,...this kind of government by a single person being most liable to inconveniences, and aptest to degenerate into tyranny, as sad and long experience hath taught us.[18]

The year 1685 saw the persecution of Covenanters increase when the death penalty was prescribed not only for preaching at a conventicle but even for attending one. This, of course, did not prevent conventicles. In 1681, Covenanters resolved to form a united body, and societies would appoint deputies to meet in a quarterly general meeting.

When the long period of persecution ended in 1688 with the overthrow of the Stuart dynasty by William of Orange, the Scottish nation breathed an enormous sigh of relief and settled into an exhausted compromise with the English. It was agreed that the Church of Scotland was to be Presbyterian in government, not Episcopal. However, the strictest Covenanters, or "Cameronians" (from Richard Cameron, a minister killed in battle in 1680), refused to join in the established Church of Scotland because it acknowledged that the king's commissioner was to set the time and place for general assemblies and could prorogue the assembly if he disapproved of its actions.[19] The Parliament of 1690 had rescinded the act that made the king the supreme head of the church, but it left much other objectionable legislation untouched. The Cameronians saw the Revolution Settlement as a betrayal of much of that for which they had bled and died.[20] Their organizational history was somewhat checkered until 1743, but even in the absence of ministers the "society people" maintained their cohesion and identity. Eventually, they adopted the name Reformed Presbyterian because they adhered to Reformed theology and Presbyterian church government, which they regarded as the pinnacle of the Reformation.

The societies and the history of persecution served as glue to unify the Cameronians, as they found themselves a small and scattered community not only in Scotland but also in Ireland and North America. They served as perhaps the principal vehicles to maintain their cohesion as a minority group. The writings of the martyrs were reprinted often, and their stories were told to their children around the evening fire. One example will suffice: Jane (Cannon) Swisshelm, born to a Covenanter family in Pittsburgh in 1815, described the efforts of her Methodist husband and his family to break her of her Calvinism; but, she said, they "found a subject that would not run. My kith and kin had died at the stake, bearing testimony against popery and prelacy; had fought on those fields where Scotchmen [*sic*] charged in solid columns, singing psalms; and though I was wax at all other points, I was granite on 'The Solemn League and Covenant.'" Not only was Christ the "Head of His Church," but likewise "Prince of the kings of the earth."[21]

The Struggle in America to 1787

The earliest Covenanters in America were those banished from Scotland. About 1,700 of them were condemned to be sold as slaves in America. Seven thousand others left Scotland voluntarily. Many of the latter went to Northern Ireland while others continued on to America.[22]

All Presbyterian denominations have some connection with the Scottish Covenanters, as they all share Scottish and/or Scots-Irish antecedents. All Presbyterians who came to America prior to 1688 were in a certain sense "Covenanters." Oliver Perry Temple, in fact, used the name to reference all Scottish Presbyterians and their descendants, including all Scots-Irish or Ulster Scots. By this overly broad definition, Temple concluded that a total of 900,000, or a third of the population of the colonies in 1775, were Covenanters (actually Scots-Irish).[23]

It is quite impossible to calculate the number of these Scottish and Scots-Irish settlers who were society people. Some of those who had been banished entered the first organized Presbyterian body in the country, apparently in the belief that after the Revolution Settlement of 1688–90 in Scotland, Presbyterianism was united. But many others continued to have their society meetings even when no ministers were available. Indeed, through the Killing Time as well as the stretches with no ordained ministers, these societies held the scattered community together in unity and purpose.

A society consisted of two or more families living in the same community. They would meet in a home for worship, consider a Bible passage, read accepted authors, propose some subject for thoughtful consideration, ask a question about Christian faith or practice, and the like, as they had been accustomed to do during the persecution. They handled necessary financial matters. They admitted and disciplined members, but in the absence of an ordained minister did not observe baptism or communion.[24]

Societies in a region kept in touch by a "correspondence" of representatives from the societies, conducting business affecting the societies jointly such as obtaining supplies of preaching and arranging for communion services when possible. The correspondence in turn elected commissioners to attend the "general meeting," or, after 1774, the presbytery. This system, developed in Scotland in the seventeenth century, continued to preserve the identity and faithfulness of the people in what was essentially a lay person's organization.[25]

These society people who kept themselves separate from the first organized Presbyterian body in America were the people who later organized "the Reformed Presbytery" and later "the Synod of the

Reformed Presbyterian Church." Known variously as "society people," "United Societies," "Cameronians," and "Covenanters," these are the people (and the church) that are here designated "Covenanter," because the name has been generally retained by them through the years. The maintenance of these societies continued for many years in America; until at least the late nineteenth century, many established congregations were divided into societies, and the midweek prayer meetings, often held in homes, were called "society meetings."

The first formal society of Covenanters in America after the Revolution of 1688 was organized at Paxtang in Dauphin County, Pennsylvania, in 1720. Further north on the Susquehanna River near Milton, Northumberland County, a society was formed by 1728. Other settlements were created in the same period in Lancaster, York, Dauphin, Cumberland, Franklin, Adams, and Fulton Counties.[26] These settlements were the forefront of the earliest westward migration. "This zone combined in part with the German zone, but in general Scotch-Irishmen [sic] tended to follow the valleys farther toward the mountains, to be the outer edge of this frontier."[27] They pushed into the Cumberland Valley, then the Juniata, then Redstone Creek (a tributary of the Monongahela River in Fayette County). In 1769, the Covenanter family of James Willson settled at the "forks of the Yough," where the Youghiogheny River joins the Monongahela near Elizabeth, Pennsylvania.[28]

Renewing the Covenants
In 1743, which was the centennial of the Solemn League and Covenant, the society people met at Middle Octorara in Dauphin County and renewed their allegiance to the Scottish Covenants, both National and Solemn League. Rev. Alexander Craighead presided. Many Colonists were suspicious of repeated efforts to bring the colonial governments under direct control of the king rather than under the companies and proprietors who had been granted royal patents for the colonies. The Anglican Church supported these efforts and expected to be the State Church in the colonies as it was in England. The Bishop of London heavily influenced colonial legislation, which further alarmed the dissenting churches in the colonies. A law of North Carolina giving Presbyterian ministers the right to perform marriages was vetoed by the king. It is not difficult to understand why Scots, and the society people in particular, were uneasy about English plans in the colonies. Some of the older members of the societies could still

remember the Killing Time in Scotland, which had ended only fifty-five years previously. "If the question of the establishment of bishops did not contribute a lion's share in causing that enmity to the mother country...it was involved in the struggle and deserves to be regarded as an important part of it."[29]

The proceedings at Octorara alarmed officials in Pennsylvania. Seeing the word "Presbyterians," Governor George Thomas sent to the Synod of Philadelphia to explain themselves. They assured him that "the Synod being utterly against any thing of a seditious and disloyal Tendency, unanimously agreed to condemn" the action, saying obsequiously that "it is with unfeigned Grief we hear that any who ever appeared under the Character of Presbyterians should propagate Principles which have a Tendency to promote Disloyalty and Sedition among the Inhabitants of this Province....We shall always inculcate upon our People an unshaken Loyalty to the Government."

The governor replied, "[I]t is a very particular Satisfaction to me, that you have taken this publick Opportunity of expressing your Loyalty and steady Attachment to His Majesty's Person and Government, as well as a just Detestation of Principles so manifestly tending, not only to promote Disloyalty, but to subvert all Order and Government."

In 1752, Craighead settled in Augusta County, Virginia, and in 1755, he migrated to Sugar Creek, North Carolina, where he ministered to at least seven Presbyterian congregations in Mecklenburg and adjacent counties. In July 1766, an Anglican missionary wrote that he was well informed "that the inhabitants of Mecklenburg are entire dissenters of the most rigid kind, that they had a Solemn League and Covenant teacher settled among them; that they were in general greatly averse to the Church of England, and that they looked upon a law lately enacted in this province for the better establishment of the Church as oppressive as the Stamp Act, and were determined to prevent its taking place there."[30]

Another step toward Covenanter activity in the Revolution began with the arrival of the Rev. William Martin from Kellswater (near Ballymena, County Antrim, Ireland) to Charleston in 1772, with five shiploads of his parishioners and neighbors. Some Covenanters already lived in Chester District, and here Martin brought his colony, where a number of them settled on bounty lands.[31] William Martin was an outspoken man, a characteristic that necessitated his leaving Ireland. In June 1780, he preached a sermon that, it is said, so inspired the surrounding country to resist the English troops that it contributed to the victory at King's Mountain on October 7. In the meantime, Martin was arrested by the British and imprisoned at Rocky Mount and Camden; in December he was taken to Winnsboro to appear before General Lord Cornwallis. Tories burned his church; after the war, his congregation built another church two miles east of the one destroyed by the Tories.[32]

Covenanters made organizational progress during this period as well. On March 10, 1774, three ministers and some elders met in Pennsylvania and constituted the Reformed Presbytery: John Cuthbertson, Matthew Linn, and Alexander Dobbin. Cuthbertson had arrived from Scotland on August 5, 1751. From then until 1790, he rode and walked 69,255 miles, preached on 2,452 days, baptized and married hundreds. He spent much of his time on the road, living the frontier life. He attended a "Patriotic Association" meeting during the Revolution and led the people in a solemn oath to support the colonies. He rebuked people for immorality and other sins. He held services in tents or groves, in private homes, and in barns. He did not share his era's views on race; he once married a white man to a woman of mixed race and at least once received a Black girl into church membership. Believing as he did in the biblical account of creation, he, like other Covenanters, also believed that all mankind was descended from Adam and Eve and so were brothers and of equal value in the sight of God. During the war, he made an extended tour of western Pennsylvania to visit a number of families who had settled beyond the mountains.[33]

For some twenty years, Cuthbertson was the lone Covenanter minister in the colonies, and at length sent a representative to Ireland to ask for assistance. This appeal bore fruit when Matthew Linn and Alexander Dobbin came from Ireland in 1773. The establishment of the Presbytery in 1774 was momentous for the Covenanters. It was nearly a century since the first Covenanters had arrived in North America. During all these years they had continued to meet together in societies without the leadership of ministers, but at last they had an ecclesiastical organization conforming to what they believed was the scriptural plan.[34]

In the War of Independence, Covenanters willingly carried their share of the burden. So far as is known, not a single Covenanter was a Loyalist. To them, the war meant the breaking of the yoke that had been about their necks for centuries. They had a vision of a free and Christian nation. They believed that once free from the old yoke this nation would come forth purged of other yokes, such as the burden of slavery. In the spirit of John Knox, they expected that the nation would live up to its declaration that "all men are created equal; that they are endowed by their creator with certain inalienable rights; that among these are life, liberty, and the pursuit of happiness."

Jefferson had, in fact, included in his original draft of the Declaration a protest against slavery, a paragraph which was stricken at the insistence of South Carolina and Georgia:

[George III] has waged cruel war against human nature itself, violating its most sacred rights of life and liberty in the persons of a distant people who never offended him, captivating and carrying them into slavery in another hemisphere, or to incur miserable death in their transportation hither. [T]his piratical warfare, the opprobrium of *infidel* powers, is the warfare of the *Christian* king of Great Britain. [De]termined to keep open a market where MEN should be bought and sold, he has prostituted his negative for suppressing every legislative attempt to prohibit or to restrain this execrable commerce. [A]nd that this assemblage of horrors might want no fact of distinguished die [color], he is now exciting those very people to rise in arms among us, and to purchase that liberty of which *he* had deprived them, by murdering the people upon whom *he* also obtruded them: thus paying off former crimes committed against the *liberties* of one people, with crimes which he urges them to commit against the *lives* of another.[35]

Of course, neither the Covenanters nor the rest of the Colonists knew of Jefferson's attempt. The Covenanters naïvely took at face value, however, the Declaration's assurances of the equality of all men, and on July 2, 1777, they swore their full support for the cause of the War of Independence. Many members served in the revolutionary army or militia.

"But when the victory was won and the Americans settled down to construct foundations for their new nation, contrary to the hopes and prayers of the Covenanters they seemed to have forgotten God. There was, in the new Constitution, no mention of dependence upon that 'Divine Providence' who had been invoked to secure the blessings of liberty."[36] During the Constitutional Convention, Benjamin Franklin reminded the delegates of the debt the new nation owed to "a superintending Providence in our favor," but the convention refused to approve so much as prayers during its sessions.[37]

The Reformed Presbyterians at that point were again disorganized because all their ministers in the North had merged with the Associate Presbyterians in 1782 to form the Associate Reformed Presbyterian Church. There was no official church court to speak for them authoritatively, but they maintained their separate existence in the historic societies. In May 1798, the Reformed Presbytery of America was reconstituted at Philadelphia.[38]

From the very birth of the Constitution, the Reformed Presbyterians objected to its flaws. First, they said, it failed to acknowledge God or Christ as the source of the nation's liberty; second, it protected human slavery by requiring the capture and return of fugitive slaves; third, it permitted the importation of slaves to continue for twenty years; and fourth, it even gave slavery preferential consideration by means of the "three-fifths clause." One of the Covenanters' early actions was to authorize a testimony, which stated in relevant part:

> There are moral evils essential to the constitution of the United States, which render it necessary to refuse allegiance to the whole system....It establishes that system of robbery, by which men are held in slavery, despoiled of liberty, and property, and protection. It violates the principles of representation, by bestowing upon the domestic tyrant who holds of his fellow-creatures in bondage, an influence in making laws for freemen, proportioned to the number of his own slaves. This constitution is, notwithstanding its numerous excellencies, in many instances inconsistent, oppressive, and impious.
>
> Since the adoption of the constitution in the year 1789, the members of the Reformed Presbyterian Church...have refused to serve in any office which implies an approbation of the constitution, or which is placed under the direction of an immoral law. They have abstained from giving their votes at elections for legislators or officers who must be qualified to act by an oath of allegiance to this immoral system.[39]

Their first objection was that the Constitution made no mention of God or of Jesus Christ, which was central to their political philosophy.[40] The other three of their four objections to the Constitution became widespread among abolitionists some years later: since the document protected slavery—it permitted the importation of slaves for twenty years and it required the capture and return of fugitive slaves—it might in fairness be called a proslavery document. The three-fifths rule, which worked to the advantage of slave owners and the disadvantage of everyone else, was anti-democratic. In the early 1840s, many abolitionists began to turn to political action, voting for third-party candidates such as James G. Birney, who, they hoped, would alter the Constitution so as to eliminate slavery. On the other hand, William Lloyd Garrison and others, and much like the Covenanters, condemned the Constitution as being so proslavery and thoroughly controlled by slaveholders that sincere abolitionists should not vote in political elections at all.[41] Garrison described the Constitution as, in the words of the prophet Isaiah, "a covenant with death and an agreement with hell." At a Fourth of July celebration in Framingham, Massachusetts, in 1854, he publicly burned a copy of the Constitution. One of the founders of the American Anti-Slavery Society, Rev. Beriah Green of western New York, told Birney in 1852, "This hog-haunted, so called government I abhor as an atrocious conspiracy, and submit to its demands just as I would to the demands of a band of robbers."[42]

Moreover, Southerners themselves saw in the Constitution a bulwark of the slave system. Two examples are illustrative. James Chesnut [sic] Sr. joined the Confederacy reluctantly, saying, "...I wanted all the power the United States gave me—to hold my own." A member of the Virginia secession convention told that assembly, "It is nothing but the prestige and power of the General Government now that guarantees to the slaveholder his right."[43]

As events unfolded from 1789 to 1866, it became clear that the Covenanters' analysis of the Constitution in its relation to slavery eventually became the view of the country as a whole.

The Covenanters' attitude of dissent from any government of church or state—whether in Scotland or America—that does not conform to the standards of Scripture is the basic principle of the Covenanters and provided the driving force behind their antislavery work. Their objections to the new Constitution of the United States were parallel: it violated the rights of both God and man. Their immediate reaction was separation and protest, conditioned by nearly two centuries of harsh experience.[44] In this complex context, we turn to their relationship with the institution of human slavery in the United States.

3

The Sum of All Villainies

The Institution of Negro Slavery in North America

In Ramah there was a voice heard,—weeping, and lamentation, and great mourning; Rachel weeping for her children, and would not be comforted." Mr. Haley and Tom jogged onward in their wagon, each, for a time, absorbed in his own reflections. Now, the reflections of two men sitting side by side are a curious thing,— seated on the same seat, having the same eyes, ears, hands and organs of all sorts, and having pass before their eyes the same objects,—it is wonderful what a variety we shall find in these same reflections!

As, for example, Mr. Haley: he thought first of Tom's length, and breadth, and height, and what he would sell for, if he was kept fat and in good case till he got him into market. He thought of how he should make out his gang; he thought of the respective market value of certain supposititious men and women and children who were to compose it, and other kindred topics of the business; then he thought of himself, and how humane he was, that whereas other men chained their "n******" hand and foot both, he only put fetters on the feet, and left Tom the use of his hands, as long as he behaved well; and he sighed to think how ungrateful human nature was, so that there was even room to doubt whether Tom appreciated his mercies. He had been taken in so by "n******" whom he had favored; but still he was astonished to consider how good-natured he yet remained!

—"Select Incident of Lawful Trade," *Uncle Tom's Cabin*, by Harriet Beecher Stowe

Origins and Nature of American Slavery

On June 9, 2020, Senator Tim Kaine of Virginia stated on the floor of the U.S. Senate, "The United States didn't inherit slavery from anybody. We created it. It got created by the Virginia General Assembly and the legislatures of other states. It got created by the court systems in colonial America that enforced fugitive slave laws." To what extent Senator Kaine represents a common view among the American citizenry is unclear. What is clear is that his astounding comment represents an inexcusably shallow and incorrect view of slavery, both in the United States and elsewhere.

Throughout most of recorded history, people who lost wars or raids and their dependents were routinely subjected to involuntary servitude. Hugh Thomas, historian of the Atlantic slave trade, has summarized a common experience of mankind with the remark that "[m]ost settled societies at one time or another have employed forced labor; and most peoples...have experienced years of servitude."[1] Slavery played a major role in the economic and social life of ancient Mesopotamia, Egypt, India, China, Greece, and Rome, and while in northern Europe it slowly evolved into serfdom, in the Mediterranean and Muslim worlds it continued in its traditional forms for many centuries. Indeed, it was not abolished *de jure* in Saudi Arabia until 1962, and exists today *de facto* in many places.[2]

Beginning in the late thirteenth century, Europeans began to explore the west coast of Africa, trading for gold, ivory, and other commodities, including slaves. By the fifteenth century, the Portuguese, who dominated this trade, were introducing African slaves into Iberia. (African slaves had been common enough previously, but those were brought via land routes by Muslim traders.)[3] Christopher Columbus, on his second voyage to the New World in 1493, developed a plan to send Native Americans to Spain as slaves, but Queen Isabella refused her permission.[4] The first industry established by Europeans in the New World was raising sugar cane, which requires a large labor force, and the Indians did not thrive under the conditions created by their new masters. Around 1500, African slaves were introduced in Hispaniola, the first of a deluge of captives brought to the Western Hemisphere in the next three centuries.[5]

Seymour Drescher, a noted historian of slavery in the Atlantic world (and winner of the prestigious Frederick Douglass Prize in 2003), has observed that slavery was in fact the default setting in most of the world at the time: "Personal freedom, not slavery, was the peculiar institution." In 1772, Arthur Young estimated that only 33 million of the world's 775 million inhabitants could be called free.[6]

The first African slaves to be brought to what is now the United States arrived with the Spanish occupation of Florida in the early sixteenth century.[7] In the English colonies, African slaves did not arrive in Virginia until 1619, aboard two English pirate ships, the *Treasurer* and the *White Lion*, the latter of which was flying a Dutch flag. These slaves, purchased in Angola, had been captured from a Portuguese slaver, the *São João Bautista,* bound for Vera Cruz.[8] There was, however, no law respecting slavery in the English colonies, and the earliest bonded laborers, whether African or European, were treated as indentured servants—that is, their servitude ended after a specified length of time, at which they were considered to have "worked off" the costs of bringing them to the colony.[9]

A few other Black slaves seem to have come from England as slaves of English nobles who acquired property in Virginia.[10] Beginning with James I (1603–25), the English monarchs licensed and encouraged the traffic in slaves, and throughout the seventeenth century, the English share of that trade increased. The great need for labor in the colonies of the vast new continents and the existing practice of slavery among the Native Americans were temptations too strong for the Christian conquerors, and they quickly adopted this expedient.[11]

In Latin America, in spite of the mildness of Spanish legislation compared with the Black Codes of other nations, the treatment of slaves was often barbarous, with exhausting working conditions, inadequate clothing, housing, food, and drink, and indescribable punishments. The planters and masters there considered it more economical to work the slaves until their productivity was spent and then replace them with newly imported "stock."[12] Consequently, the death rate of Negro slaves in Latin America was substantially higher than in the southern United States.

During the period 1500–1870, of the 9,735,000 Negro slaves brought into the Western Hemisphere, Brazil received 38 percent, the British and French Caribbean 17 percent each, Spanish America 17 percent, other Caribbean colonies (Dutch, Danish, and Swedish) 6 percent, and the United States 6 percent.[13] The slave population of the United States, in contrast to Latin America, grew primarily (and, after 1808, almost entirely) through natural increase. By 1825, the United States contained about 1,750,000 slaves—36 percent of the slaves in the Western Hemisphere.[14]

Slavery grew rapidly in North America. For example, in 1671 there were 2,000 Black slaves in Virginia and 6,000 English

indentured servants, out of a population of 40,000.[15] By 1700, the
Negro population of Virginia had grown to 16,000, and by 1800, to
nearly 347,000.[16] Nor was this growth confined to the South. Slaves
were introduced into Massachusetts and New York with the earliest
settlers. Vessels were fitted out for the slave trade in Northern ports.[17]
Every colony had slaves. There was sentiment, however, in all of the
colonies against the trade, and various steps were taken in attempts
to prohibit the traffic. In 1772, Virginia asked George III to stop the
importation of slaves into that colony, but the request was denied.
Soon after the Revolutionary War, various states outlawed both slavery
and the slave trade. In 1780, Massachusetts abolished it immediately,
and Pennsylvania provided a gradual emancipation.[18] In 1794, New
York followed suit. Delaware, Maryland, Virginia, North and South
Carolina, and Georgia continued to maintain the institution of slavery.
However, when enslaved persons in Northern colonies were freed by
law, many owners did not free but sold their slaves to the South.[19]
The North could not claim innocence when discussing the origin and
early history of slavery in the country. But it was in the South that the
institution took root and grew until it was an indispensable part of its
economy and the basis for its political life.

From 1790 to 1820, the slave population in the United States
increased 91.5 percent. In Virginia, it increased from 292,627 to
425,163. South Carolina's increase was from 107,094 to 251,783. In
Georgia, it jumped from 29,264 to 149,656. Louisiana, in the same
period, mounted from 3,011 to 69,064. Tennessee increased from
13,584 to 80,107; Kentucky from 12,430 to 126,732; and Mississippi
from 3,489 to 32,814.[20] By 1830, there were 773,303 slaves and
1,703,948 free white people in the Border States. The rest of the South
had 1,231,084 Black slaves among a white population of 1,953,660.
In 1860, immediately before the Civil War, there were between 3.5
and 4 million slaves in the South, when the white population of the
region was approximately 9 million.[21] Of this number, only 2,300
owners had from fifty to one hundred slaves each; 350,000 owners
possessed from one to ten each, while the great majority of white
people were not slave owners at all. Yet this small aristocracy of great
planters decided the policies of the South. No more than 500,000
people had any substantial profit from slavery, yet the South was
united in upholding the system. The great cotton planters ruled the
South.[22]

Doubts and Certainties about Slavery

Reformed Presbyterians were not the first people to discern a contradiction between the teachings of Christianity and the existence and practice of slavery. While Covenanters were among the vanguard of the Abolition Movement in the nineteenth-century United States, many Europeans had been active in tearing down the universal acceptance of slavery for several centuries. Those efforts were not ecclesiastically based, but laid a humanitarian foundation on which the later Abolitionist Movement could build.

> Two hundred years ago, three-quarters of the world's population were in bondage of one kind or another. Eighty thousand were trafficked every year from Africa to the New World. Ship owners, slave traders, sugar exporters, chocolate makers and plantation owners were earning fortunes....Slaves and other subjugated people have rebelled throughout history, but the campaign in England was something never seen before: it was the first time a large number of people became outraged, and stayed outraged for many years, over someone else's rights.[23]

The liberation of slaves and the agitation that nourished that movement began as early as the Middle Ages, when some countries provided that serfs who ran away to cities became free. Almost as early as Europeans introduced slavery into the New World, it became a point of contention.

In 1552, the Spanish Jesuit Bartolomé de las Casas, in protesting against the treatment of Native Americans, recommended the enslavement of Africans instead, although he later regretted that advice. Several Dominicans wrote against the enslavement of Africans as well as Indians. But by the seventeenth century, the Spanish and Portuguese colonies suppressed every objection to slavery and to the treatment of slaves.[24]

In the British and French colonies, meanwhile, white indentured servants and Scottish, Irish, and Native American prisoners of war might be held in lifetime servitude much like African slaves, including the raising of cane in the Caribbean islands. The struggle to free the serfs in England started in the sixteenth century under the Tudor kings. There had long been some sense that freedom was the natural or created status of mankind and slavery was a social construct with no basis in nature or logic.

During the eighteenth century, English and French writers urged the abolition of slavery. In *Utopia* (1516), Thomas More had offered several suggestions to ameliorate the treatment of bondsmen in England. The early public arguments against slavery had to wait: they were made by Puritan ministers more than a century later. In the same period, Aphra Behn published her influential 1688 novel *Oroonoko: Or, The Royal Slave.*[25] The first known antislavery publication in what became the United States was Judge Samuel Sewall's *The Selling of Joseph* (Boston, 1700), but it had little effect. One of the fathers of the Enlightenment, Montesquieu, in his *L'Esprit des Lois* (written ca. 1727, published 1748), found certain practices intrinsically evil: despotism, slavery, and intolerance. Book XV of this *Spirit of Laws* is devoted to arguments against slavery and includes a list of sarcastic or satirical "reasons" to justify the enslavement of Africans. Influenced by both the Enlightenment and Christian theology, John Wesley issued his *Thoughts on Slavery* (1774).[26] Accounts of the experiences of slavery by Africans in Britain made the realities of the slave system part of the consciousness of the public.[27] The organization of the Society for the Abolition of the Slave Trade in 1787 provided an institutional structure for efforts against both the slave trade and slavery itself. These efforts, however, seemed to focus only on slavery in Great Britain and not in its American colonies.

Slave Life

As slavery permeated Southern economy, social structure, and politics, an enslaved person's quality of life varied according to his or her enslaver and overseer. Some owners were kind and generous; others were cruel. It was natural that critics opposed to the whole system paid particular attention to accounts of cruel and tragic incidents, while those who defended the institution stressed the gentler side. Both sides of the argument depended primarily on anecdotal evidence, and both sides found more than enough of that.

Frederick Douglass, who escaped from slavery, saw nothing of generosity or gentleness in the system. According to Douglass, for example, the holiday season was given to the slaves, not because the owners loved the slaves and wished to see them happy, but because they knew it would be dangerous to work them during the holidays. The holiday season was a safety-valve to help keep the slaves in subjection.[28] Negroes were believed to be happy by nature, and slave singing was pointed out as an indication that the slaves were indifferent to their lot in life. Douglass said that on the contrary, their singing was no sign of joy or contentment, but a release for their unhappiness: "The songs of the slave represent the sorrows of his heart; he is relieved by singing only as an aching heart is relieved by tears."[29] There were those who said that the slaves, if given a choice, would prefer to stay with their masters. Perhaps some of them would have preferred shelter and support to the responsibilities of freedom. But

> the whole trend and tenor of the slave codes rested upon the well-grounded belief that the normal frame of mind of the Negro was a desire for freedom; and this belief is supported by the countless instances of fugitives who had no better reason to give for running away than that obstinate desire to be free which the white people counted among their chief claims to the admiration of mankind.[30]

Indeed, from the relatively high number of slave rebellions in the United States prior to 1863, it is very clear that thousands of Black slaves chose to risk their lives in a bid for freedom rather than to remain in bondage, whatever its conditions. More than 250 slave rebellions involving ten or more slaves are recorded. Slaveholders who feared slave uprisings were not paranoid but prudent.[31]

The desire to be free was Frederick Douglass's experience. Given the privilege of hiring himself out by the week, he tasted freedom, became more restless than ever, and finally escaped.[32]

There were occupational distinctions among slaves. The naïve view of the Northern abolitionists saw a simple dichotomy between house servants and field hands. It is true that the butler or cook had privileges that were not enjoyed by the field hands. The coachman could travel with his master, but the field hand worked from dawn to dusk—not only, however, in the stereotypical cotton field, but in a variety of agricultural work: raising food crops, caring for livestock, building fences and buildings, etc. Both in the cities and the countryside, slaves also held a large share of the skilled trades and crafts (blacksmiths, carpenters, masons, etc.).[33] After the 1831 slave rebellion led by Nat Turner, who could read and write, many of the slave states enacted laws prohibiting teaching literacy skills to slaves, free Black people, and children of mixed race. These laws, however, were frequently defied.[34]

The legislature of each slave state enacted a Slave Code to control the slaves. Some laws protected them from excessive abuse. Their lives, for example, were theoretically protected. Albert Bushnell Hart notes both the rule and the exception: "All slave-holding states made the malicious and unnecessary killing of a slave a capital offense, but the master was allowed to exercise authority sufficient to protect his life and enforce his commands; and the Tennessee laws of 1836 specifically provided that 'any slave dying under moderate correction' could not be held to be murdered."[35] The definition of *moderate* was, of course, the crux of the matter. Frederick Douglass told of the brutal beatings administered by overseers on the plantations where he had worked. A young woman, for example, was tied up to a joist and whipped until she was covered with blood, simply because she had kept company with a young man of a neighboring plantation. The overseer wanted her for his own purposes.[36] It should be noted that in the colonial era the *criminal* codes of all countries permitted such harsh punishments, as will be seen below.

It is difficult to determine just how severe this system had become before it was finally destroyed. In the absence of statistics, both proponents and opponents relied on anecdotal evidence. The abolitionists sought out cases of brutal severity to "prove beyond question that there were many awful instances of barbarity which public opinion did not check."[37] Hart recorded that "[a]s late as 1808 slaves were burned alive by order of a court in Charleston; and for supposed complicity in setting a fire in Augusta in 1830, a slave woman was executed and quartered."[38]

Slaves could be whipped for any reason the overseer or owner might imagine: fishing with a seine, for example, or being found on horseback without written permission. Frederick Douglass tells of a slave who ran when whipped and waded into a pool of water. The overseer ordered him back, but the slave just stood where he was. The overseer gave him the count of three to return or he would shoot him. Still the slave remained. The overseer "blew his head off." A woman killed her slave girl for not waking up when the baby she was minding cried. Neither the overseer nor the woman was held criminally liable.[39] In another incident, a woman with a whip forced a little slave girl to the roof of the house, where the terrified child fell off and was killed; the woman then "chained her cook to the wall, till the woman, in utter despair, set fire to the house, and the fire company discovered the miserable story."[40]

Slaves were defined in the laws of most slave states to be "chattels personal," in the same category as livestock, furniture, books, etc., although, in Louisiana, they were considered real estate—i.e., immovable, bound to the land, as were serfs. As chattel, slaves were commodities—objects, not persons—and subject to sale at any time.[41] Private sales were common, and this involved no public exhibition. In some cases the owner showed some regard for the preferences of his slave—for example, a request to be sold to another plantation in order to be reunited with a family member. Public sales by auction, however, were better known in the North, sales in which slaves, horses, cows, hogs, and other livestock were advertised together. The slave auction room, maintained in each Southern city, presented to many minds one of the most repulsive aspects of slavery. Slaves were examined much as animals were, with prospective purchasers checking the teeth, musculature, and other physical qualities. Young mixed-race women of great beauty were bought by single young white men. Families might be separated. When estates were settled, slaves might be sold if the heirs were unable or unwilling to continue in the family business. With the growth of the cotton industry, and with the end of the legal importation of slaves in 1809, the price of slaves began to rise. In 1798, a field hand sold for $200; in 1822, the price had risen to $300. By 1830, the price had doubled to $600. In 1840, a good hand sold for $1,000. "In 1859, at Savannah, prime women sold at $1,100 to $1,200; men as high as $1,300."[42]

The indignities of the auction block made lasting impressions on those sold. Potential buyers questioned the enslaved people, had them stripped naked and carefully examined them like horses or cattle, from their head to their feet, sometimes with excessive touching or feeling, and sometimes demanded physical exercise to assess strength and agility.[43] Slaves from age twelve or so to thirty-nine were the most valuable in terms of work and breeding potential, and when they were "brought to market" they were graded, the top being No. 1 or prime, much as USDA inspectors today rate beef as prime, select, or choice.

Persons were also classified by ancestry to provide a precise code of discrimination and rights: those from entirely Black ancestry were Negroes; those with one Black and one white parent were mulattoes, those with one Black and three white grandparents were called quadroons, and those with one Black and seven white great-grandparents were dubbed octaroons. The last two terms, however, are now considered racist and are no longer used. South Carolina defined an additional class: mestizos, defined as "the issue of a negro and an Indian, and is subject to all the disabilities of a free negro and a mulatto."[44] These are generally included in the phrase, "and other free persons of color."

Slaves who escaped from bondage were pursued with dogs, guns, whips, and ropes. The rugged part of Alabama was a favorite hiding place for runaway slaves. The slaves on nearby plantations would help them find food at night. A white man told Frederick Law Olmsted that he had seen people who had come 200 miles to look for their slaves. Then he said,

> 'I suppose 'twould seem kind o' barbarous to you to see a pack of hounds after a human being?' 'Yes, it would.' 'Some fellows take just as much delight in't as in runnin' a fox. Always seemed to me kind o' barbarous sport.'...(A pause.) 'It's necessary, though....On these small plantations, n****** ain't very often whipped bad; but on them big plantations, they've got to use 'em hard to keep any sort o' control over 'em. The overseers have to always go about armed. Their life wouldn't be safe, if they didn't. As't is, they very often get cut pretty bad.' 'In such cases, what is done with the Negro?' 'Oh, he gets hung for it—if he cuts a white man; that's the law; "intent to kill," they call it; and the State pays the owner what he's worth, to hang him.'[45]

The severity that accompanied slavery was seen to be an integral part of the system. Even those travelers who painted the bright side of the picture argued the necessity of such severe measures. A. B. Hart summed it up:

> ...[I]t was rather a continuance of a state of things not exactly comfortable, but without which slavery could not exist; barbarities, fierce and sanguinary punishments, lynchings, did not seem abnormal to the slave-holders; and if slavery itself was allowable in a Christian and enlightened community, any method necessary to keep it up was justified. The indictment of slavery was that it was a deliberate refusal to go along with the rest of the world in the enjoyment of a more humane spirit than that of the eighteenth century.[46]

In the minds of white Southerners, they had not built this system, but had inherited it. Like having a wolf by the throat, they dared not let go.

Emphatically, slaves were exploited, abused, and mistreated in many ways. Although what follows is in no sense to be understood as a defense or even extenuation of slavery, one cannot claim to understand the slave system, nor the antislavery crusade, nor indeed the historical image of Black Americans, without considering evidence that undercuts certain aspects of the traditional understanding of American slavery. For example, it is widely believed that the plantation regime was so dehumanizing and demoralizing that Black slaves developed extreme laxity in work habits, sexuality, and family affection. All enslavers were degraded brutes; all enslaved people were docile victims of unbridled brutality. These stereotypes cry out for more accurate pictures of the situation.

In 1974, two economic historians, Robert W. Fogel of the University of Chicago and Stanley L. Engerman of the University of Rochester, published the results of their cliometric (that is, based on historical data) study of slavery, in which they argued that the slave system in the South was handsomely profitable for the enslavers—that is, slave farms were more productive, per unit of labor, than Northern farms. Southern planters were logical in their organization, so as to maximize profits and control losses. A part of the study focused on the lives of the slaves, arguing that the economic lives of enslaved persons, as revealed in historical data, were comparable to the economic lives of many free citizens of the North. This politically charged argument contains facts that are needed in order to present a balanced and accurate picture of slave lives.

Consider first the evidence about the sale of slaves. Data reveal that such sales and the forced separation of slave families were much less common than often claimed. While the period from 1790 to 1860 saw a great shift in the Negro slave population from the southern Atlantic states to the central and western Southern states (Alabama, Mississippi, Louisiana, and Texas), about 84 percent of the slaves moving westward went with their owners.

In the fifty years from 1810 to 1860, only 127,000 slaves were *sold* from the east to the west, or an average of about 2,500 per year across the South as a whole. In New Orleans, the largest slave market in the southwestern states, more than 84 percent of sales over age fourteen were unmarried individuals. Of the remaining 16 percent, six percent were sold with their spouses and an estimated 25 percent were widowed or voluntarily separated. Thus, while interregional slave sales undeniably resulted in the destruction of a number of slave marriages, the practice was rather less widespread than abolitionist anecdotes suggest.[47]

By the same token, the breeding of slaves for market—the most lurid and titillating aspect of antislavery propaganda—was so extremely uncommon that many thousands of hours of research by professional historians have failed to produce a single authenticated instance of a human "stud farm." Ongoing plantations very seldom sold a slave, either one they had purchased or one born on the plantation. For example, on nineteen plantations with a total slave population of 3,900, a total of seven slaves were sold over a period of ninety years, ending in 1865.[48]

Second, consider the care of slaves. It is often asserted that slaves were fed only corn and pork, because surviving instructions to overseers specify the daily quota of these commodities to be distributed to the slaves. These foodstuffs, however, were the two most important that could be preserved for year-round consumption, and it was necessary to ensure that the supply would last the entire year. Seasonal foods such as vegetables and fruit were consumed when they were in season. Some foods would spoil quickly: beef, mutton, chicken, and milk, for example, and had to be eaten close to the time of slaughter or harvest. Salt, sugar, and molasses were frequently purchased for slave consumption. Slaves were usually assigned garden plots and might also hunt and fish for additional comestibles. As Fogel and Engerman have shown, the average daily food consumption of slaves in 1860 exceeded the average of the entire U.S. population in 1879, had higher energy value (calories), and, astonishingly, exceeded the 1964 recommended daily levels of protein, calcium, iron, and vitamins A and C.[49]

While the slave population was counted in every U.S. census, that of 1860 also included data on slave houses. In those returns, the average slave home on large plantations contained 5.2 persons. In the same year, the average free household contained 5.3. Thus, most slaves, like most free people, lived in single-family homes. Occasionally, very large plantations provided dormitories for unmarried men and women, but the single-family household was the rule. Data on the condition of slave houses were not collected, and information is spotty. There seems to have been a wide variation in quality: from three- or four-room cottages of wood-frame, brick, or stone, with glazed windows and up to 800 square feet of living space, to windowless single-room log cabins with earth floors or planks resting directly on earth. These houses were comparable to the housing of most free workers at the time, and in fact superior to the crowded, filthy tenements of urban workers.[50]

The medical care received by slaves was likewise comparable to that available to the free population in general, although primitive by modern standards. The health of their slaves was a major concern of most slave owners, and hospital care was provided for the sick. Larger plantations often had substantial hospitals, and smaller ones simply provided a cabin for the sick; but in all cases, the owner was concerned to provide rest, medical care, and special diets, as well as to reduce the danger of contagion. Many provided a nurse and one or more midwives, and physicians were available—although with the existing state of medical knowledge, the cure (bleeding, purging, opium, etc.) might be worse than the disease. The owners frequently emphasized the importance of hygiene for the slaves: cleanliness of person, clothing, bedding, and cabins. Pregnant women received the best health care, including lighter work loads. Their confinement normally lasted four weeks, followed by two weeks of light work near the slave quarters. During the first year, the mother was excused to nurse the child during work hours, at first, four times a day, and after five to seven months, twice a day. The mortality rate for slave mothers in 1850 was one per thousand, which is quite low in absolute terms and lower than the death rate for Southern white mothers. While the infant mortality rate was significantly higher than that for white American infants nationwide, it was virtually identical with that for Southern white infants.[51]

Moreover, while life expectancy for slaves in the U.S. in 1850 was thirty-six years (12 percent below the expectancy for white Americans, which was forty years), it was equal to that of the citizens of France, Italy, and the Netherlands, and substantially greater than the twenty-four years' expectancy for urban industrial workers in the U.S. and United Kingdom.[52]

Consider in the third place the function and structure of the family in the slave system. The family was the administrative unit for the allocation of food, clothing, and shelter. It was an important element in maintaining labor discipline—by encouraging strong family attachments, planters reduced the danger of individual slaves' running away.

By permitting families to have *de facto* ownership of houses, furniture, clothing, garden plots, and small livestock, planters created an economic stake for slaves in the system. Moreover, the size of the stake was variable. It was possible for some families to achieve substantially higher levels of income and of *de facto* wealth ownership than others. The size and quality of houses and the allotments of clothes as well as the size of the garden plots differed from family to family.[53]

The family was also the principal means of increasing the slave population and the principal site for the rearing of children. Slave owners provided rewards and sanctions to promote stable families among the slaves: cash grants were given, marriages were celebrated, adultery and divorce were punished. Within fairly wide limits, the states left the issues of regulating slave behavior to the planters, including marriage. Thus, while the states' Slave Codes provided that slave marriages did not have legal standing (because that would limit the owners' absolute property rights in the slaves), the planters were free to permit and encourage them.[54]

After the end of the war, thousands of formerly slave couples registered their marriages in the appropriate courts; in Vicksburg, Mississippi, ten of the 4,638 couples who registered from 1864–1866 had been married for more than fifty years.[55]

Consider, fourth and finally, the punishment and rewards experienced by slaves. The most common and best known punishment was whipping, although others were also used, such as confinement and the deprivation of various privileges, as well as sale, branding, and execution. Whippings might be mild or severe; many slaves never received a whipping, but others might receive multiple whippings. This too, however, must be seen in perspective. Until the nineteenth century, whipping was considered a perfectly normal form of punishment, not only for criminals but also for others who shirked their duties. The whipping of wives, for example, was condoned in some quarters. Armed forces frequently whipped those who violated military discipline. While Frederic the Great banned flogging in the Prussian army in the eighteenth century, it was not prohibited in the U.S. Navy until 1855, and the British Navy continued the practice well into the nineteenth century.[56] (It was legal under the British penal code until 1948.) Slave owners could not, of course, use the capitalist disciplinary tool of firing a worker who was indifferent, lazy, or dishonest; but in their desire to discipline workers, they did not want to lose the use of their slaves' labor any more than necessary.

Planters wanted from their slaves more than the minimal effort needed to avoid getting whipped. They saw the need to provide incentives that would motivate the slaves to hard work and personal responsibility: prizes, unscheduled holidays, substantial year-end bonuses, patches of land on which they could raise cash crops, and the like. Some planters even created profit-sharing schemes for their slaves. Slaves also had opportunities to rise within the social and economic hierarchy that existed under bondage and might be able to earn enough money to buy their freedom.[57]

It must be emphasized again that while the data cited by Fogel and Engerman provide a more nuanced account of the life of U.S. slaves than tradition suggests, the brutal fact of bondage remained. The data do nothing to mitigate the fundamental *moral* evil of slavery, or to reduce in retrospect the necessity of abolishing slavery, or to justify the attitudes and practices of racial prejudice practiced both before and since emancipation. Indeed, as will be seen in succeeding chapters, had the data discovered by Fogel and Engerman been known in the era of slavery, the efforts of the Reformed Presbyterians would have been little different from the course actually pursued, because their *primary* objection was not to the treatment of slaves but to the very existence of slavery.

4

This Outrage on the Rights of Men

The Antislavery Movement to 1830

Hugh McMillan, reared in the Reformed Presbyterian Church in Chester County, South Carolina, recalled in a letter of 1855 his experiences of 1816 and his relief to hear of the proposal to permit freed slaves to emigrate to Africa:

> The hand of slavery in [South Carolina] and in other States, was constantly making the door of emancipation more narrow and more difficult to open....The subject of slavery, which always pressed heavily on the church, appeared to be becoming more weighty, inasmuch as emancipation was becoming encumbered with increasing difficulties. The question often occurred, 'What shall I say to the slaveholder?' If I say, 'emancipate,' he replies, 'it is impossible; I cannot free the slave here; and I cannot remove him out of the State. And could I do it, I have my doubts as to the propriety of doing so—the propriety of casting an uneducated family or individual, upon society at large without any one to feel for their situation!'
>
> While I was somewhat perplexed with these thoughts, from day to day, I was cheered to see, that while the hand of slavery was closing the door of emancipation, the hand of Providence was opening it. The door of Colonization was opened; I felt no longer at a loss in replying to the slaveholder who said 'I am willing to give you my slave, if you can free him, and make him better than he is with me!' To the plan of Colonization, and to the noble examples occurring in those days, I referred and said, 'go and do likewise!'[1]

The Christian Basis

While the American crusade to abolish slavery is often attributed to economic and sectional factors, it arose from a biblical foundation.

Even though it took sectional interest to bring about the final blow, it required the recounting of the horrors of slavery and the prophetic voice of condemnation to penetrate the consciousness and the conscience of the North. Writing more than half a century after the war, Pulitzer Prize-winning historian James Ford Rhodes wrote,

> The teachings of Christ and the Apostles actuated this crusade, and its latent power was great....[B]y stirring the national conscience, they made possible the formation of a political party whose cardinal principle was opposition to the extension of slavery, and whose reason for existence lay in the belief of its adherents that slavery in the South was wrong.[2]

In the colonial period, antislavery sentiment was common. In 1701, the town of Boston proposed "putting a period [time-limit] to Negroes being slaves" (i.e., that they be considered to be indentured servants), but nothing came of it in the legislature. During the colonial period, the Virginia House of Burgesses passed twenty-three acts aiming to suppress slavery and the slave trade, but all received royal vetoes.[3]

Churches, too, were concerned. In 1774, the Philadelphia meeting of the Quakers disowned any member engaging in the slave trade, and in 1776 disowned any slave owner who refused to free his slaves. In 1794, the Presbyterian General Assembly stated that the biblical condemnation of "man-stealers" includes "all who are concerned in bringing any of the human race into Slavery, or retaining them therein."[4] The General Committee of the Baptists of Virginia in 1789 adopted the resolution "that slavery is a violent deprivation of the rights of nature, and inconsistent with republican government, and therefore we recommend it to our brethren to make use of every measure to extirpate this horrid evil from the land...."[5] One of the rules of the first edition of the Methodist *Book of Discipline* (1784) was, "Every member of our Society who has slaves in his possession, shall, within twelve months after notice given to him by the assistant, legally execute and record an instrument, whereby he emancipates and sets free every slave in his possession." As this was unheeded by the membership, another statement appeared in the *Discipline* in 1796: "The preachers and other members of our Society are requested to consider the subject of negro slavery...that the Conference may have full light, in order to take further steps towards eradicating this enormous evil from that part of the Church of God with which they are connected."[6] The Conference's suggestion of "further steps" probably meant the *gradual* emancipation of slaves. The Christian message against slavery was being proclaimed in many churches before 1800— but behavioral change was not enforced in any of them, at least in part because of the fear of losing proslavery members.

Colonial legislatures and churches were not the only voices expressing disapproval of slavery. A number of individuals, particularly from the elite, condemned the institution of slavery during the colonial and revolutionary periods. George Washington wrote in a letter in 1786, "I never mean, unless some particular circumstances should compel me to it, to possess another slave by purchase, it being among my *first wishes* to see some plan adopted by which slavery, in this country, may be abolished by law."[7]

In his last will and testament, President Washington expressed the desire to free all of his slaves. Of the 317 slaves on the plantation, he could free his own 123 but not the 153 of Mrs. Washington's dower (the one-third of the personal property of her first husband, which reverted to the Custis estate upon her death), and in addition, the slaves were intermarried. His own slaves were eligible to be freed after Martha's death, but when her friend Dolly Madison pointed out to her that it was to the slaves' advantage for her to die soon, she prudently freed them effective January 1, 1801.[8]

Thomas Jefferson, too, although a slaveholder, wrote against slavery on several occasions. In his *Notes on the State of Virginia,* he described the practical moral problems raised by its existence. He attempted in the draft Declaration of Independence to list the slave trade among the offenses of George III. In a number of his letters, he refers to his wish to end the slave system, and it is noteworthy that, in a time when Black slaves were customarily referred to as "goods and chattels," "property," or "human cattle," Jefferson refers to them as "citizens" and "brethren."[9]

> And can the liberties of a nation be thought secure, when we have removed their only firm basis—a conviction in the minds of the people that these liberties are of the gift of God? that they are not to be violated but with his wrath? Indeed, I tremble for my country when I reflect that God is just; that his justice cannot sleep forever; that considering numbers, nature, and natural means only, a revolution of the wheel of fortune, an exchange of

situation is among possible events; that it may become probable
by supernatural interference! The Almighty has no attribute which
can take side with us in such a contest.[10]

Jefferson, nonetheless, believed strongly that Black people were
inferior to white people in nearly every respect: beauty, abstract
thought, and imagination (poetry, painting, and sculpture). They
were stronger, he said, in ability for physical labor, in requiring less
sleep, in tolerating heat, and in not feeling or remembering "their
griefs and afflictions."[11]

James Madison, the "father of the Constitution," advocated abolition of the slave trade to prevent "dishonor to the National character." During the debates on the Constitution, Madison said that "it is
wrong to admit into the Constitution the idea that there can be property in man."[12] Similar sentiments were expressed by James Monroe,
Patrick Henry, John Randolph, Governor Thomas Randolph, Henry
Clay, Cassius M. Clay, Senator Thomas Hart Benton, and many other
prominent Southern leaders of that era.

Early Actions of the Covenanters in America

If the first Reformed Presbytery, existing only from 1774 to
1782, left minutes of its meetings, they have not survived. Rev. John
Cuthbertson recorded in his diary the fact of its organization on
March 10, 1774. For May 23 and 24 of the same year, he simply said,
"Presbytery met both days." His record of each subsequent meeting
is recorded in the same laconic tone, with no mention of the actions
taken. Some indication of his concern about slavery may be drawn
from his statement of October 21, 1751 (his first year in America),
that he had "conversed with Joseph Tate concerning the equality of
the race." It is noteworthy that Cuthbertson used the singular form
race to indicate a belief that all human beings are members of the
same human race. Soon after the organization of the Presbytery he
"baptized...Bess McBride—negro."

On October 17, 1780, Cuthbertson wrote that he had "married
Newport Walker and Jean Broadley, negro mulatto." Another Black
congregant was baptized later. The scarcity of slave names among his
careful list of those he baptized and married during his forty years in
America suggests that few, if any, among the Reformed Presbyterians
in colonial Pennsylvania possessed slaves at that time.[13] Most of the
slaves in Pennsylvania at the time were concentrated in and around

Philadelphia, while Covenanters were generally found on the western frontier. Cuthbertson had no hesitation in administering Christian rites and sacraments to Black persons.

In 1782, a majority of Reformed Presbyterians (including all three of its ministers) and of Seceders (Associate Presbyterians) merged to become the Associate Reformed Presbyterian Church, and the Reformed Presbytery became disorganized. Some members in each of the constituent churches saw the union as a sad compromise, however, and remained outside it until they could reorganize.

Slaves were held by some Covenanters in the Carolinas before 1800, and a few were held in New York. In 1792, Rev. James McGarragh and Rev. William King were sent by the Scottish Reformed Presbytery to inspect the affairs of the congregations in the Carolinas. William Martin, who had been previously suspended for intemperance, was restored to office. James McKinney arrived from Ireland in 1793. Both Martin and McGarragh were suspended in 1795 for intemperance, leaving King the only Reformed Presbyterian minister in the South, while McKinney was preaching throughout the Northeast.[14] According to the *Reformed Presbyterian Testimony*, adopted in 1806, it was apparent that King had "applied the principles of the Church, as now understood, to this great evil in his own bounds." King was too ill to attend the meeting reorganizing the presbytery in America, and died the same year, 1798.[15]

In Ireland, meanwhile, rebellion was brewing, and the English were acutely aware of the rebellion in Saint Domingue, which would result in creating the nation of Haiti in 1803. They kept a close eye on anyone suspected of supporting resistance organizations such as the United Irishmen. Alarmed at the prospect of rebellion and foreign interference, they commenced a harsh counter-insurgency campaign. After the great Irish Rebellion in 1798, a reign of terror spread across the island, with further rebellions occurring from 1799–1804.

Although the movement had broad support among the Irish of all persuasions, many of the leaders of the United Irishmen were Protestants, and some Reformed Presbyterians were suspected of involvement. It is not surprising, then, to discover a strong flow of immigration from Ireland to the United States in the wake of these troubles. Among those who came in the fall of 1797 were Rev. William Gibson and two students of theology, John Black and Samuel B. Wylie. James McKinney and William Gibson, with ruling elders, constituted anew the Reformed Presbytery of America in May 1798 at Philadelphia. Another student of theology, Alexander McLeod, was taken under care of the presbytery at this time, as was Thomas Donnelly, who had been studying theology under William King in South Carolina.[16] These were the leaders in the denomination when the question of slavery was brought up in earnest in 1800.

The issue faced the fledgling organization, and not only its congregations in South Carolina, when Alexander McLeod received a call from the congregation in Coldenham, New York, also known as Walkill.[17] McLeod declined the call, giving as his reason that some of the members owned slaves. He soon published what he called a "discourse" titled *Negro Slavery Unjustifiable,* a firm and full argument against slavery. At his declining the call, action resulted immediately: "The Presbytery, now having the subject regularly before them, resolved to purge the church of this dreadful evil. They enacted that no slaveholder should be retained in their communion."[18]

Recall that the Philadelphia Conference of the Friends (Quakers), as well as the Presbyterians, Methodists, and Freewill Baptists had adopted similar sentiments earlier than 1800, but with no mechanism of enforcement—some members of each continued to hold slaves. The Associate Presbyterians, or Seceders, like the Reformed Presbyterians a small Presbyterian body with roots in Scotland, adopted the prohibition in 1811 but backed away from it. Part of the Associate Reformed Presbyterian Church in 1830 adopted a resolution favoring emancipation "as soon as opportunity in the providence of God is afforded to slave owners..." The remainder of that denomination, however, continued to accept slaveholders, leading to a division in that church in the 1850s.[19] Nearly all of the major Protestant denominations experienced regional splits in the decade leading up to the Civil War. John McKivigan, pointing to these facts, concludes, "The significance of the Quaker, Freewill Baptist, and most Scottish immigrant sects lay in their demonstration to northern Christians that a denomination could refuse fellowship to slaveholders and still prosper."[20]

At the same meeting of the Reformed Presbytery, Samuel B. Wylie and James McKinney were appointed to visit the congregations in the South and "regulate the concerns of the Church in that part of America." The minutes of the meetings held by these two ministers and the elders chosen at various stops are dated from June 27, 1800, to April 7, 1801.[21] These are the earliest extant official records of the actions of the Presbytery regarding slavery. Meanwhile, Alexander

McLeod met with the committee on November 7, 1800, and when the call was presented to him "he hesitated and requested until the next day to make up his mind." The next day, "The Committee again resumed the business of Mr. McLeod's call, and after some reasonings with him on the subject, he consented to accept it only conditionally."[22] The committee then went west to Pittsburgh, then south, arriving at the Rocky Creek Meeting House in Chester District, South Carolina, for their first meeting there on January 28, 1801. They received a paper from the Reformed Presbyterians of South Carolina requesting that Thomas Donnelly and some elders be ordained. They also requested that another minister be sent to serve with Donnelly and that the committee take up the cases of the two ministers who had been suspended by the Scottish Committee in 1795.[23] The suspension of McGarragh was continued. The case of William Martin was problematic; with advancing age his alcoholism was exacerbated, but now there was the equally serious charge of selling a slave. The charge read,

> That he sold, some time since, a negro man then in his possession, thereby doing everything in his power to prevent himself from ever having in his power to liberate a poor, wretched fellow mortal, in any other period of his life, putting this price of blood among his substance, while he left his fellow mortal to languish out the last moments of his life under the galling chains of slavery, without one scanty ray of hope of ever obtaining deliverance any other way but by the hand of death; and all this after the determination of the courts and church to which he belonged had marked African enslavement with the strongest degree of abhorrence.[24]

After long and solemn consideration, the Presbytery's Committee voted unanimously to depose William Martin from the ministry.[25] At the committee's next meeting, February 11, 1801,

> A petition came in requesting a reconsideration of the business respecting slaveholders, as far as that species of traffic might be supposed to affect Christian Communion, and that such steps might be taken, in the premises, as should place the whole affair on such a moral basis as the principles of our common confession seem imperiously to demand. It was agreed, prior to the further consideration of this subject, that all slaveholders in the

communion of the church should be warned to attend the next
meeting of Committee; and that then the merits of the petition
aforementioned shall be particularly attended to.

When the committee met next, on February 18, 1801,

The consideration of the state of the enslaved Africans was
introduced this day into the Committee....It was unanimously
agreed, that enslaving these, our African brethren, is an evil of
enormous magnitude, and that none who continue in such a
gross departure from humanity and the dictates of our benevolent
religion, can have any just title to communion in this church.
Moreover, in order to point out the modes of carrying this matter
into execution, it was agreed to send the following note to the
persons concerned, who are here this day, *viz*: 'Sir: You are hereby
informed that none can have communion in this church who hold
slaves. You must therefore immediately have it registered, legally,
that your slaves are freed before sacrament. If any difficulty arises
to you in the manner of doing it, that you are desired to apply
to the Committee of Presbytery, who will give directions in any
circumstances of a doubtful nature in which you may be involved,
in carrying this injunction into execution.'[26]

Thomas Donnelly and two ruling elders were appointed to inquire
into the specific circumstances of each of the slaves to be liberated and
the current legal form of emancipation, "that the instructions of the
Reformed Presbytery in purging out this accursed thing from among
them, may be carried into the most speedy effect."[27] W. M. Glasgow
reported that "the Committee were no less surprised than delighted
to find with what alacrity those concerned came forward and complied
with the decree of Presbytery. In one day, in the small community of
Covenanters at Rocky Creek, not less than three thousand guineas
were sacrificed upon the altar of principle."[28] It appears that the
order of the Presbytery was generally complied with. D. S. Faris later
described the exceptions:

It is said that of all those that gave bonds, only four persons
failed to carry out their obligations. One of these, James Kell, was
afterwards taken in the act of adultery with his own slave; a second
died a vile drunkard; and a third was reduced to abject poverty,

and was caught stealing the nails to make his wife's coffin. Thus the brand of Cain was put upon the sin of slavery....The blessing of God followed those that turned from their sin, and some of their children and grandchildren became ministers and elders in the church. Some of the slaves then freed also became members of the church...[29]

It is very likely that the alacrity with which most of the Reformed Presbyterians in South Carolina freed their slaves was because King and Donnelly had both been teaching against slavery for some years previous to the prohibition.

The full Presbytery met at Coldenham, New York, on July 3, 1801, and noted that "...on the subject of slavery, Mr. Beatty promised to have the freedom of the three negroes belonging to him registered in the county court, as soon as may be, *viz.:* Sally and Candace, at the age of 25 years, and Dick, at the age of 28."[30]

Immediately following this promise by one of the elders of the congregation at Coldenham, the call from that congregation was again presented to McLeod; he accepted and was ordained and installed pastor of the congregations of Coldenham and New York City on July 6, 1801.

The resolve of the congregation and the presbytery was tested when a man who apparently had been in regular attendance refused to comply with the ruling. On November 23, 1801, the Coldenham Session took the following action:

> It was resolved that the Moderator make a short statement in writing of the principals [sic] of the Presbyteries [sic] Act respecting slavery—and that two of the Elders, Messrs. Beatty and Slater, Converse with him upon the Subject so that the Matter may be brought into a Judicial Settlement at the next meeting of Session in April 1802.[31]

On May 5, 1802, the session declared that the man in question had no regular connection with the church at the time the call was made out for McLeod or when he was ordained and installed as pastor. The man

> evidenced no design to comply with the Presbyteries [sic] Act anent Slavery; nor to be in full communion with the church. After

much conversation it was unanimously determined to have no
further trouble with him in any Judicatory unless he himself make
application for the priveleges [sic] of the Church. He is therefore
to be Considered in no case as a member of this Church untill
[sic] then.[32]

Thus, it appears that there were some individuals affiliated with
the Reformed Presbyterian Church in the years before 1801 who
had absorbed some perspectives of the culture around them, and
whose ideals of liberty and equality consequently did not extend to
Black people. They also reveal, however, that there was a widespread
conviction that slaveholding was sin and a determination to eliminate
the evil of slavery from the church. Once the matter was brought
before the courts of the church for a decision, it was settled decisively
and permanently. Any who were unwilling to free their slaves at that
time left the communion of the church, and no slaveholder was
subsequently admitted.

In the Doctrinal section of the original *Reformed Presbyterian
Testimony,* chapter 28, "Of Civil Government," the following
statements are condemned as *errors:*

That it is lawful for civil rulers to authorize the purchase and sale
of any part of the human family, as slaves.

That a constitution of government which deprives unoffending
men of liberty and property is a moral institution, to be recognized
as God's ordinance.[33]

In declaring that the U.S. Constitution was not God's ordinance,
the church's position might appear to be in conflict with Romans 13:1,
"Let every soul be subject unto the higher powers. For there is no
power but of God: the powers that be are ordained of God." Christians
are adjured to render general civil obedience to the government
under whose protection they live. Certainly the Roman Empire—the
government in view in Romans 13—was not governed by biblical
standards of either statehood or morality. From their earliest days in
Scotland, Covenanters had believed that Christians were only justified
in disobeying if the civil government made requirements contrary
to the Word of God: "We ought to obey God rather than man"
(Acts 5:29). It is clear from their subsequent record that Reformed

Presbyterians did not deny the legitimacy of the government in other areas than slavery—they obeyed the laws pertaining to other spheres of life such as taxes, real estate, felonies, and misdemeanors; but in light of the general tenor of Scripture, they did not feel bound to obey a law that seemed to them so clearly contrary to Scripture.

In 1861, virtually at the beginning of the Civil War, the denomination added a paragraph to the same chapter, which read,

> The holding of human beings, of whatever race or colour, as slaves, being in every aspect opposed to the word of God, and inconsistent with the principles of the gospel of Christ, a gross infringement upon the rights of man, and so a sin against God, should be held and treated by national authorities as a crime. Nor can any constitution of government be just or moral which does not provide against the commission of such a crime within its jurisdiction.[34]

This paragraph is buttressed by a number of passages of Scripture, such as, "He that stealeth a man and selleth him, or if he be found in his hand, he shall surely be put to death" (Exod. 21:16).

At the same time, two additional *errors* were noted:

> That man can hold property in man.

> That slaveholders may be admitted to the communion of the Church.[35]

By 1808, the Reformed Presbytery had grown sufficiently to justify a larger organizational structure. On May 24, 1809, the Synod of the Reformed Presbyterian Church in North America was constituted at Philadelphia, and ratified all the acts of the Reformed Presbytery.

The Work of Some Covenanter Ministers, 1795–1830

Thomas Donnelly

Thomas Donnelly's entire ministry was spent in South Carolina, maintaining a firm and active testimony against slavery. For a meeting held at the home of John Kell of Rocky Creek at some point before 1798 (and well before the presbytery's prohibition), Donnelly, then a student of theology, served as clerk, and recorded:

What humane mind but will mingle his tears with those of his fellow mortals, when he sees them shut out from every source of rational happiness, banished far from their native home, torn from their dear relations, and wallowing in the most abominable uncleanness, while every means of meliorating their condition is artfully kept from their view, by their insolent and murderous masters....Alas!! When shall God arise for the cries of the oppressed?[36]

The slaves of the neighborhood certainly knew the attitude of "Mass' Donnelly," and many of them went to hear him preach when their masters allowed. Some slaveholders occasionally attended as well. One morning he was preaching about the road to heaven and said that it was "too narrow for slaveholders to drive along with their coaches and slaves." The slaveholders present walked out of the church, much to the amusement of the slaves who were present. In later years, his denunciations were overlooked. "Oh, it is only old Donnelly; let it go." Another man saying the same things, however, would have been tarred and feathered.[37]

James Faris

James Faris, raised in his native Chester County, graduated from South Carolina College at Columbia in 1816 and then became principal of Pendleton Academy, "a flourishing classical school patronized by John C. Calhoun, and in which several congressmen and eminent legislators were educated."[38] He was a successful teacher and within six years had saved $2,000. He resigned in 1822, began to study theology with Rev. Donnelly, and was licensed to preach in 1824. He was seriously troubled about the condition of the slaves and decided to do what he could to help. He planned to buy a slave with the purpose of setting him free. He had in mind to buy the janitor of the school for this purpose, but another slave was about to be sold "down the river"—i.e., to a plantation in the deep South; and at his pleas, Faris instead bought this slave, named Isaac. The Bill of Sale read:

> HOPEWELL, S.C., Nov. 29, 1819
>
> Sold to Mr. James Faris my negro man Isaac, for six hundred dollars, and I do hereby warrant and defend the property of the said negro man Isaac to the said James Faris his heirs and assigns forever.
>
> (Signed) A. PICKENS (Seal)[39]

Emancipating a slave required a simple legal procedure before 1820, but in that year a tighter law was enacted requiring a specific action of the state Legislature for each case. Faris and Isaac were thwarted by the change in the law. Faris petitioned the legislature for permission to free this slave. The petition was denied. Isaac signed a bond to work off his purchase price, actually paid $100 toward it, and Faris forgave the balance. In May of 1825, Faris went to Philadelphia to study theology, took Isaac with him, and there gave him his freedom.[40] Isaac did not fare well in Philadelphia. His employer there, a Mr. Boyd, caught him in bed with a white servant girl and was appalled to discover fornication in his own house.[41] Apparently Isaac also had habits of laziness that prevented his ever having a productive life. All the same, Faris wrote, "I am not disappointed. It was not because I thought him an honest and deserving man that I brought him here. It was to do my duty, and I hope I have done it in this particular."[42]

Faris's petition to the South Carolina Legislature attests to the mindset of this young schoolteacher and to his boldness in speaking truth to power:

> To the Honorable the Senate and house of Representatives of the State of South Carolina,
>
> The petition of the undersigned humbly showeth,
>
> That your petitioner believes that every man is born free and has a right as soon as he has discharged the expenses of his minority to dispose of himself according to the laws of morality and equitable policy. In agreeableness to this principle of natural and republican equity, your petitioner is of the opinion that, that system of slavery which deprives a fellow man of liberty, which invades domestic happiness, dissolves the relation of husband and wife, robs the child of its natural guardian, and leaves the comfort, the labour, and the life of an unoffending fellow being at the disposal of an arbitrary master is a most unrighteous establishment. The gross ignorance of the slaves, and the consequent immoralities of which they are guilty, which plunges them into eternal perdition, and renders them a terror to their master, and all around him: and also the many acts of wanton cruelty exercised by masters, or their representatives, upon slaves would but shock the feelings of your humane assembly. The notoriety, however, of the evil, certainly, calls loudly for a remedy, which it belongs to you to apply, that the vengeance of a righteous Providence may be averted from our

guilty land, relief afforded to suffering humanity, and confidence restored to all our relations in life by humane and equitable regulations.

While your petitioner entertains such sentiments concerning slavery as a system, he himself is the owner of a slave, whom he is desirous to emancipate, and restore to the blessings of freedom. This slave whose name is Isaac is about 27 or 30 years of age, is industrious, disposed to live peaceably and is capable of procuring to himself a livelihood by honest means: and if set free will be subject to the laws for keeping in subjection his people of colour. On such a supposition no possible danger can be apprehended by the public from your authorizing his emancipation.

Your petitioner therefore humbly prays, your Honorable Body, to take his case into consideration, and grant him the privilege of emancipating his slave Isaac, and of becoming guardian for him, that he may have it in his power to do a duty to his fellow man, and relieve his own conscience, and your petitioner shall as in duty bound, forever pray,

James Faris[43]

Some years later, while Faris was pastor of the Bethesda congregation at Bloomington, Indiana, a South Carolinian named David Crossin, wanting to free a large family of slaves and unable to do it under South Carolina's restrictive law, willed them to Faris for that purpose. They were offered the choice to go to Liberia, but chose Indiana: "Even there they had to be formally sold, and security given for their good behavior."[44] So, for several years, Faris supervised their welfare.

James Renwick Willson

Among the most powerful preachers and controversialists in the history of the Reformed Presbyterian Church was James Renwick Willson, born April 9, 1780, near the "forks of the Yough," where the Youghiogheny River joins the Monongahela. In 1805, he graduated from Jefferson College in Canonsburg (since 1865 incorporated into Washington and Jefferson College in Washington, Pennsylvania), then studied theology privately with John McMillan in Canonsburg and with Alexander McLeod in New York. After being licensed to preach, he taught school in Bedford, Pennsylvania from 1809 to 1815, when he took charge of a classical academy in Philadelphia. In 1817, he became pastor of the Reformed Presbyterian congregations of Coldenham and Newburgh, New York, where he remained until 1830. For three years, he served the congregation in Albany, then returned to Coldenham from 1833–40. He was chosen professor of theology in 1836 and in 1840 moved to Allegheny, Pennsylvania (now North Side, Pittsburgh); to Cincinnati from 1845–9; and to Northwood, Ohio from 1849–51, when he retired. He lived for two years with his son, James M. Willson, in Philadelphia, and spent summers in Coldenham, where he died September 29, 1853.[45] His sermons, diaries, and other writings through the years display a wide breadth of both interest and knowledge, but never the slightest uncertainty about moral issues of the day.

In a sermon preached December 6, 1819, for example, he spoke of the guilt of the United States in rejecting Christ's authority, in which he said, "Witness their guaranteeing by the constitution, the right to hold man in involuntary bondage; their numerous laws fortifying this outrage on the rights of men...."[46]

Before this sermon could be published, the Missouri Compromise had passed through Congress, and Willson added this footnote to a paragraph in which he had condemned the Constitutional Convention for framing the constitution with no homage to God:

> Nor does it appear that the lapse of nearly half a century, has produced any reformation; as even now, a decision has passed in Congress, in favor of the abhorrent practice of slavery; an evil repugnant to the finest feelings of humanity, and acknowledged, by themselves, to be contrary to the claims of religion and morality; but irrepealable, because agreeable to, and sanctioned by, the constitution of the United States.[47]

In the early years of the Republic, not only did its territory and population expand, so did the print media. The number of magazines grew from 12 in 1790 to 489 in 1840.[48] Small as their denomination was, Reformed Presbyterians readily took to the press to unify their scattered communities and to attract others to their point of view. In 1822, J. R. Willson started the first periodical to be published by a Reformed Presbyterian in America, *The Evangelical Witness*. In this, he published articles on history, theology, and travel, and clippings from current news at home and abroad. In the first volume, he printed the "Causes of Fasting" adopted by the Pittsburgh Presbytery when it had appointed a "day of fasting and humiliation." The causes were many. Sins of members of the church were set forth unstintingly. The sins of the nation as well were confessed by the Reformed Presbyterians as citizens of the nation, so that they might be free from the judgment that would surely come. One among the many national sins was, of course, slavery, of which the presbytery said:

> The rights of man, though the boast of America, are not regarded. Unoffending men are doomed to hopeless slavery. 'That all men are born free and equal,' is echoed on every tongue. While to the disgrace of humanity, and in opposition to the professed principle, thousands are born slaves. Ah! our brethren, the sons of our father and our mother...[49]

That this was not a boast of self-righteousness is made apparent in the next statement: "In the last place, let us bewail the *plagues of our own hearts.* Who can say, I have made my hands clean? Let us lament *our leanness...*"

In the October 1823 issue, Willson published an article on "Statistics of the Slave Population of the United States," containing a table showing the changes in the various states from 1790 to 1820.[50] In a separate essay, "Slavery in the United States," Willson sounded a clear call to the nation to face and eradicate this evil.

In the decade of the 1820s, the antislavery movement in the United States appeared to have exhausted itself. In the 1820s and 1830s, the major denominations not only refused to speak out against slavery, but prohibited even discussing the subject. They feared that attacks on slavery and the exclusion of slaveholders from church communion would promote violence and disunion and disrupt the arrival of the millennium as anticipated in the dominant postmillennialism view.[51] After the war, a Methodist minister approved his denomination's opposition to the abolitionists by pointing to their "un-Christian temper, and a disposition to prompt and summary justice not in harmony with the laws and plans of God." Some doubted that the Black slaves were ready to be free, or even had the capacity to function as free citizens.[52] Thus in "the plans of God," domestic tranquility trumped mere morality.

But the Covenanters, who had broken decisively with slavery in 1800, never hesitated to condemn it completely. In his essay of October 1823, Willson spoke out strongly:

The stain upon our national character is annually becoming more dark, and its impolitic, cruel, and immoral nature, is constantly developing itself in the detestable course pursued by its advocates and friends. South Carolina stands preeminent among her sister states in an odious policy, in reference to the sable and unfortunate sons of Africa. By her constitution, article 1ˢᵗ, sect. 6ᵗʰ, she requires, among other qualifications, as indispensable, that each of her representatives be the owner of, at least, 'ten negroes'! No matter how devoted to the liberties of his country he may be; no matter how moral he may be; no matter how wealthy he may be; no matter how enlightened and enlarged his political views may be; he can have no place in her legislative counsel, unless he shall hold in slavery ten human beings, ten immortal spirits, as free by the laws of heaven as himself![53]

He called attention to an act passed by the South Carolina legislature the previous winter that required the governor to arrest every free Black person, including those arriving by ship in any port in the state, even including sailors in the navy and merchant marine, and to "sell them into absolute slavery." He pointed out that the act had been ruled unconstitutional by Justice William Johnson of the U.S. Supreme Court. Then he ridiculed the act this way:

To *prevent* the intercourse of enlightened negroes with their slaves, let not such negroes be banished, but *sell* them, *retain* them, and *associate* them with the South Carolina slaves! It really seems that slavery produces fatuity of intellect, as well as callousness of the moral sense, in those who practice it.[54]

It was not his purpose, he said, to hold a particular state up to ridicule, but simply to show the tendency of "this abominable traffic in human flesh, and bones, and blood, and souls, to embroil and degrade, if not ultimately to ruin, our beloved, and otherwise happy country." He took an emphatic stand against a proposal current in Illinois to become a slave state, in violation of the Northwest Ordinance of 1787.

Should the people of that new commonwealth be so infatuated, as to dare to blot their constitution with the assertion of the immoral and degrading claim of slavery, as a right, it is devoutly hoped there will be virtue enough found in the northern and middle states to

enforce, *at the point of the bayonet, if necessary,* the fulfilment of the
solemn compact of 1787, by which the people of that region are
forever incapacitated to introduce slavery. (Emphasis added.)

Willson spoke presciently of the reaction to come:

> The issue will be tremendous. Humanity may be pressed, but its
> spring is not easily broken. The day of its reaction,—and that day
> will come,—will present terrible scenes. And where is the friend of
> human right, that, in case of a servile war, would expose his life,
> in attempting to reduce to a continued bondage the unfortunate
> African, struggling for rights which he never forfeited, which
> he could not alienate, and which God has guarded for him by
> penalties unspeakably awful...[55]

In an oft-repeated anecdote, a woman is reported to have asked
Willson if it were true that the Reformed Presbyterians did not admit
slaveholders to the communion table. Willson answered, "Yes, madam,
it is true; we do not even admit horse thieves."[56]

Willson found that *The Evangelical Witness* had readers in the
South. There were replies from journalists and letters to the editor
from private individuals. One respondent wrote, "...we think there
is too much vehemence manifested on the subject of slavery. The
intelligent part of the southern section of the United States, have long
regarded slavery both as a moral and political evil, as it exists in our
country. We see the disease, but where is the remedy?"[57] The writer
blamed the North for introducing slavery into the colonies and quoted
Scripture commanding slaves to obey their masters. Willson replied to
each argument, expressing a wish that "our southern brethren may be
relieved from this curse." With regard to the introduction of slavery,
he pointed out that the first slaves in English-speaking North America
were purchased in a Southern port, Charleston. "The North has not
left this legacy to the South; they have acquired it for themselves."
He reminded readers that the South had refused to ratify the Federal
Constitution unless "that odious guarantee was contained in its
provisions." He admitted that both North and South shared guilt. He
had no intention of inducing slaves to disobey, but denied that the
type of slavery practiced in the South was sanctioned in the Scripture
his respondent had cited. He wrote that if Southerners really wanted
a remedy, only one existed. If they would emancipate their slaves at

once, "a God of mercy and wisdom would aid them, and difficulties would vanish." He explained the action of the Covenanter Church in 1800 and how their members south and north had emancipated their slaves. "Let others go and do likewise."[58]

In 1838, Willson delivered *An Address on West India Emancipation*, reporting that all the slaves on Antigua had been emancipated on August 1, 1834, without any trouble whatever; on the contrary, agricultural productivity, land values, and public morality and safety all improved.[59]

Willson thus presented the doctrine of immediate emancipation as the only real solution to the problem, almost a decade before other abolitionists considered it, rather than gradualism or colonization, to be an option.

5

We Have, in Fact, Always Been an Abolition Society

The Antislavery Movement after 1830

One evening in 1834, James Milligan was on one of his frequent antislavery lecture tours and facing a hostile crowd. The Vermont pastor felt a personal stake in opposing the cruelties of slavery: in 1801, as a sixteen-year-old boy in Scotland, he had seen a boyhood friend, a cook in the British army, receive five hundred lashes for the crime of having flour smudged on his uniform at inspection. His friend died as a consequence, and Milligan vowed an enduring hatred of the whip.

His burning antislavery lectures took him across New England, lecturing for the cause of the slaves. One evening, he was in an unnamed town in New Hampshire. The hostility of the audience was palpable, but he had been pelted with rotten eggs before and was not deterred. Milligan fearlessly denounced slavery as sin and predicted the judgment of God against the United States for this iniquity. Voices in the audience began to murmur, "Get the tar ready." At length, a man shouted, "You've just earned yourself a coat of tar and feathers!" The audience cheered, and some men removed their coats and started toward the platform. Unruffled, Milligan called out, "Hear me out! If you will only pay attention until the end, I'll help pay for the tar and the feathers!"

At this, the audience roared with laughter. They listened, he finished his speech, and there was no further mention of tar and feathers. The next day, Milligan left town on the stagecoach and found that one of his fellow passengers was Congressman Franklin Pierce, a genial proslavery Democrat. "Mr. Milligan," said the congressman, "I heard your address last evening. I must say I admire your presence of mind when the issue of tar and feathers was raised. I have no doubt that you would have received the ornamental coat, which you richly deserved; but you appeared too willing."[1]

Milligan had come to America in the year after his friend's death, and spent time in Pittsburgh and Philadelphia before becoming a Reformed Presbyterian pastor, first in Coldenham, New York, and then in Ryegate, Vermont. The brutal punishment of enslaved people in America ensured his everlasting opposition to slavery.

Americans in the early republic had a variety of reasons to be uncomfortable with the institution of slavery, whether because of the injustice of inequality, its effects on white society, or the failure to live up to the Declaration of Independence. Initially, very few regarded slavery as sin, though many regarded it as wrong. The first solution to be actively proposed and promoted was to colonize freed slaves in "their homeland" of Africa. Antislavery activists slowly realized that the goal of colonization organizations was simply to rid America of its Black people, and in response to that racism, formed new organizations to work toward emancipation, sometimes (but not always) combined with the goal of racial equality. Antislavery advocates also differed among themselves over the best way to accomplish their goals. Some favored *gradual* emancipation, whereby enslaved people would be freed after working long enough to repay their enslavers' investment and costs of maintenance.

Others demanded *immediate* emancipation for all enslaved people. These in turn differed over whether enslavers should be compensated for the value of their property, since emancipation would amount to a government taking of private property. Later, abolitionists disagreed over tactics. Most relied on *moral suasion* to move society forward, but by the mid-1850s, in light of the Compromise of 1850, the Kansas–Nebraska Act of 1854, and the Dred Scott decision of 1857, it was clear that persuasion was not accomplishing the goal. Some, such as John Brown and the Radical Abolitionist party, felt that *violence* was the only effective alternative. Reformed Presbyterians were always immediatists (despite naïvely flirting with colonization in its early stages), and although none engaged in Brown-style violence, some sympathized with him.

Intramural Struggle

While the church was unanimous in its opposition to slavery, it did not agree about the proper course of action to take.[2] On the one hand were those who believed that a passive witness was the only biblical course; on the other hand were advocates of an active organized opposition. In favor of passivity was the concept that, by the action of God, the millennium would come soon. Like countless other postmillennialists of the time, many Reformed Presbyterians expected that Christ would return to establish his millennial kingdom in 1866. This implied that the church's responsibility was to maintain its own purity and bear faithful testimony rather than to take organized action against evil.[3] Operating in tandem with this was the belief that the church was the only institution ordained by God to act in the world, so that voluntary associations for moral reform of any sort were inconsistent with church membership. Believers should not "enter entangling associations with ungodly men, and with those in connection with backslidden churches."[4] The Illinois Presbytery went so far as to describe voluntary associations as "the ebullitions of the deranged moral elements of society."[5]

This view, of a purely passive witness, was never adopted by the majority of the church, although the rift continued throughout most of the century and was not confined to the issue of slavery. Many members were thankful to see the increasing number and influence of "active associations…to liberate the captive and unhappy slave from the oppressive bondage under which he groans."[6] The most prolific preachers and writers of the denomination fit into the activist side in this discussion and preached and wrote on a wide variety of public and moral issues.

Colonization

It was with good cause that enslavers feared slave violence. The British colonies in North America experienced major slave rebellions in 1663, 1712, 1739, and 1741. The first slave revolution to succeed in the modern era was in Saint-Domingue, which began in 1791 and led in 1803 to the establishment of Haiti as the first republic ruled by former Black slaves. In the slave revolt itself, thousands of Black and white people died. In 1800, inspired in part by the revolution in Saint-Domingue, a slave named Gabriel planned a slave rebellion in Virginia, but torrential rains interfered, the rebellion was nipped in the bud, and Gabriel and twenty-four others were executed, with no further bloodshed.[7] Additional uprisings occurred in 1811 in Louisiana, in 1822 in Charleston, South Carolina ("Denmark Vesey's Uprising"), and in 1831 in Southampton County, Virginia ("Nat Turner's Rebellion"), among others. All of these prompted increased paranoia among Southern white slaveholders and led to ever-tighter legal restrictions on slaves.

These rebellions, and the rumors and fears of new risings, strengthened the resolve of the enslavers to enforce slavery and repress Black activism, and simultaneously discouraged the early abolitionist sentiment. They were taken as evidence that the Black race was dangerous, violent, and savage. Certainly, murdering masters and their families in their beds, as Nat Turner and his followers did, was more than alarming. Congress had passed the first Fugitive Slave Law in 1793, to implement the Constitution, Article II, Section 4, but Northerners evinced little interest in enforcing it. In the wake of revolts by the enslaved, more white people feared "an increasing domestic danger," more pointed out that the economic and social status of free Black people was unsatisfactory, and more slave owners began to realize that they indeed held a wolf by the ears. If a way could be found to get both slaves and free Black people out of the country, perhaps the Republic would be safe once again.[8]

Therefore, in December 1816 and the early months of 1817, a group of men met in Washington, D.C., to create an organization "to promote and execute a plan for colonizing (with their consent) the Free People of Colour residing in our country, in Africa, or such other place as Congress shall deem most expedient."[9] They adopted the name The American Colonization Society. Their attitude, and that of most of their early supporters, was expressed by William H. Fitzhugh of Virginia in 1826 (by which time opposition was growing): "But we entertained a hope...that this operation, properly conducted, would *in the end,* remove from our country every vestige of domestic slavery, without a single violation of individual wishes or individual rights."[10]

The dangers of freeing the enslaved, however, were not confined to violation of rights or fear of reprisal; the amalgamation of the races was a widespread fear. Thomas Jefferson suggested colonization in his *Notes on the State of Virginia*—but for clearly racist reasons, based on the "general inferiority" of the Black race. After describing how the conditions of slaves in ancient Rome were much worse than those of the slaves of Virginia, Jefferson added, "Among the Romans emancipation required but one effort. The slave, when made free, might mix with [freemen], without staining the blood of his master. But with us a second is necessary, unknown to history. When freed, he is to be removed beyond the reach of mixture."[11] Jefferson's concern, therefore, was to maintain the racial purity of the white population. He was not alone in his opinion.

The first president of the Colonization Society was Bushrod Washington, associate justice of the Supreme Court and the nephew of President Washington. Others in the leadership included Henry Clay, Andrew Jackson, and Francis Scott Key. Its official publication was *The African Repository*, which sent agents to Africa to select a site for a colony. Congress in 1819 gave encouragement to the movement by providing that Black slaves captured while being illegally imported into the United States were to be returned to Africa. One hundred thousand dollars was appropriated to carry out the intentions of Congress.

Many joined the colonization movement under the impression that Black people desired it, an impression given by scattered efforts in this direction. In 1787, the English reformer Granville Sharp established a colony for freed Black people in Sierra Leone. The same year, a Dr. Thornton made the same proposal in Boston and in Providence, Rhode Island. In 1789, Rev. Samuel Hopkins of Newport, Rhode Island, proposed to Granville Sharp that free Black citizens from New England be sent to Sierra Leone, and in 1790, Ferdinando Fairfax of Richmond, Virginia, proposed that "Free People of Colour" be colonized in Africa. Associations of free Black members in Rhode Island and Indiana favored colonization; those in Rhode Island, in fact, raised money and sent an agent to Africa to search for a site.[12] Under these circumstances, some Reformed Presbyterians welcomed this effort. While the minutes of the Reformed Presbyterian Synod do not survive from this period, it has been suggested that some Christian supporters were influenced by the biblical examples of the Hebrews who, when delivered from bondage in Egypt and Babylon, returned to the Promised Land. This, of course, would ignore the very real differences in their circumstances: the Africans had been neither a single ethnic/linguistic group nor a single faith community. Nor had they ever had a single homeland.

Others hoped that colonization as a safety valve would lead enslavers who were afraid of the possible consequences of emancipation to free their slaves. William Lloyd Garrison and the Quaker abolitionist Benjamin Lundy advertised for Black slaves with agricultural skills to colonize in Haiti; they also considered establishing colonies in Canada and Texas. Thus "if an asylum could be found for them, and their removal assured," no master who might be inclined to emancipate his slaves "could have excuse for not doing so."[13] Neither Lundy nor Garrison saw then what they later believed to be the real (i.e., racist) roots of the Colonization Society.

Nor did some of the Covenanters. At its founding in 1823, Alexander McLeod was second vice president of the New York Colonization Society.[14] James Faris joined the society while he was principal of the Pendleton Academy in South Carolina, but soon decided that its intentions were not good and abandoned the organization.[15]

The society's plans did not work out as advertised. In ten years, from 1820 to 1830, only 1,162 people were resettled. Many of those who emigrated died of malaria and other diseases in the unaccustomed subtropical climate. Free Black people generally did not want to be shipped out of the country where most of them had been born. They soon saw that "the colonization scheme was a benevolent and soft-spoken swindle."[16] More important, perhaps, was the fact that, despite the assurances that emigration would be voluntary, it was all too often compulsory. Freed Black slaves were subjected to discriminatory legislation in both slave and free states; they were physically abused in order to secure their consent to emigrate, and Southern proponents of slavery were quite frank in discussing the need to use force to coerce emigration.[17]

Within less than a decade, Reformed Presbyterians moved against the Colonization Society. The society had received the endorsement of the Synod in 1828 with the clear stipulation that removal from the United States was to be only with the consent of the emancipated—which was, in fact, part of the society's constitution—and only to "such places as the emancipated shall choose."[18] In 1836, petitions came to the Synod from Vermont and Ohio asking for a change in that endorsement. Synod responded that the Colonization Society "has manifested a total disregard of those principles on which it received the approbation of this court. This court never did give its approbation to the colonization society considered as opposed to manumission; on the contrary, it was on the supposition that it would be favorable to abolition that we gave it our countenance....[T]he Reformed Presbyterian Church...has in fact always been an abolition society.... We withdraw the approbation given the colonization society, and transfer our approbation and patronage to the cause of abolition."[19]

Members of the church were urged to cooperate with abolition societies to encourage the cause of abolition and to uphold "the paramount authority of the divine law in regard to social relations and actions." They were delighted that an antislavery periodical had recently published an article that contained the statement, "The sacred scriptures are the standard of morals for governments as well as for individuals," and then rejoiced that men of talent, moral worth, and influence "are helping us to propagate that great truth which is the seed bud of all our [defining characteristics] as a professing people."[20]

The transfer of approval was so worded as to guard against further embarrassing entanglements. Synod approved "the cause of abolition" rather than any specific societies. The denomination considered itself to be among the first abolition societies in America.

Antislavery Societies

Americans' readiness to join voluntary organizations for virtually any purpose was a characteristic noted by Alexis de Tocqueville early in the nineteenth century, and the antislavery movement exemplified this readiness in spades. Benjamin Lundy, a Quaker abolitionist originally from New Jersey, had traveled widely, speaking freely against slavery and organizing local antislavery societies as early as 1815. Previously, a society had been formed in Pennsylvania in 1773; by 1808, societies existed in New Jersey, Kentucky, and New York, and were organized in Delaware in 1809, in Tennessee in 1814, in Ohio and North Carolina in 1816, in Maryland in 1817, and in Virginia in 1822. More than one hundred local societies existed during this period. The 1817 formation of the American Colonization Society, whose ostensible purpose was to facilitate eventual emancipation of the enslaved people in the United States, attracted initial enthusiasm. By 1830, however, this enthusiasm had waned among those who wanted an end to slavery. When William Lloyd Garrison resigned from the Colonization Society, he joined forces with Lundy in printing the latter's journal, *Genius of Universal Emancipation*, in Baltimore. Their partnership exemplified one of the divisions within the Abolition Movement: Lundy was a gradualist, but as Garrison worked on the paper, he (Garrison) became convinced of the need for immediate and complete emancipation, so became an immediatist.

Coinciding with this change, at about this time (1830), a decided shift occurred in the whole abolition crusade, as it transitioned to a more aggressive position. Garrison and Lundy continued to work together amicably, but after Garrison served a brief time in jail for his writings, he returned to his native Massachusetts and established his own weekly newspaper, *The Liberator*. From the start in January 1831 until its final issue in December 1865, it was undoubtedly the most influential antislavery periodical in the nation, despite a relatively small paid circulation. On June 1, 1832, Garrison published his only book, *Thoughts on African Colonization: or An Impartial Exhibition of the Doctrines, Principles and Purposes of the American Colonization Society, together with the Resolutions, Addresses and Remonstrances of the Free People of Colour*.[21] This produced an immediate and dramatic effect, despite the strenuous efforts of the American Colonization Society (ACS) leaders at countermeasures. By November of that year, he had them on the ropes, with their spokesman writing that "no Christian would deliberately sacrifice the substantial interests, both of individuals and the community, to any unsubstantial theory of the rights of man."[22] In the same year, Garrison founded the New England Antislavery Society and in 1833, helped to organize the American Antislavery Society.

Immediatism

In the meantime, other events were also working to transform the antislavery movement. In 1829, a free Black man from North Carolina named David Walker published his *Appeal to the Coloured Citizens of the World* in Boston, threatening that enslaved and free Black people would rise up to murder the slave owners.[23] In 1831 came Nat Turner's Rebellion, in which a number of enslaved persons attempted to carry out Walker's injunctions. The South, naturally, was alarmed, and the fears of the enslavers multiplied, as did the measures to repress the slaves further and to prevent Walker's *Appeal* from being spread in either South or North. Thus, although Garrison, Wendell Phillips, and other Northern abolitionists remained committed to peaceful change, the tone of general public discourse rose to a higher pitch. Garrison had already described the U.S. Constitution as "dripping… with human blood." By 1854, at a Fourth of July counter-celebration at Framingham, Massachusetts, Garrison culminated his address for the day by burning publicly the Fugitive Slave Act and the U.S. Constitution. "So perish all compromises with tyranny," he cried.[24]

The new, more militant tone of abolitionism after 1829 met with immediate resistance in the South. Garrison demanded immediate and absolute emancipation, and he made no distinction between the enslaver who treated his enslaved persons with the greatest cruelty and the one who treated them kindly. Increasingly, he made no distinction between Southerners who owned slaves and those who merely lived in their states and supported the slave system with their votes and their taxes; he came to see no distinction between them and Northerners

Wendell Phillips, a Boston Unitarian, was a well-known radical abolitionist and speaker.

James Milligan was an RP pastor known for antislavery lecture tours.

William Lloyd Garrison, a notable Boston Unitarian, founded the American Antislavery Society. He described the U.S. Constitution as "dripping... with human blood." All three portraits above are from Looking Back from the Sunset Land *by N. R. Johnston*

who supported a wicked Constitution by voting in elections. The Covenanters, of course, had been immediatists since 1800 and had refused to vote since 1789; they too believed that the foundational sin of slavery was not physical cruelty but the ownership of one human being by another. At about the same time, their coreligionists, the northern Associate Reformed Presbyterians, "declared slave owning a civil issue and rejected the moral grounds of the Abolitionists."[25]

The new societies—the New England and the American Antislavery Societies—grew rapidly. By 1840, there were at least 1,454 local and state antislavery societies, most of them well-financed and prosperous. Another sixty-five had appeared and disappeared before 1840.[26] Many Reformed Presbyterians subscribed to *The Liberator* and many joined these societies. For example, James McLeod Willson, pastor of the First Reformed Presbyterian Church in Philadelphia, was president of the Union Antislavery Society of Philadelphia, organized June 12, 1838.[27] Some members of his congregation opposed his involvement, not because they were proslavery, but because, as we have seen, they considered it to be inconsistent for Christians to unite with unbelievers, or even members of other denominations, in societies for the promotion of any cause, however worthy, and that such groups outside of the organized church diminished the authority of the church. Curiously, James R. W. Sloane, one of the most active Covenanter ministers in the antislavery cause, opposed voluntary associations and never became a member of an antislavery society. James M. Willson, however, maintained the right of Christians to cooperate as citizens with other citizens in such good works as the antislavery movement, especially when the Christian church as a whole was so divided.[28] Many did so. John Fisher and S. M. Willson were secretaries of auxiliary societies in York, New York, and Craftsbury, Vermont respectively.[29] Rev. James R. Willson and Rev. David Scott were official delegates to the 1839 convention of the society.[30] Rev. Thomas Sproull was corresponding secretary of the Pennsylvania Antislavery Society.[31]

This difference of opinion within the Reformed Presbyterian Church might be seen by some as a separation between what Max Weber called the "ascetic" and "mystical" points of view. Both groups, however, were committed to the vision of the transformation of society; that is, both were "ascetic," wanting to see society reformed along biblical lines. Those who opposed joining these societies believed that the church and its members should not co-labor with those who differed with them on other theological issues, but wait passively for God to act in the millennium. The Synod initially waffled but eventually decided in favor of careful cooperation with other believers.

The Synod of 1838 contented itself with reminding members that "the testimony of this church is directed against, not only the practical evil of slavery, but also against the immoral principles in the constitution of the United States, by which this wicked system is supported." Therefore, "from all associations which propose, by any act homologating [ratifying] the constitution of the United States, to remove the evil of slavery, it is our duty and determination to stand aloof."[32] In other words, any association that affirmed the Constitution was to be avoided by Reformed Presbyterians.

After a small group of anti-cooperationists, led by Rev. David Steele and one other minister, defected, the Synod of 1841 clarified the denomination's position by resolving "That our ministers and people be admonished to refuse uniting unnecessarily in associations with the erroneous and wicked, when a bond of confederation is required to be signed implying identity with such persons."[33]

Nevertheless, some Reformed Presbyterians remained closely allied with the leaders of the abolition societies. Some went so far as to believe that the Lord had raised up William Lloyd Garrison to take the place of a number of ministers and members who separated from the denomination in 1833—the very moment when Garrison and the Antislavery Society "took the same attitude towards the Constitution that the Old Light Covenanters held, to rally to the testimony and fill up the gap."[34] Those who had left the fellowship "professed to have obtained 'new light' in regard to the relation of the government to the system of slavery." These "New Lights" had adopted the Southern view that the U.S. was not actually a national government, but a confederation of sovereign states, each responsible for its peculiar institutions, and that the Constitution did not *actually* endorse slavery.[35]

It was Garrison's attitude toward the Constitution that drew Reformed Presbyterians toward him. He, like the Covenanters, had reached the conclusion that the Constitution was essentially proslavery. This was a contentious point among abolitionists, as James Oakes has shown.[36] Quoting Isaiah 28:15, he called it "a covenant with death, and an agreement with hell." Such strong language was not unfamiliar to Reformed Presbyterians; their *Testimony* in 1806 affirmed that because the Constitution deprived innocent people of their liberty and property, it was not to be considered as an ordinance of God (i.e., not established by him).[37]

Horace Greeley later listed four distinct categories of antislavery people in the North preceding the Civil War: (1) the Garrisonians, who considered the Constitution to be a proslavery document and refused to vote under it; (2) the members of the Liberty Party, who regarded the Constitution as proslavery, but swore to uphold it, and supported only antislavery candidates for office; (3) "Various small sects and parties;...some of the sects agreeing with the latter in interpreting and revering the Bible as consistently antislavery, while refusing with the former to vote"; (4) those who "refused either to withhold their votes, or to throw them away on candidates whose election was impossible, but persisted in voting, at nearly every election, so as to effect good and prevent evil to the extent of their power."[38] The Reformed Presbyterians would be included in the third group.

An interesting light on Greeley and the Garrisonian/Covenanter attitude toward voting was revealed in a letter he wrote to Rev. James R. Thompson of Newburgh, New York, not long before the election of Abraham Lincoln. Greeley wrote:

> OFFICE OF THE TRIBUNE
> New York, Sept. 2, 1860
>
> Dear Sir:
>
> I consider every hour that I can keep my eyes open devoted to the election of Lincoln until after November 6th. I will not make engagements prior to that time. I may be able afterwards to comply with your request.
>
> Is your Church one of those that *talks* against Slavery but refuses to *vote* against it? If so, I must regard it as a barren figtree.
>
> Yours,
> Horace Greeley[39]

During the campaign, Greeley was impatient with anyone who would not help to elect Lincoln. He believed that the first and third groups of abolitionists were fruitless, since they refused to vote at all, while the second threw their votes away by voting for men who had no chance of election. Only the fourth had his approval.

Reformed Presbyterian churches were always available for abolition speakers. When the English abolitionist George Thompson (1804–78) visited in 1834–5, the Garrisonians had difficulty finding venues for meetings to hear Thompson; a few Methodist churches were still open to them at that time, but the denomination officially suppressed any efforts to discuss slavery. Initially, no place in Philadelphia could be found, until the First Reformed Presbyterian Church was made available, and it was reported that so many people crowded into the church to hear him that the gallery floor collapsed.[40] Pastor James M. Willson stood by his side after threats had been received that the building would be burned down.[41]

Mob Violence

That such violence was no idle threat was proven shortly afterward. When George Thompson was scheduled to address a meeting of the Female Antislavery Society in Boston, a reward of $100 was offered for the first individual who would seize him and bring him to the tar kettle before dark. The mob erroneously took Garrison and pulled him through the streets at the end of a rope until he was rescued by the mayor of Boston. In 1836, a similar incident occurred during a series of riots in Cincinnati, in which the printing office of James G. Birney (editor of the abolitionist weekly *The Philanthropist*) was burned twice in one month, and proslavery forces offered a reward of $1,000 for his capture.

Other violence ensued. On November 7, 1837, a Presbyterian minister, Rev. Elijah P. Lovejoy, was deemed to have criticized slavery once too often. His printing presses in St Louis had been twice destroyed; he then moved to Alton, Illinois, where his presses were thrown into the Mississippi three times. On November 7, he was killed by the mob in Alton, and his fourth press was broken into pieces and thrown into the river. In a riot in Philadelphia, forty-four houses were damaged or destroyed by proslavery mobs. In 1838, the abolitionists in Philadelphia built Pennsylvania Hall for their meetings, only to see it burned to the ground by a mob before its dedication was complete.[42]

Covenanter ministers accompanied Garrison and his associates on lecture tours and faced mobs with them. The pastor at Topsham, Vermont, Nathan R. Johnston, toured the state with Garrison and Samuel May.[43] Later, in his reminiscences, Johnston quotes personal letters he had received from Garrison, Wendell Phillips, Samuel May, Charles C. Burleigh, and other abolitionists. Garrison wrote to him in 1874,

Be assured that I had not forgotten you, and therefore I needed no reminder of our acquaintance years ago, when there were so few to lift up their voices against 'the abomination of desolation,' and so many to defend it as compatible with Republicanism and Christianity. In your own person and position, you acquitted yourself so courageously, faithfully, and uncompromisingly, that you will always deserve to be honorably remembered in connection with the anti-slavery struggle. It gives me great pleasure to proffer you afresh my warmest regards and best wishes.[44]

Another Vermont minister who was a close friend of Garrison was James Milligan, whose braving a hostile crowd has been recounted already. When George Thompson came to America to lecture, Milligan "bought a chaise on purpose to escort the illustrious English philanthropist in a lecture tour over New England."[45]

Rev. J. R. W. Sloane of New York's Third Reformed Presbyterian Church was frequently on the same platform with Garrison. Oliver Johnson, a friend and biographer of Garrison, later wrote to Professor William Milligan Sloane of Columbia about his father:

It was the fashion then to denounce Garrison and his associates as infidels and blasphemers, whose real purpose was the destruction of Christianity and civil government; but Mr. Sloane, knowing these accusations to be false, did not hesitate to come to our platform as often as we needed him, and give us the benefit of his voice and influence.

Another of the well-known abolitionist ministers, Dr. George B. Cheever of the Church of the Puritans in New York's Union Square, wrote,

Dr. Sloane was one of the most faithful and courageous opponents of slavery....On occasion of the vast assemblage in Cooper Institute, in behalf of John Brown's widow and family, he did speak, out of the depths of righteousness and truth, in the midst of a howling mob, with a severity and calmness of rebuke, and a demonstration of the hideous iniquity of slavery, as a sin against God and man, demanding immediate abolition.[46]

Other Reformed Presbyterian ministers also met with violence. William Sloane, the father of J. R. W. Sloane, was one such. John Black Johnston, the founder of Geneva College in 1848, was once dragged from his horse and had ribs broken. Armour McFarland, pastor at Utica, Licking County, Ohio, and then of the Jonathan's Creek congregation in Muskingum County, lectured throughout Ohio and often encountered hostility. James Wallace and Hugh Stevenson were once set upon by a mob whose shouts could be heard three miles away. A. M. Milligan, by then pastor at New Alexandria, Pennsylvania, was rotten-egged and burned in effigy both in Greensburg and at Elders Ridge, Indiana County, for condemning slavery as sin.[47]

An aside in the biography of Garrison by his sons summed up the consistent reputation of Covenanter ministers in the pre-Civil War era: "...we have the testimony of an earnest Covenanter (and therefore antislavery) clergyman..."[48] If Reformed Presbyterians were not all actual members of the Garrisonian abolition "societies," they were at least close allies. The common elements uniting them were, first, the belief that slavery was a sin and it was sinful to compromise with it; and second, the conviction that the U.S. Constitution was a proslavery document.

6

The Constitution Is the Magna Carta of Slavery

Covenanter Antislavery Doctrine

The Church Anti-Slavery Society, holding its annual meeting in Boston's spacious Tremont Temple in 1860, listened in rapt attention as the distinguished speaker thundered against the defenders of slavery. "It is not...upon the abuses of slavery that we insist: there are no abuses of slavery, as there are none of murder, none of adultery.... It is of itself inherently sinful, a *malum in se* [evil in itself] at once to be repented of and abandoned." So the Rev. James R. W. Sloane, pastor of the Third Reformed Presbyterian Church in New York, exhorted his enthusiastic audience. This theme was a consistent note in the antislavery doctrine of the Covenanters, as well as a foundation of the interdenominational Church Anti-Slavery Society.[1] While this belief was far from universal among abolitionists, it was shared by many and had been embodied in the platform of the Free Democratic Party in 1852: "Sixth. That slavery is a sin against God and a crime against man, which no human enactment nor usage can make right; and that Christianity, humanity, and patriotism alike demand its abolition." At the same time, the eminent Princeton theologian Charles Hodge, while opposing slavery, refused to say that it was in itself a sin.[2]

Having looked in the previous two chapters at the activities of some of the leading Reformed Presbyterians in the antislavery movement and the deep-seated consistency in their opposition, one may well ask, "*Why* were they (and other Americans) so strongly opposed to a practice that was embedded in custom and constitution? Were there *reasons,* or were they, in the words of Timothy L. Smith, simply 'numbered among the screwballs'?"

Varieties of Antislavery Reasoning

To combat slavery, its foes had access to an assortment of lines of attack, all of which were used by some in the movement at various times. Reformed Presbyterians used some common approaches and at least one distinctive approach. It seemed that each of the enemies of the "peculiar institution" found some arguments persuasive and others unconvincing. Not surprisingly, the advocates of slavery found none persuasive until the final argument—war. Only when used in combination, and only when the issue was forced by the Slave Power, did these arguments finally tip the national scales of justice toward the center. In the memorable words of Mark A. Noll, "For the history of theology in America, the great tragedy of the Civil War is that the most persuasive theologians were the Rev. Drs. William Tecumseh Sherman and Ulysses S. Grant."[3]

The earliest antislavery arguments in America were ethical. During the colonial period these were seldom mentioned, in part because there were thousands of indentured servants who worked off their indebtedness and then were free to leave. Puritan ministers and judges saw no inconsistency in owning Black slaves.[4] Only when the Enlightenment brought about conversations on the natural rights of mankind did a widespread sense of unease about perpetual slavery emerge. The Revolutionary generation wrote that "all men are created equal," but failed to consider the racial meaning of "all" or to include women in the distribution of divinely created equality. It is also noteworthy that both friends and foes of slavery usually did not distinguish between the issues of slavery and race; as we shall see below, Reformed Presbyterians were among the first white abolitionists to make this distinction and to reject the widespread belief in the alleged inferiority of Black people—for example, they admitted Black people to church membership on an equal footing and sanctioned interracial marriage.

A related issue in Enlightenment sentiment was both moral and social: the debilitating or coarsening effect of the slave system on young white men and women. They grew up expecting to command and to be obeyed; they were schooled from childhood in cruelty; their finer sensibilities were calloused by regular exposure to legally sanctioned suffering. Adolescent and adult white males expected to command the favors of female slaves. White youth were, to use a popular modern expression, "victims of the system." Moreover, since a significant part of their inheritance and fortune was invested in slave property, they were helpless to change or abolish the system. Thomas Jefferson explained these social disadvantages of the system in his *Notes on the State of Virginia*, Query XVIII.

J. R. Willson was among the most powerful preachers and controversialists in the history of the Reformed Presbyterian Church. He knew Harriet Beecher Stowe. After all slaves on Antigua had been emanicpated in 1834, he presented the doctrine of immediate emancipation as the only real solution to U.S. slavery.

Alexander Mcleod, an RP minister who became an influential abolitionist speaker, declined a call to a congregation in New York because some of the members owned slaves. Soon after, he published Negro Slavery Unjustifiable, *a firm and full argument against slavery.*

Covenanters made a similar point, although it was incidental and was never a central part of their argument. The first major Reformed Presbyterian spokesman for abolition was Alexander McLeod, who in his 1802 discourse *Negro Slavery Unjustifiable* quoted Jedidiah Morse and his comment on the debilitating effect of slavery: "...slavery is the bane of industry. It renders labour among the whites not only unfashionable, but disreputable."[5] In 1860, J. R. W. Sloane pointed to the coarsening effects of slavery on its defenders and on society in general.[6]

A third type of argument against slavery was humanitarian, which was not quite synonymous with moral reasoning but was an appeal to human sympathy. It emphasized the cruelties inflicted on slaves in the form of whippings and other humiliations, sexual exploitation, the destruction of families, and the deprivation of literacy and of the Bible. The appeal to Christian compassion was clear and strong. The unprecedented success of Harriet Beecher Stowe's *Uncle Tom's Cabin* (1852) showed that compassion could successfully move people toward abolition.[7] McLeod had insisted in 1802 that Christians had a moral responsibility to empathize with the sufferings of the slaves, as well as with those who suffered from other causes, and Stowe's novel "put legs on" the idea.

Covenanters spoke emphatically about the humanitarian outrages of slavery. The volatile J. R. Willson recorded in his diary that he had read *Uncle Tom's Cabin* "by Dr. Beecher's daughter, the wife of Professor Stowe late of Lane Seminary." He had known the Lane faculty when living and teaching in Cincinnati from 1845 to 1849, and he describes his reaction: "She is [a] plain, domestic woman. So unobtrusive, I never expected that [she] could write a book evincing so profound a knowledge of corrupt human nature. Her tender sympathy with the deep sorrows of the slaves is above all praise."[8]

While emphatically sympathetic to the slaves' suffering, Covenanters recognized that cruelty was not merely an abuse of the slave system but an essential element, because it seemed to be necessary in order to control the slaves. Fundamentally, however, "the sin consists in the relation" (ownership/servitude) and not in the cruel behavior primarily.[9] Because slavery was a *malum in se*, a sin in itself, cruelty was an ancillary sin.

A fourth type of argument was economic rather than moral or theological. First, it was sometimes thought that slave labor was less expensive than the hire of free labor and so provided an unfair economic advantage to slave owners. This was apparent if a small farmer, for example, owned no slaves and so was compelled to hire laborers, or to rely on the help of his wife and children in the fields, or to reduce the scope of his farming operations, while his slave-owning neighbors flourished and extended their farms by using "cost-free" slave labor. It was also apparent that when a factory owner could buy or rent slave labor at a lower cost than hiring free workers for the same jobs, he depressed the market for free laborers.

Plenty of evidence showed, however, that the economy of the slave South was less productive than that of the non-slave North. In 1789, Jedidiah Morse had insisted that "From repeated and accurate calculations, it has been found that the expense of maintaining a slave, if we include the purchase-money, is much greater than that of maintaining a free man; and the labour of the free man, influenced by the powerful motive of gain, is at least twice as profitable to the employer as that of the slave."[10]

In the mid-nineteenth century, Hinton R. Helper—an abolitionist from Georgia—adduced statistics to show how far the free states exceeded the slave states economically. In 1850, the sixteen free states had a total valuation of real and personal property of $4.1 billion, including, of course, no unfree people, while the 15 slave states had $2.9 billion total valuation, including 3,204,313 slaves. The free states had total revenues of $18.7 million; the slave states, $8.3 million. Public expenditures in the free states totaled $17.1 million in all; in the slave states, $7.5 million. He estimated that the value of the hay crop alone of the free states in that year had a retail value of $331 million, which was more than four times the value of all the cotton produced in the United States in that time.[11]

Helper also compared pairs of states that had grown or failed to grow from the census of 1790 to that of 1850, showing how far the free states exceeded their slave state counterparts: New York and Virginia, Massachusetts and North Carolina, and Pennsylvania and South Carolina. In 1856, the real and personal estate valuation of New York City alone was $511 million—far more than the entire state of Virginia.[12] It was perfectly clear, said Helper, that slavery did not produce prosperity or foster production.[13]

Some advocates for slavery tried to turn the argument about efficiency on its ear. True enough, they said; owning slaves, which entailed the responsibility to provide food, clothing, shelter, and medical care, cost more than the slave earned in production. Slave owning was economically counterproductive. Thus, slave owners should be reckoned benefactors of mankind, providing philanthropically for a helpless and incapable race and generously sacrificing their own well-being for the good of the Africans and the protection of white society. It hardly needs to be said that this argument is laughably specious, but some advocates of slavery found it appealing.

In the fifth place, the North had a powerful and legitimate political argument against "the Slave Power" in the "federal ratio," by which three-fifths of the slaves were counted in the population for purposes of representation in Congress and the Electoral College. This ratio represented a major compromise in the Constitutional Convention between the two principal sections, the slave states and the non-slave. The slaves could not vote, of course, and were regarded by state law in the South as chattels; counting 60 percent of them as though they were *people* significantly skewed political power in favor of the slave states.[14] The extra representatives spoke, not for the slaves nor the poor whites, but for the slave owners. Northerners asked rhetorically if they could not count three-fifths of their cattle or horses, but their arguments were brushed aside. The slave states used their power to the fullest in national politics by blocking attempts to limit the expansion of slaveholding, by insisting on the admission of new states that permitted slavery,[15] and by dominating the presidency, the House of Representatives, and the Supreme Court. They even skewed the Senate, which consists of two senators from every state. Since Congress had fixed no minimum population for the formation of a new state, a number of new slave states were thinly populated. In the 1850s, six of the slave states had a combined free population of 189,791, fewer than Pennsylvania, yet of course had twelve senators to Pennsylvania's two.[16] This political imbalance gave rise to the term "the Slave Power" in political discussions, periodically creating crises in government, which in turn required further compromises—especially those of 1820 and 1850.[17]

In addition to these ethical, social, humanitarian, economic, and political arguments was a sixth line of reasoning: biblical. While this kind of argument was unacceptable to many people in the nineteenth century, and while the defenders of slavery offered literalistic biblical arguments to support their views, biblical and theological reasoning were foundational to the antislavery thinking of many Americans, including the Covenanters.[18]

Origins of Reformed Antislavery Doctrine

Biblical opposition to human slavery did not originate in America, or in the eighteenth or nineteenth century, but can be found at least as early as the fifth century, in the work of Augustine of Hippo. In *The City of God* (412–423 AD), Augustine quoted Genesis 1:26: "Let them have dominion over the fish of the sea, and over the fowls of the air, and over every creeping thing which creepeth on the earth." He pointed out that:

> [God] did not intend that His rational creature, who was made in His image, should have dominion over anything but the irrational creation—not man over man, but man over the beasts. And hence the righteous men in primitive times were made shepherds of cattle rather than kings of men...for it is with justice, we believe, that the condition of slavery is the result of sin....The prime cause, then, of slavery is sin, which brings man under the dominion of his fellow.[19]

It was left to later generations to build a system that would ensure slavery did not endure. Throughout the Middle Ages, slavery slowly evolved into serfdom but flourished in Muslim lands. Extensive systems of capture, enslavement, and sale of slaves were developed by Vikings, Mongols, Tatars, Saracens, and other non-Christian forces, and Crusader orders captured a number of Muslims and used or traded them as slaves.

By the fifteenth century, however, the historic sources of slaves dried up and Europeans, especially the Portuguese, began to import slaves from Africa, until the majority of enslaved people in Iberia were native Africans. The treatment of slaves and the possibilities of manumission (the release from slavery) varied widely with both geography and time, but the basic institution endured. England had formally abolished slavery in 1102, but by the seventeenth century, when the colonial empire emerged, slavery was adopted as the most expedient way to reap the benefits of the new colonies. The great landowning families in Britain often became the great landowning families in the Americas, creating a need for new and plentiful supplies of laborers.

In this context, then, the arguments for and against slavery developed, and the last of these to develop was the biblical or theological argument against it.

Alexander McLeod

The essence of the biblical or theological argument was that slavery was a sin, condemned in Scripture and contrary to the principles of the Christian life. This was always at the core of the Reformed Presbyterian opposition but was not exclusive to them: other denominations, and indeed the Church Anti-Slavery Society, also used the same terms in condemning slavery. The earliest systematic exposition of the Covenanter position was Alexander McLeod's *Negro Slavery Unjustifiable*.[20] Even before that publication, however, McLeod's firm antislavery conviction influenced the Reformed Presbytery to prohibit slavery in the denomination. McLeod, a native of Scotland, had come to America in 1792 at the age of eighteen. Graduating from Union College in 1798, he studied theology privately. In 1800, he was called as pastor of the congregations of Coldenham and New York, but he declined on the ground that there were slaveholders among those at Coldenham who had signed his call. This was the stimulus; the presbytery acted unanimously to prohibit slaveholders from membership.

The text for McLeod's discourse is Exodus 21:16: "He that stealeth a man, and selleth him, or if he be found in his hand, he shall surely be put to death." This, he says, was a political law for the Hebrew nation, but because it is grounded in the moral law it is "obligatory still on every subject of moral argument." It is based on the eighth commandment, "Thou shalt not steal." If a person who steals such possessions as money is guilty of sin, a person who steals another's father, brother, wife, or child cannot be innocent. Moreover, as a person who knowingly buys stolen property is held complicit in the theft, so one who buys, holds, or sells a stolen person also shares in the guilt.

Perpetual slavery, he says, is inconsistent with the "natural rights" of man, by which he means the rights conferred by God at creation, rather than the rights that Enlightenment thinkers understood as the essence of humanity. McLeod thus distinguishes clearly between Christianity and the secular philosophy of the Enlightenment. Man is created a free agent and as such has a right to exercise that freedom. The "rights of man," in other words, "are not inherent, but derived from God" by virtue of the divine act of creation. A person's life and faculties are the gifts of God, and no one has a right to take them unless he has forfeited them by crime. The opposite principle would be absurd: everyone would have a right to sell and enslave everyone else, so that law becomes raw force and justice becomes cunning—a Hobbesian nightmare of "all against all."

Slavery, moreover, contradicts "the general tenor of sacred scriptures," including Jesus's command to "do unto others as you would have them do unto you" (Matthew 7:12). By asserting the inferiority of Black persons, slavery violates the reality of creation expressed in Acts 17:26: "God has made of one blood all the nations of the earth." McLeod thus embraces the biblical account of monogenesis; that is, that all people descend from an original couple, Adam and Eve. This had been the accepted orthodoxy throughout Jewish and Christian history.

Slavery, says McLeod, clearly violates four of the Ten Commandments. The fifth requires that children obey their parents "in the Lord," but under slavery, children are taught to obey the master rather than their parents in everything. The sixth not only prohibits taking the life of another, but by implication requires people to preserve and protect the lives of others. Under slavery, however, the lives of the slaves are at the absolute whim of the master, despite the provisions of the states' Slave Codes that certain arbitrary killings of slaves were punishable. The lives of slaves were held to be of no value beyond their appraised or market price. The eighth commandment, which prohibits stealing, is violated because slavery robs the slave of the fruit of his labor, except for whatever food and clothing is granted by the master. Finally, he says, the tenth commandment, which forbids covetousness, is violated because the slave owner is avaricious: he employs servants without wages, enriches himself from the coerced labor of others, and sells his slaves to the highest bidder for financial gain.

McLeod also says that slavery contradicts the gospel of free grace, that is, the slaves are in the same position—in sin—and the same need—for salvation—as the owners. There is no use pretending that the owner is morally better than the slave; they are brothers, equal in their standing before God.

Finally, McLeod identifies six pernicious consequences of the slave system:

1. It destroys the finer feelings of people and hardens their hearts to cruelty and blood. He quotes Thomas Jefferson's *Notes on the State of Virginia* to this effect.

2. It debases part of the human race by degrading them physically and psychologically and destroys their mental powers by refusing them education and denying them opportunity to exercise judgment.

3. It encourages licentiousness and debauchery when slaves are encouraged or required to "be fruitful and multiply" but are not permitted to marry.

4. It destroys natural affections when slave owners father children by their slave women and then deny paternity, raise these children as slaves, and even sell them.

5. The domestic tyranny of the masters is a training ground for civil tyranny, because owners are totally unaccustomed to being thwarted or disobeyed.

6. Sooner or later, slavery brings down the judgment of God on societies and individuals.

McLeod also answers a number of commonly offered arguments in favor of slavery. The first was the claim that Africans are inherently inferior to Americans and Europeans, and "it is just" for the more intelligent to rule the less intelligent. They are miserable in Africa anyway, the reasoning went, and are no worse off being enslaved here. But, says McLeod, the inferiority of the Black race is "greatly exaggerated" and is the result of circumstances—i.e., they have been willfully and forcefully held in ignorance. Even if they *were* less intelligent, which he emphatically rejects, it does not follow that they should be enslaved; they still would have the same fundamental God-given rights to liberty and self-determination.

The second and closely related argument was that Black people are a different race of people from white people; they clearly cannot be descended from the same pair, Adam and Eve. McLeod here emphasizes his belief in monogenesis. The belief that some races of mankind are superior or inferior must, perforce, depend on a theory of polygenesis—descent from multiple original couples. As early as 1774, the Englishman Edward Long had developed a racial hierarchy in which native Africans were situated between Europeans and orangutans. As late as 1906, a Congolese "Pygmy" named Ota Benga was placed in a cage in the Bronx Zoo and labeled "the missing link" between orangutans and "the white race."[21]

In the mid-nineteenth century, this argument was expanded into "scientific racism." Samuel George Morton, "the father of physical anthropology," measured the cranial capacities of hundreds of skulls and found that on average, Caucasians had the largest brain cavities and Africans and Australian aborigines the smallest. On this and other bases, Morton concluded that the races of mankind were different species.[22] As the most readily available response for antislavery Christians, McLeod pointed first to Acts 17:26: God "has made from one man every nation of mankind to live on the face of all the earth, having determined allotted periods and the boundaries of their dwelling place." McLeod then points out that there are individual differences within every species. Climate, diet, and other variables, particularly over a long span of time, explain the differences observed among people. "[A]gain, he turns to the device of reversing the argument: if it were true, it would prove too much, as any nation might claim superiority of rank over any other, and once again, violence would be the only basis for law."

Third, a popular and seemingly biblical argument in favor of slavery was that Black people were cursed because they are descendants of Ham, according to the account of Noah's family in the book of Genesis. McLeod makes short work of this argument. First, the curse was directed to Canaan, the son of Ham, according to Genesis 9:25: "Cursed be Canaan! The lowest of slaves will he be to his brothers." Even if Africans had been descended from Ham, they were almost certainly not descended from Canaan, because Genesis 10:19 identifies their territory as Syria–Palestine. That is, they were among the nations expelled from the Promised Land when the Israelites conquered it. There is nothing in the biblical account to indicate that *all* of Canaan's descendants were condemned to perpetual and eternal slavery. Moreover, the curse was a prediction and not a rule of duty, according to McLeod. God has given many people over to slavery in the course of history, but the tyrants and murderers who ruled over them—such as Egypt, Babylon, and Rome—were held accountable by God. Finally, if the "curse of Ham" argument were to hold water, every slaveholder would need somehow to prove that he is descended from Shem or Japheth and not from Ham in order to avoid being enslaved himself.[23]

The fourth objection to ending American slavery was that God permitted the ancient Israelites to hold slaves. True enough, answers McLeod; but quite irrelevant to modern nations and the modern style of slavery, which is absolute and permanent. Like other ancient peoples, under the prevailing customs of war, the Hebrews could use prisoners captured during war as slaves. Israelites themselves could be sold into servitude under two conditions: theft and insolvency. Even a thief could not be sold into servitude so long as he had enough property to repay the theft. If an Israelite was impoverished and indebted, he could be forced into servitude, but not "with rigour" or "ruthlessly"

(Leviticus 25:43, 46, 53). In either case, the maximum term of service was six years, and when a debtor was set free, his master was required to give him some livestock to go into business again (Deuteronomy 15:12-15). Foreigners could be acquired as slaves, but the same laws were applied to them that applied to the Hebrews: "one manner of law as well for the stranger as for one of your own country" (Leviticus 24:20; 25:35). In the case of the Canaanite tribes who were displaced by the Israelites when they claimed the Promised Land, the Israelites were specifically appointed to punish those peoples for their sins. God's command was to exterminate them; but if they voluntarily submitted, they were only reduced to servitude, and the Israelites were forbidden to abuse them—"use them harshly" (Exodus 21:26).

Additionally, McLeod continues, the Israelites had no right to send ships to distant lands to steal or buy, chain, and torture people who had done them no harm. They had no precedent for that, no divine approval, and no instances in their history.[24] Therefore, he concludes, even if the kind of slavery in the Old Testament had been the same as that visited on Africans in the modern era, "the practice of modern nations would remain unjustifiable."

The fifth objection offered by the advocates of slavery was that in the New Testament, Christ and the Apostles do not condemn slavery as it existed under Greek and Roman law. That, says McLeod, is untrue as well as irrelevant. Untrue because Paul, in 1 Timothy 1:10, condemns "man-stealers," often properly translated "slave traders." In 1 Corinthians 7:21, he advises slaves to procure their freedom if they can; but if not, to continue patiently. In Colossians 4:1, he directs masters to treat their servants justly, mercifully, and with fair wages. Note that the proslavery argument that slaveholding is moral because it is not condemned in the New Testament is at best an argument from silence. The argument is irrelevant because it would not be reasonable to construct a system of ethics upon all the realities of Roman society that are not expressly condemned in Scripture. The unspeakable cruelties of Nero, for example, are not specifically prohibited but were not for that reason ethically permissible.

A sixth argument in favor of slavery said, in effect, "Yes, the practice is wrong; but here they are. We found them as slaves, and we can't do anything about it." McLeod rephrases the argument to make its absurdity plain: these advocates say, "A long continuance of evil-doing will change the nature of wrong into right." If the first stealer and the first buyer sinned in enslaving their victims, the one who continues the crime continues the guilt. The best reparation is to set the slave free at once. The slave owner cannot afford this financially; therefore, count the wages earned by a slave's labor, and when he has earned enough to pay the purchase price with interest, set him free and pay him just wages as long as he chooses to continue to work for you.

Christians, says McLeod, have a moral responsibility to empathize with the sufferings of the slaves; this is not a situation to be contemplated coolly or merely theoretically. The slaves are our brothers, human beings who are to be commended to the God of mercy and comfort. Christians must do anything in their power to alleviate the sorrows of the slaves. Ministers have a duty to preach and teach on the subject, speaking the truth in apt circumstances.

Legislators and statesmen must exercise their responsibilities to work quickly to correct this evil practice. McLeod does not underestimate the challenges:

> Every plan is accompanied with difficulties. To export them to Africa would be cruel. To establish them in a separate colony would be dangerous. To give them their liberty, and incorporate them with the whites, would be more so. The sins of the fathers, it is to be feared, will be visited on their children. But it is more safe to adopt any one of those plans than continue the evil. By a national repenting and forsaking, we may find mercy.[25]

At the beginning of the century, then, McLeod dismisses the idea of colonization. The many deaths from subtropical diseases among those "repatriated" to Africa bear out his first point. His statement that establishing freed slaves in a separate colony "would be dangerous" must be understood in McLeod's terms. Many of his contemporaries believed that the Black race was not mentally or emotionally capable of operating a political entity. Considering his other statements about Black persons, that does not seem a feasible explanation for McLeod. Rather, as Covenanters were to demonstrate before, during, and after the Civil War, slaves who had been held down in ignorance and illiteracy needed education before attacking broader societal challenges such as public administration. As for incorporating them into a predominately Caucasian society at that point, McLeod's concern is clearly based not on Jefferson's fear of racial mixing but rather on the expectation that the freed slaves might exact well-deserved revenge on their former masters and their children.

When the Reformed Presbyterian Synod endorsed the American Colonization Society in 1826, they appeared to support the first feasible way to work in concert with others toward the eventual elimination of slavery. Within a decade, it was clear that the Synod's trust was misplaced. Most American Black people did not want to leave the land where they had been raised; emigration of Black people was not truly voluntary; slave owners were not, in general, disposed to free their slaves for emigration or any other purpose; and the reason that proslavery people encouraged colonization was to remove the dangerous examples and influences of Black freemen to prevent their influencing the slaves to dissatisfaction or rebellion. Realizing all this, the Synod of 1836 recommitted itself to Alexander McLeod's preferred vision: immediate emancipation.[26]

Throughout the antislavery era, Reformed Presbyterians consistently emphasized the biblical/theological theme that slavery is a sin. An unsigned essay in *The Reformed Presbyterian* in 1838, titled "Slavery in the United States a National Sin," argues that because holding people in slavery is sinful, and because it is protected by the federal Constitution, the whole nation is guilty, that is, all the citizens who belong to a nation so constituted. The slave states are guilty of slavery, and because the free states have joined with them in the federal Constitution, they too are guilty. True, the essay argued, the union did not create slavery, but they gave it national sanction. The reasoning is simple and logical: "If it is wrong for an individual to hold slaves, it is wrong for a state to permit him to do so....But, if it is wrong for a state, it is equally wrong for a number of states to recognize it, in their national confederacy." Moreover, the continuing admission of slave states makes the sin a national one. Slavery in the District of Columbia cannot be blamed on a state; it is the act of the national government. When opponents of slavery argue the sinfulness of slavery, many of its proponents turn not to defend against this charge but to fall back on its constitutionality, a redoubt from behind that they are able to resist every attack.[27]

Covenanter Theory of the State

Upon reading the views of McLeod and other Reformed Presbyterians who addressed such social issues as slavery, the twenty-first-century reader is conditioned to react against the language of "sin," "evil," and "judgment" and of "wicked" rulers as being theocratic. But such language is based soundly in a distinctive political theory with roots in Reformation Scotland. In modern popular rhetoric, *theocracy* is defined as "government by clergy," although the correct term for the latter would be *hierocracy*. This misuse of *theocracy* conjures up images of inquisitions, witch trials, and the imposition of Old Testament laws.[28] Were the abolitionists, and the Reformed Presbyterians, in particular, theocratic? In today's popular sense of the word, no. Nor would they have been comfortable with today's dominion theology or Christian reconstructionism.[29]

Theocracy, however, has several legitimate meanings. At root, it means *a state that is thought to be ruled by a sovereign God or gods.* The term has not been rigorously defined, essentially because it does not specify a governmental system or structure parallel to monarchy, oligarchy, or democracy. Instead, it "designates a certain kind of placement of the ultimate source of state authority, regardless of the form of government."[30] Covenanter political theory, particularly articulated in Samuel Rutherford's *Lex, Rex* (1644), has tended to embrace democracy or republicanism because those forms better comport with scriptural principles about human nature and the need for mutual accountability. Covenanters did not have positive experiences with kings who claimed to rule by divine right and thus to be above correction or restraint. Rather, Reformed Presbyterians believed that every government must acknowledge the authority and law of Jesus Christ in its foundation (constitution) and seek to make its laws conform to the will of God, but that church and state each must pursue its God-given functions under God, free of control by the other.[31]

Why, then, did they place such strong emphasis on slavery as a national *sin?* Why did they so strongly criticize U.S. presidents who were not Christian believers? Is there a sense in which they could be called theocrats?

From their beginnings, Covenanters laid particular stress on the Christian doctrine of "the mediatorial dominion of Christ." In this view, Christ was held to be the supreme ruler of the world in two different senses. First, as the Creator and a member of the Trinity, his authority is part of his nature, that is, original and underived. Second, because of Christ's work as the God-man intermediary and the redeemer of mankind, God the Father had *appointed* him ruler of all creation. Therefore, the laws and the magistrates must govern in conformity with his principles (the principles of Scripture), but it does not authorize them to control the church or to impose Christianity on its citizens.[32] As noted, this doctrine does not support or require a particular form of civil government, least of all a hierocracy. The denomination's current statement accurately summarizes their historic theology of the State:

> God has given the exercise of all authority to the Lord Jesus Christ. Christ is the Divine Lawgiver, Governor and Judge. His will concerning the purpose of civil government and the principles regarding its functions and operation are revealed in the written Word of God. The Holy Spirit enables even unregenerate rulers to fulfill their proper functions. A true recognition of the authority and law of Christ in national life can only be the fruit of the Spirit's regenerating power in the lives of individuals.[33]

That is to say that Christ, as the Mediator between God and man, is *at present* the supreme ruler (governor) of all nations, whether they acknowledge that fact or not. Even rulers who are non-believers can function properly in their civil capacities; for example, establish and enforce laws that defend the nation, protect the poor and powerless, and maintain justice. Recognition of the supremacy of Christ and of Divine Law cannot be imposed by coercion or other human action, however, but will happen only by the Holy Spirit's acting to regenerate (convert) a majority of the citizens.

This doctrine was the bedrock upon which Covenanter antislavery activity was predicated. They were calling the United States to honor Christ by obeying what Scripture teaches about slavery.

The Sin of Racism

For many on all sides of the controversy, the question of slavery and the question of race were inseparable.[34] That is, if (as appeared to literalists) the Bible justified slavery, then it was clear to them that the Black people were the race suitable for enslavement. But the long history of the Covenanters showed that for them the underlying, fundamental issue was not slavery but freedom.

Their ancestors had been denied freedom in Scotland, more recent ancestors had fought for freedom in America, and, in the plan of God, freedom was the norm for human life. Anything that prevented human beings from freedom was therefore sin and to be opposed, whether religious oppression, political oppression, or physical and economic bondage. The principle that they expressed—that "man cannot hold ownership in man"—was held to be true regardless of skin tone, intellectual ability, or any other consideration. That those who were enslaved in the United States were of African descent was obvious, but it was not central to the Reformed Presbyterians' antislavery argument.

The Reformed Presbyterian argument against racism relied heavily on points that Alexander McLeod had argued in 1802, one of which was the creation account in Genesis and Paul's statement in Acts 17:26, "God hath made of one blood all the nations of the earth." The corollary was that therefore, all people are brothers, all created by the same God and given the same fundamental rights and responsibilities. This left no room for enslaving one race, no room for enslaving any race in perpetuity, and no justification for either shame or arrogance about one's race or national origin.

While it would be folly to pretend that individual Reformed Presbyterians were never guilty of holding racist views or of denigrating African Americans or other minorities, it is remarkable how often the nineteenth-century Covenanter sources specifically repudiate such views and denounce them as sinful, just as slavery is sinful. This was manifested in behavior as well in principle. Rev. Hugh Park McClurkin, born in 1821 near Rocky Creek in Chester County, South Carolina, recalled his boyhood:

> Our fathers abounded in love. They were known and read of all men as fast friends of the slaves. My father's house was a rendezvous for the colored people, especially on Saturday night. They came on their way to 'wife's house' to get my father to take them on horse-back part of the way, particularly if the creeks were high. During the time their masters allowed them to work for themselves they made [corn-] husk collars for horses and mules ([farmers] seldom had any other kind in those days), also baskets, in which the cotton was picked; and on Saturday night they brought loads of these to my father's house, that he might sell them.[35]

After describing how "Mass' Donnelly" (Rev. Thomas Donnelly) was loved by the slaves in the area for his personal qualities as well as his fearless criticism of the slave owners, he continues:

> On one occasion [when a small boy] I was frightened by the noisy demonstrations of a very black woman and man; but when the

man learned it from my father, he came kindly to me, laid his hand on my head, and said, "God bless you, my little child; if all the white folks were 'feard of us as you are, it would be good times for us poor black folks." He uttered this with tears rolling down from his big white eyes over very black cheeks. He then said, he hoped "the time would come afore long, when poor black folks would be *people*, just like white folks, and not be treated as cows or mules, and when white folks would work for themselves." This forever removed from me all fear of colored folks, and made me a lover of them. This same man was owned by Rev. John Hemphill of the A[ssociate] R[eformed] [Presbyterian] Church...[36]

One of the most emphatic opponents of the sin of racial prejudice was Rev. James R. Willson. While he was pastor at Coldenham, New York, the congregation included several families of free Black individuals. He wrote of knowing Black citizens in the area who were "not only citizens, but men of property, morality, and intelligence, highly respected by their white neighbors." He was glad to see them join at the communion tables of Northern churches.[37] The first Black man to join that congregation was Jephtha Williams. When he died in 1851, he had been a member for thirty-two years, and "his conversation, prayer, and example, have been blessed of God to bring into the church more than sixty souls of his coloured brethren, and thirteen families." Part of the reason he left the Goodwill Presbyterian Church to join the Covenanter congregation was his discovery that Black congregants could be buried in the Coldenham churchyard, unlike the Goodwill church.[38] The relevance of Williams's decision is shown in *The Covenanter* magazine's reprinting with approval a remark from the *National Era* that "with the prejudice against free people of color, no freed Negro could gain self-confidence."[39] The Coldenham assembly evidently included enough members whom Williams judged to be without prejudice that he was able to join the church with enthusiasm.

Willson acted promptly to stamp out prejudice when it appeared. In late 1839, the Coldenham consistory (Session) adopted a require-ment that all of the Black worshipers sit in the balcony during services, and Willson reacted vigorously. A verbal tongue lashing was followed by a written statement of "Reasons of Protest," which employed both reasoning and biblical argument. He enumerated thirteen reasons why their action was sinful.

First, he said, "You deprive the coloured members of a right that God has given them." He quoted Ephesians 2:6 and 9: "You are no more strangers and foreigners." Second, "You dishonor the adopted sons and daughters of the Almighty." Third, "You dishonor Christ. He admits them to sit at his communion table and yet you dishonor him by your act declaring that those who eat and drink with Him shall not sit on the same floor with you, lest you be defiled. What! Christ's guests defile you!"

The consistory's resolution, he claimed, "is in favor of slavery." If the church may deprive Black persons of *any* of the equal rights that God has given to them, then the state may likewise deprive them of *all* their rights. In addition, he said, "The slave holder despises them and enslaves them because they are black; you despise them and deprive them of a seat below because they are black." In a similar vein, the consistory "look on them with contempt because they are black, contrary to the entreaty of the spouse in the Song [of Songs, 1:6]."

In the seventh place, he claimed that the consistory was guilty of overreaching by trying to "prescribe what shall not and what shall be preached."

Eighth, he said, the action was cruel. The elderly, as well as infirm Black mothers and their babies, would not be able to sit near the stove and so would be unable to attend church in bad weather. Ninth, the action was "altogether unprecedented," by which he obviously meant "in this congregation" or "in this denomination." The major American denominations provided ample precedent in both the South and the North, but Willson was clearly framing the argument to isolate his opponents.

In the tenth place, Willson wrote, the text of the resolution might be interpreted to prevent Black applicants from sitting beside white applicants to be examined for communion.

Eleventh, the resolution was offensive to other Reformed Presbyterian congregations. He cited First New York congregation, where there was no racial segregation, and asked, "Are you richer, more refined, more tasteful, more delicate, more holy than they?"

Twelfth, because "notorious sinners" might sit on the main floor if only they are white, the consistory was giving more honor to the ungodly than to followers of Christ.

Finally, Willson alluded to the discussion in the consistory meeting, citing a comment that the "the peace of the congregation would be disturbed" if Black worshipers were allowed to continue sitting on the main floor. "Is that God's peace in his church which is procured by depriving the disciples of Christ of their rights?" he asked. "Are all the poor, who do not pay much into your coffers, to be trodden down because of their poverty?"[40]

At or near the same time, Willson began to write an undated essay titled "The Liberia of the Sanctuary," which does not appear to have been completed or published. It covers much the same ground as his protest against the act of the Coldenham Session. He used Liberia as a metaphor for the plan in "some" (unnamed!) white churches to banish Black people to the balcony, making clear his low opinion of the motives and purposes behind the American Colonization Society. He called racially segregated communion tables a "Negro Botany Bay," a reference to the English penal colony in Australia. He added, "This is not done in any Reformed Presbyterian congregation. The coloured worshipers happily sit among the white people in the 1st and 2nd Reformed Presbyterian [churches] in the city of New York."[41]

An additional charge that he brought against segregation in the church is, "You charge [accuse] God foolishly. Who made your brethren black? It was the God that made both you and them." He mocks the excuse that integrated seating might offend some people. "Who?" he asked. "The profane drunken rabble who have made the mobs…[and] the purse-proud, haughty formalists." Should the church really alter its biblical principles to avoid displeasing such people?[42]

The record contains nothing further about relegating Black worshipers to the balcony.

The mid-1840s found Willson teaching in the Reformed Presbyterian Theological Seminary, then located in Cincinnati. Consistent with the denomination's position and Willson's convictions, the tiny seminary had a racially integrated student body, in the person of Charles L. Williams, a son of the Coldenham congregation. Black students generally had little opportunity for formal education, even in the North; a professional school with a racially integrated student body was highly unusual in 1845.[43]

James R. W. Sloane

Perhaps the most capable and respected Covenanter spokesman in the generation after James R. Willson was James Renwick Willson Sloane, born in 1823 in Topsham, Vermont, and raised near Cadiz, Ohio, and Coulterville, Illinois. After graduating from Jefferson

College in Canonsburg, Pennsylvania, he taught school in Kentucky, acquiring firsthand experience with the culture of the slave states. He soon returned to Ohio and graduated from the Reformed Presbyterian Theological Seminary (at that time located in Northwood, Logan County, Ohio).

After serving as president of Richmond College and then of Geneva College, and then a short term as pastor of Rushsylvania RP congregation, he was called to pastor the Third New York congregation and served there from 1856–1868. Although his pulpit skills were highly regarded in Ohio circles, it was in New York that he came to attention on the national stage, both as a leading preacher in the city and as a fearless abolitionist. His sermons were published or summarized in the *New York Times* and the *Tribune*, and as a speaker he often shared the platform with other leading abolitionists, including William Lloyd Garrison, Wendell Phillips, Henry Ward Beecher, and George B. Cheever.[44] He was not a flamboyant orator, but the power of his stage presence is illustrated in an incident at Cooper Union in 1859.

After the execution of John Brown in Virginia, abolitionists in New York and New England began a fund for the benefit of Brown's widow and surviving children. They held a large meeting on December 15 for this purpose. Cheever spoke first, and almost immediately proslavery protesters began to shout, hoot, and hiss, eliciting counter cheers. Thirty policemen in the hall were unable to control the situation. Just as Cheever was closing, an additional seventy-five policemen arrived and spread around the hall. Wendell Phillips was the next speaker and was able to complete his remarks. He was followed by Rev. Hiram Mattison, a Methodist pastor who because of poor health was unable to make his voice heard above the din of the hall. Sloane was the final speaker and the *New York Tribune* reported, "The Rev. J. R. W. Sloane came forward; and in the course of his address he succeeded, by describing the characteristics of the turbulent element which had disturbed the meeting, in quieting the rioters, and, in fact, caused many of them to *hang their heads, and leave the room!*"[45]

While Sloane seems to have published no books, a number of his sermons and other speeches were published, which preserve the public record of one of the most capable Covenanter spokesmen for the cause of the slaves.

Only about a year after coming to New York, Sloane was invited to give the address at the 1857 annual meeting of the New York Anti-

Slavery Society. Under the title "Slavery in Church and State," he dealt chiefly with the influence of slavery in the nation and in many of the churches. In an uncharacteristically colloquial attack, he referred to "the miserable booby [sic] theology of the slaveholding churches."[46] He explained the sharpness of this attack as a reflection of the contempt he had heard, even among slaveholders in Kentucky, for ministers who attempt to justify slavery on the basis of the Bible. He used both biblical and classical allusions in order to transition to discussing some of the effects of slavery on the state:

> When the founders of this nation gave [slavery] a place in the government, they sowed the wind that we might reap the whirlwind. Its vine is of the vine of Sodom and the fields of Gomorrah; its grapes are grapes of gall, and its clusters bitter. The dragon's teeth have produced a crop of armed men. What has this system done for the American people that they should so love and cherish it? It has turned many of the most fertile and attractive portions of our country into a barren waste. It has covered the vast domain over which it extends with a fearful mental, moral, and spiritual darkness....It has degraded the poor white population of the South to the level of the slaves themselves. It has corrupted the church, deprived it to a very great extent of its moral power...[47]

Sloane also attacks the press and politicians for the influence of the Slave Power in stifling opponents and muting any negative discussion of the peculiar institution. Yet, he says, the politicians at any rate can do nothing about it because as a condition of public service they have taken an oath to support the Constitution, which clearly provides the legal foundation for slavery. The slaveholding members of Congress, he says, are at least consistent, while the Free Soil senators and representatives are not. So deeply is slavery embedded in the Constitution that

> Slavery is the central power of the system; the attractive and radiating centre of the entire influence of the country. It has sunk its roots deeply into the national soil; extended its boughs from ocean to ocean, while the tree of Liberty withers and droops and dies under its deadly shadow....It has become the great national disease pervading the entire body politic; preying upon the vitals, tainting all the blood, and threatening the very existence, of the nation...[48]

To talk about simply limiting the spread of slavery, Sloane said, has been worse than idle, because the Slave Power has been busy meanwhile extending its influence. "The North has been made a hunting ground," and with the 1850 repeal of the Missouri Compromise and the Supreme Court's 1857 declaration that the Missouri Compromise was unconstitutional in their Dred Scott decision, "the entire public domain has been thrown open to slavery."[49]

The only way out of the situation, then, is to follow the principles of the Anti-Slavery Society. He begs his listeners to come out of the churches that tolerate slavery and slaveholding, and come out of the federal Union as it stands. That Union is going to be dissolved, and if abolitionists do not dissolve it, it will dissolve itself.

Three years later, on May 29, 1860, Sloane addressed the second annual meeting of the Church Anti-Slavery Society in Tremont Temple, Boston. Taking as his title "The Church and Slavery," Sloane focused on the churches and ministers who defended slavery, rebutting in some detail their arguments. One of the theses advanced by these apologists, as it had been by the Colonization Society, was that slavery provided an opportunity to reach Africans with the Christian gospel. Well, Sloane asks ironically, if slavery is useful for evangelism, why do we not extend its blessings to, say, the Chinese, the Indians, or the Japanese? There were at the time diplomats from Japan visiting in Washington, said Sloane; why not capture and enslave them, and then when they are elderly and unable to work, send them back to Japan to convert their countrymen?[50]

Sloane's next point, noted at the beginning of this chapter, was that "there are no *abuses* of slavery, as there are none of murder, none of adultery..."

A third defense offered on behalf of slavery was that the breaking up of slave families, while it might unfortunately be unavoidable at times, was rare. On the contrary, said Sloane: it is an essential element of the system. If masters were unable to sell men, women, and children separately, the market would collapse and the system be rendered unworkable. Of his experiences during several years in the South, he says, "I found no plantations with a dozen or more slaves which were not made up of fragments of families." In slavery, he pointed out, the obligations of family relationships—husband and wife, parent and child—are impossible to perform. The very nature of the slave system, then, requires constant trampling on the seventh commandment, which prohibits adultery.[51] Finally, Sloane pointed to

The Great Hall of Cooper Institute (today Cooper Union) was the scene of a major disturbance in 1859, when J. R. W. Sloane calmed a crowd gathered to benefit the family of John Brown. (Wikimedia Commons, public domain.)

Dred Scott was a slave who sued for his freedom. The court instead ruled that he was not a citizen of the United States and had no right to sue in its courts. The Dred Scott Decision opened many people's eyes to the true evil of slavery.
Image is from 1857. (blackpast.org, public domain.)

the demoralization of the enslaved: "This is the terrible reality that haunts the slave from day to day; his manhood gone, his aspirations all crushed in the birth; no sun of hope rises upon his dark horizon as he looks upon the vista of future years, —slavery for himself and for his children, and children's children, not to one or two or a thousand, but to all generations."[52]

Sloane pointed repeatedly in his work to the complicity of Christian churches in supporting, defending, and perpetuating slavery. As one deeply committed to the cause of the Christian gospel everywhere in the world, he said, "If there is one reason for which more than another, I hate this system, it is the foul disgrace and dishonor which it has brought upon our holy religion."[53]

A parallel address on "The State and Slavery," probably delivered the same year (1860), is one of the most clearly political of Sloane's preserved speeches. He analyzed the sad plight of the nation. The cause is not political or legal, he says, and neither is it Northern radicals versus Southern fire-eaters; rather it is that "we cherish a system at war with all laws of natural justice." Therefore, the remedy does not lie in political parties, or in the election of a Republican president; rather, "The only remedy is to get rid of the mischief." He gave advice to politicians, merchants, editors, and ministers on how to defeat slavery.[54]

At the end of 1860, Sloane preached on "The Character and Influence of Abolitionism," a direct reply to a sermon under the same title that had been given by Rev. Henry Van Dyke of Brooklyn, attacking abolitionists and defending slavery biblically.[55] After objecting to Van Dyke's definition of an abolitionist, Sloane demolished Van Dyke's arguments justifying slavery from the Bible. The Hebrew language, he said, contains no word for slave or slavery in the modern sense, but speaks of servants and bond servants who were to be treated considerately and by the same laws as everyone else. Although slavery was part of the Greco-Roman world, Jesus, he said, clearly preached liberty: "Christ's first sermon was an abolition discourse, from an incendiary publication called the 'Prophecy of Isaiah,' an antislavery book of the Old Testament." Sloane pointed out that slaves were admitted to membership in the church in the Apostolic period, but there is no proof that slaveholders were.[56]

Van Dyke had attacked abolitionists on the ground that they misrepresented and abused the proslavery position. Sloane replies that the misrepresentation and abuse had come from the other side: "Sometimes it has come from dainty hands—pulpit, press, and platform." But all too often, he says, the arguments have been physical, nontheological and nonlogical—antislavery advocates "have been mobbed, hooted, hissed, pelted with unmerchantable eggs, exposed to popular violence, and to every indignity and danger; politically, socially, religiously ostracized; denounced as Infidels, Socialists, Jacobins, and whatever else might be considered odious and contemptible."[57]

It is worth noting that after Van Dyke's death, his sons Henry and Paul compiled a memorial volume, and in the biographical portion felt impelled to offer this explanation for some of their father's actions:

> [A]fter the lapse of a quarter of a century, whatever may be thought of the position that he took, one thing is clear: it was taken honestly...and it was maintained fairly....On two points his position has been misunderstood by some, though never by those who knew him. He was not a pro-slavery man....[H]e never thought that slavery ought to be perpetuated. It is true that he was not in sympathy with the methods of early abolitionism; and he expressed his opposition with frankness. He did not believe that the Bible condemned slavery as a sin in itself, and therefore he would not be forced to say so.[58]

The sermon to which J. R. W. Sloane replied, however, was preached in late 1860, after Lincoln's election, and thus expressed scorn for more than "early abolitionism." Moreover, Van Dyke's arguments that the Bible warrants slaveholding go beyond a mere refusal to state that slavery is sin, since he might theoretically retreat to a position (as others did) that, for example, Scripture is ambiguous on the subject, or that slavery is undesirable for other reasons, or even that slavery is a positive good. Perhaps the Van Dyke sons are more to be commended for filial devotion than for candor.

Almost a year later, and well after the war had begun, Sloane preached a sermon which was printed in full in the *New York Times* the following day.[59] His text was Exodus 5:1: "Thus saith the Lord God of Israel, 'Let my people go,' and his theme was the need for emancipation of the slaves. He drew several parallels between Egypt at the time of Moses and the United States in its contemporary crisis: the prevalence of oppression, solemn warnings and calls to repentance and reformation, and leaders "deaf to every call and every warning." The nation, he says, has the duty to "proclaim the emancipation of the African slaves throughout the United States." He explains four reasons why this ought to be done as soon as possible:

1. It would be an act of justice to the slaves;
2. God has given us a favorable opportunity now;
3. It is "absolutely essential to the preservation of the country"; and
4. "It is necessary in order to secure a moral basis for the war and a claim upon the sympathy of foreign nations."

Sloane points to the impossibility of restoring the *status quo ante bellum*: "Revolutions never go back, and if these States are ever to be restored, it will be as free, and not as slaveholding States. However great the difficulties may be on the side of emancipation, there are absolute impossibilities upon the other." He acknowledged that his first point will not persuade those whose only concern is expediency, and while emancipation ought to be carried out in the name of morality and justice, it is by the grace of God that such men are advocating a correct action although from a wrong motive.

Still later in the war, Sloane's theoretical basis had developed to include what had become perhaps the most common religious rallying cry for the Union side: that Secession and the Confederacy constituted rebellion against God. As George M. Frederickson has noted, "Sermons on the sin of rebellion or revolution outnumbered those on slavery."[60] Because Reformed Presbyterians had always maintained that the U.S. Constitution was sinful in its refusal to acknowledge God or Christ, and that a law contravening God's Word (i.e., slavery) was no proper law, seeing rebellion against the Constitution as sin was not prominent in Covenanter writings. However, in August of 1862, Sloane was invited to give an address to two Literary Societies at his alma mater, Jefferson College, and in the course of that address took up the theme of rebellion as sin.

Although his message "The Three Pillars of a Republic" is cited by Frederickson among a number of antirebellion sermons, it was not a sermon but an academic address expounding a Covenanter view of the nation and the war. The first pillar of a republic, said Sloane, is *religion*, and the U.S. Constitution falls short: "Our government is no more Christian than it is Jewish or Mohammedan." If the United States hopes to come through this rebellion, he said, "I demand—in the name of God I demand—that while attempting to put down the slaveholders' rebellion by force of arms,—that as a means to that end we put down our own rebellion against the Lord and his anointed."[61] The consequences of the nation's rebellion are clearly the judgments of God: "There is for nations, as for individuals, an immutable morality. Any departure from this standard is as sure in the one case as in the other to incur the penalty of the divine judgments."[62] Clearly, Sloane was not among the unthinking admirers of the Constitution.

Sloane's second pillar is *law*. He begins aggressively, "The present rebellion is an infamous revolt against all law, human and divine, and as such should be suppressed at whatever cost of blood and treasure." The Northern states have permitted the South everything that they demanded and "a monopoly of the most honorable and lucrative offices of the State," and now the South "are arrayed in arms against the Constitution which they swore to support and defend." Lest Northerners feel smugly superior, however, he also condemns the "black laws" of the border and free states.

The third pillar of a republic is *liberty*, which is enjoyed in the free but not the slave states. The latter are aristocracies "in which the members take precedence based on the number of human beings that they are able to buy, hold, sell, or breed." The results are to impoverish the soil and "to degrade and madden, brutalize and barbarize, the community which practices the unnatural enormity."[63]

Sloane, in short, regarded the fundamental rebellion to be that of the U.S. Constitution against God and his law, and the rebellion of the Confederate states as essentially an unprovoked act of ingratitude.

The United States is being punished by God for its sins against him, and the Confederacy for its sins against the republic as well as against God. In this way, J. R. W. Sloane was able to combine the two most prominent religious justifications for the war: that rebellion against the Constitution is sin and slavery is sin. Thus the Covenanter Church, strongly evangelical and aggressively nonpolitical, found itself inexorably drawn by its history and theology into the political arguments at the beginning of the war.

7

The Duty to Refuse Compliance

Covenanters and the Underground Railrooad

Early in 1851, Nathan R. Johnston of the Covenanter Church in Cincinnati was deeply involved in one of the most infamous incidents in abolitionist history. Seth Conklin, a white man very active in smuggling fugitive slaves, was guiding the family of Peter Still to freedom. Quaker Levi Coffin had arranged for Johnston to drive them to a safe stop. Johnston accompanied them and spent the night with Conklin and the Still family at the home of elder David Stormont near Princeton, Indiana.

The next day, the fugitives were arrested twenty-three miles north of Vincennes and hurried back to Evansville, on the Ohio River, by a United States Marshal. The slave owner, a man named McKiernan, had come to get them. They took Conklin along with the fugitives on a river boat. Stormont and Johnston, hearing of the arrest, rode quickly to Vincennes but were too late. Johnston then went to Evansville and on down the river until he learned that Conklin's body had been found in the Ohio River near Paducah, "drowned, with his hands and feet in chains, and his skull fractured."

The man who had orchestrated this escape was William Still (1821–1902), a prominent Black abolitionist from Philadelphia and the brother of Peter Still. The plans had been laid with care. Conklin wrote to William Still from Princeton on February 18, 1851, saying that he had traveled two hundred miles to investigate Stormont before making the arrangements with him. He said that no one had ever been lost from Stormont's to Canada, though some had been lost between the Ohio River and Stormont's. "The wolves have never suspected Stormont."[1] This apparently ended at some time, because at one point his life was threatened by proslavery sympathizers. Stormont sat up all night with a rifle while his wife kept a wash boiler of hot water. The next morning, they found that horses had been tied on a nearby hill during the night, but for some reason the riders had not come near the house.[2]

Myth and Reality

The story of the Underground Railroad is one of the most dramatic—and romanticized—in American history. The term refers to a largely informal network of people and houses or other sites that were used to help slaves who escaped from their masters and fled north to freedom. Because slavery had been abolished in Canada (gradually from 1793 and completely in 1834), that was the fugitives' ultimate destination in many cases. Following the Civil War, a skein of legends grew up around this rescue network, aided by the fact that government efforts to enforce the Fugitive Slave Laws had made record keeping dangerous.

A constitutional requirement and three federal statutes created the problem: the Constitution (Article IV, Section 4), the Ordinance of 1787 ("Northwest Ordinance", Article 6), and the Fugitive Slave Acts of 1793 and 1850 required the return of escaped slaves to their owners. Under the terms of these, slaves who escaped to non-slave states were subject to recapture and return, without jury trial and without a right to testify. In addition, anyone who aided a slave in escaping could be fined $500 and imprisoned for a year.[3]

When free states found ways to circumvent or mitigate the Act of 1793, Congress amended it in 1850, requiring federal marshals and deputy marshals to apprehend fugitive slaves. A marshal or deputy who failed to do so was to be fined $1,000 (to go to the owner), and if the fugitive escaped, the marshal or deputy was responsible for the full market value of the slave. Marshals could draft any able-bodied male into a *posse comitatus* and require him to assist in capturing and transporting fugitives. Anyone who hindered recapture, or who rescued or otherwise assisted fugitive slaves, was to be fined $1,000 and imprisoned for six months. Instead of requiring circuit or district judges to sign certificates to send the accused south, special commissioners were appointed. Commissioners before whom owners or their agents appeared received more money ($10) for sending a Black person back to (or into) slavery than for freeing him ($5).[4]

If and when the act was enforced, the consequences were dire, both for the fugitive and for anyone who helped him or her. Thus, not only the escaping slaves but also anyone who helped them were exercising nonviolent civil disobedience and were risking their persons,

Cincinnati, Ohio, RPC members were part of the Underground Railroad. The photo is from The Covenanter Witness *June 18, 1930.*

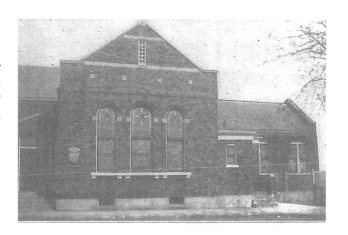

Nathan R. Johnston was an RP minister who worked with Levi Coffin and William Still to help escaping slaves cross the Ohio River as part of the Underground Railroad. He is also the author of Looking Back from the Sunset Land.

William Still was a Black abolitionist from Philadelphia who orchestrated many slaves' escapes, often aided by Covenanters. The portrait is from Looking Back from the Sunset Land *by N. R. Johnston.*

their property, and even their lives in the process. Free Black citizens were subject to kidnapping and sent to servitude. The cards were stacked against all Black people and their friends.

The question was, as Henry David Thoreau saw it, "What is to be done?" He criticized those who refused to take action against slavery:

> There are thousands who are in opinion opposed to slavery and war, who yet in effect do nothing to put an end to them; who, esteeming themselves children of Washington and Franklin, sit down with their hands in their pockets, and say that they know not what to do, and do nothing....What is the price current of an honest man and patriot today? They hesitate, and they regret, and sometimes they petition; but they do nothing in earnest and with effect.[5]

The solution, for many Americans, was the Underground Railroad. Shortly after the war's end, people began to collect narratives and other information about the railroad. Among the earliest publications was William Still's *The Underground Rail Road: A Record of Facts, Authentic Narratives, Letters, Etc. Narrating the Hardships, Hair-breadth Escapes and Death Struggles of the Slaves in their Efforts for Freedom.*[6] While the railroad rapidly assumed a place in American folklore, not until 1898 did a major study by a professional historian appear, Wilbur H. Siebert's *The Underground Railroad from Slavery to Freedom.*[7] Since then historians, novelists, folklore collectors, journalists, and others have published a plethora of materials on the subject, in the course of which fact and fantasy have become commingled. In 1961, Larry Gara's *The Liberty Line: The Legend of the Underground Railroad* began the process of untangling the facts, while maintaining a respect for the *legend* of the railroad as a national saga.[8] As a result, serious studies on it are now more tempered. Much more attention is paid to the primary role of the slaves themselves in escaping; egregious overstatements of the number of fugitives actually aided are more modest; and legends about tunnels, secret rooms, and hair-breadth escapes are more carefully scrutinized. All of this is useful, not only toward a more accurate understanding of what went on, but also in appreciating more fully the genuine accomplishments of both Black and white people in the railroad.

The informal network known as the Underground Railroad arose, without fanfare and essentially by common consent, as a means of hastening the freedom of slaves in the South. It is difficult to assign a date for the organization of the railroad, because the best evidence shows that it was never *organized* in the accepted sense; it simply *emerged* as the slave owners became increasingly aggressive in reclaiming their fleeing property. Many non-slaveholders seem frequently to have ignored the Act of 1793, and, in the North at least, many white people were simply apathetic: they would neither give assistance to runaways nor turn them in to the authorities. With passage of the amended Act as a part of the Compromise of 1850, slave owners were emboldened to demand the return of runaways, and slave catchers could enter and search private property without a warrant.

White sentiment in the North was enraged by the new law and saw in it one more overreaching power play by the slave states; the increased abolition activity in the 1850s was in part a backlash against Southern aggressiveness. The most active years of the Underground Railroad were from 1835 to the beginning of the Civil War. Historians differ in assessing whether the Act of 1850 resulted in more or less railroad activity.

As early as 1793, at least two cases of actual resistance to that year's Fugitive Slave Act occurred, and the number grew each year. Fugitives had been aided before 1818 in New Jersey and eastern Pennsylvania. By 1820, the work had started in Ohio and Indiana. In 1826, the Quaker Levi Coffin left North Carolina, moved to Indiana, and immediately assumed a leading role in the movement. The goal from the beginning was to find safe havens for those who escaped to freedom, and generally this necessitated going to Canada. Since most abolitionists rejected colonization as a solution to slavery, it was with mixed emotions that they helped the newly liberated leave the United States. The federal government was not pleased. Secretary of State Henry Clay lodged formal protests with the Canadian government in 1826 and 1827. Both times, after long delay, the response was that returning the fugitives was out of the question. The British government affirmed the Canadian decision. When fugitives in Cincinnati sent an appeal to Canada for asylum, the reply was:

> Tell the Republicans that we royalists do not know men by their color. Should you come to us, you will be entitled to all the privileges of the rest of Her Majesty's subjects.[9]

A number of those who escaped to the North slipped back into the South in order to rescue their families and even friends. The best known of these is Harriet Tubman, who, following her own escape from slavery in Maryland to Philadelphia, made some thirteen trips back to the South and brought more than seventy slaves to freedom. During the Civil War, she worked for the U.S. Army, first as a cook and nurse, then as a scout and spy. She was the first woman to lead a military operation in the war, which resulted in the rescue of more than 700 Black slaves.

Free Black citizens in the Northern cities built organizations, often called Vigilance Committees, to assist fugitives. William Still served as the corresponding secretary of the Philadelphia Vigilance Committee, and as such he was the agent in transferring a large number of escapees from slavery to freedom. The first chapter in his book *The Underground Rail Road* recounts the ordeal of the family of his own brother Peter Still and the death of Seth Conklin.

A number of prominent Americans rendered aid to fleeing slaves; among others, Siebert mentions William Still, Levi Coffin, Frederick Douglass, Harriet Tubman, Theodore Parker, Thomas Wentworth Higginson, Salmon P. Chase, Thomas Garrett, Thaddeus Stevens, Rutherford B. Hayes, Joshua R. Giddings, Charles Sumner, Richard H. Dana, and Harriet Beecher Stowe.[10] Those who participated in the railroad were frequently snubbed socially and were unwelcome in many churches. Slave hunters with bloodhounds might surround the homes of suspected slave smugglers and watch them for days, and they were authorized to enter the houses by force. Large sums were offered to neighbors to practice espionage on the abolitionists. Slave owners and hunters disguised themselves in efforts to glean local information about fugitives and their helpers.[11]

The "members" of the Underground Railroad were forced to develop and even improvise methods of assisting the fugitives. The escaping slaves followed rivers, canals, railroad tracks, and at times the roads. They often struck out through thick woods, following the North Star or, if that were hidden, the moss on trees. In Virginia, they followed the Appalachian chain. Safe places, called "stations," were in homes, caves, barns, or sheltered spots in the woods, on river banks, or in a multitude of other places. Various methods of communication were devised, such as the call of a hoot owl or a series of knocks or raps on a door or window. Letters were sent ahead of the fugitives at times and of necessity were in veiled language. One example illustrates the point:

Low Moor, May 6, 1859

Mr. C.B.C.

Dear Sir: —By tomorrow evening's mail, you will receive two copies of the 'Irrepressible Conflict' bound in black. After perusal, please forward, and oblige,

Yours truly,
G. W. W.[12]

One very determined Black man had himself boxed up in a shipping carton in 1849 and was sent by wagon and train from Richmond to Philadelphia. Delivered to the Vigilance Committee's office and uncrated, he became an antislavery speaker, known as Henry Box Brown. Others traveled in more mundane transport: under a load of hay, or in a peddler's wagon with a deceptive bottom, or the like. Disguises were common.[13]

The effect of the Underground Railroad was more psychological than otherwise. Of course, owners did lose valuable property, but the railroad was not a major hemorrhage of the slave population.[14] At the same time, many Black men who were capable of leading rebellions escaped instead, and the railroad may thus be accurately called a safety valve for the South. It prompted a large number of Northerners to defy federal laws on the ground that those laws were unjust and offensive and that compassion for fellow human beings and obedience to the Law of God were higher priorities than submission to the law of the United States. It created in the South a fear of the abolitionists and a perhaps exaggerated realization that the Abolition Movement was effective.

Covenanters and the Underground Railroad

Bearing in mind their history, Reformed Presbyterians and others of Scottish and Scots-Irish descent loved liberty and generally gave strong support to the antislavery crusade. Siebert identified some Scottish communities as particularly active in the Underground Railroad, singling out those in Morgan and Logan Counties, Ohio, and in Randolph and Washington Counties, Illinois: "There were some New England colonies in the west where anti-slavery sentiments predominated. These, like some of the religious communities, as those of the Quakers and Covenanters, became well known centres of underground activity." Some of the slaves did not go to Canada but remained in communities where the "presence of Quakers,

Wesleyan Methodists, Covenanters or Free Presbyterians gave them the assurance of safety and assistance."[15]

Describing the operation of the railroad in Illinois, Siebert said, "The few lines known in southwestern Illinois were developed by a few Covenanter communities." Speaking generally of the unhelpful attitude of the churches toward the slaves and free Black citizens, he points to two conspicuous exceptions:

> It is a fact worthy of record in this connection that the teachings of two sects, the Scot[s] Covenanters and the Wesleyan Methodists, did not exclude the negro from the bonds of Christian brotherhood, and where churches of either denomination existed the Road was likely to be found in active operation.[16]

The frequent mention of the Covenanters in Siebert's account is an indication that they were not insignificant in the Underground Railroad. Most of the routes he had discovered were in Ohio, where he had done the majority of his research. There were also extensive lines in Pennsylvania, and some through Indiana, Illinois, Iowa, and even Kansas. Railroad traffic flowed heavily through Philadelphia to New York and thence to Albany and Rochester. A map of known Underground Railroad "stations" matches rather well with the locations of the Covenanter congregations at the time.

Urban Congregations

Large cities such as Boston, New York, Philadelphia, Pittsburgh, and Cincinnati were popular centers of the railroad because fugitives could easily meld into the population. Covenanters in the cities were also active in the operations. N. R. Johnston, at that time the "stated supply" of the Cincinnati congregation, describes one of the successful incidents of their cooperation with Levi Coffin.[17] John L. McFetridge, a Covenanter who worked in a lumber yard in Covington, Kentucky, came to Johnston at church one day, telling him of a group of slaves who had arrived in Covington and wanted help to cross the Ohio River and through the state. Johnston met secretly with one of the slaves, Patterson Randall. "I laid the whole matter," he writes, "before three well-known friends of freedom, viz. Hugh Glasgow, my host (than whom no truer friend of the slave ever walked the streets of Cincinnati), a leading colored business man, and that noble and well-known friend of human rights, Friend Levi Coffin." These four men arranged and carried out the river crossing by boat, as there was no bridge on the Ohio River at Cincinnati until the completion of John Roebling's suspension bridge in 1866. They saw them safely through Cincinnati and seven miles beyond the city to the first railroad station. Johnston and Glasgow went out the next day to see if the slaves were safe, climbing a ladder to a secret room above a double corn crib to visit them. Later the same winter, Coffin asked Johnston to arrange with the Covenanters of Indiana or Illinois to aid in the ill-fated attempt to rescue the family of Peter Still.[18]

In Philadelphia, too, the Covenanters were active. James M. Willson, pastor of First RP Church from 1834 to 1862, was President of the Philadelphia Anti-Slavery Society, and his church was a station on the Underground Railroad. Members who at the time were children later remembered "looking back and up at the balcony during services and seeing a row of black faces peering over the edge of the balcony. This gallery was frequently used as a hiding place for fugitives."[19]

Western Pennsylvania

In western Pennsylvania, one of the Covenanter congregations active in the railroad was Brookland, a rural church in northern Westmoreland County. At one time the pastor, Robert Reed, concealed a fugitive from North Carolina in his study for a week. This fugitive was "almost white"; his father was a planter and congressman. While the fugitive was there, two slave hunters rode past the house, carrying whips. Reed's wife, Mary Walkinshaw Reed, was almost paralyzed with fear. A few nights later, one of the ruling elders, David McElroy, took the fugitive to the home of Alexander White, an elder in the Rehoboth congregation in Jefferson County. Other stations in Westmoreland County included the home of Robert Sproull near Brookland and that of Rev. Robert B. Cannon in Greensburg.[20]

> Mary Walkinshaw, as a girl, saw both colored men and women at her grandfather's home. Her own home became a station for the fugitives on their perilous journey. It was just before the Civil War that Billy Shafer, footsore, hungry, and sick, came to her door. He had walked all the way from the home of Dr. Cannon, in Greensburg, in one day. She took him in and ministered unto him. She held him in her arms when he died. His last words told of his sorrow for the trouble he had caused her, and his gratitude for her kindness. The men of Brookland buried him in the old cemetery.

*Brookland, Pa.,
RPC was home
to Pastor Robert
Reed and Elder
David McElroy,
who helped hide
and transport
fugitive slaves.*

*First RPC of
Philadelphia.
Drawing from
Our Banner
1884.*

*Rehoboth, Pa.,
RPC's elders,
including
Alexander
White, were
active in the
Underground
Railroad.*

He had reached the end of life's journey. Its hardships were over. The land of eternal freedom and rest had been reached.[21]

Covenanter congregations in Lawrence, Mercer, and Crawford counties were also deeply involved. In 1853, Rev. Thomas Hanna became pastor of the Slippery Rock congregation, located at Rose Point. Hanna lived in New Castle and was active in receiving runaway slaves and forwarding them to safe places farther north in Mercer County. Other members involved included Rev. James Blackwood, George W. Boggs, John Love, David and Jane Pattison, Robert and Rachel Speer, and Matthew and Sarah Stewart. Thomas Willson, an elder in the congregation, and his wife, Margaret, farmed near Rose Point and were very active in concealing fugitives and furthering their flight. A number of members lived near Portersville, one of which was George H. Magee, an elder in the church. Magee built a wagon with a double bottom to conceal runaways, and in the basement of his house he built a small room with one door, one window, and a dirt floor. Like many homes in western Pennsylvania, his was on a steep hillside with the front door at the road level; thus, the cellar door(s) led directly out at ground level. His son John Magee later recalled an incident:

> I remember two men, supposed to be slave hunters, being entertained in my father's house overnight, when in the basement there were six slaves being hidden. The wood-burning fireplace was plentifully supplied with fuel, and my mother was carrying provisions and bedding the back way for these people. Two small children were in the group but not a sound came from them.[22]

Beaver County, with a plethora of presbyterians, was a major hub in helping the slaves who came into the state through Washington County and Pittsburgh. Covenanters of the Little Beaver congregation near New Galilee participated actively in the Underground Railroad.

Ohio

The largest and most active center of Underground Railroad activity was Ohio, which with its 358-mile border with Virginia and Kentucky was a natural locus for flights to freedom. The northern and eastern parts of the state were centers of New England activism, and the southern and southwestern parts were dotted with Quakers,

Covenanters, and antislavery immigrants from the South. Siebert points to the particular influence of three colleges that helped foster underground activity in the state: Oberlin College, Western Reserve College, and Geneva College, the last being the college of the Reformed Presbyterian Church.[23]

Northeast of Columbus, in and around the village of Utica, was one of the oldest Covenanter settlements in Ohio.[24] The earliest Covenanter settler was James Dunlap in 1805; in 1809 a society was formed. In 1813, the Covenanter congregation was organized with thirty-five members and James Dunlap and Nathaniel Kirkpatrick as the elders. During the abolition period, one of the routes of the Underground Railroad went through this settlement, and a number of local families were involved. On Main Street directly opposite the Covenanter Church stands a brick home in which were four small secret rooms to conceal fugitives. A mile south of the town was a grist mill, which at the time was owned by Thomas McNaughton, a Covenanter. There was said to be a tunnel from the mill, under the North Fork of Licking River, to a cabin in the woods.[25] A more credible version of the story says simply that the McNaughtons hid fugitive slaves beneath the floorboards of the mill. In Utica, the home of Armour McFarland, pastor from 1837–1853, served as a safe house; the fugitives were concealed in a secret space under the front steps. On a hill east of the town and overlooking the Licking Valley stood the James M. Kirkpatrick farm, while north of town was the Dunlap farm; both of these Covenanter families hid fugitives. In 2009, a local man remembered as a boy playing in a tunnel that reportedly led to the Kirkpatrick farmhouse.[26]

John Calvin Boyd was pastor of the Utica Reformed Presbyterians from 1856 to 1882 and at Sandusky, near Crestline in Crawford County, from 1847 to 1867. He was characterized as a "fearless advocate of the cause of the slave, hazarded his interests and even his life for the overthrow of human slavery." As a young man, he and six brothers had served as conductors on the Underground Railroad in Coshocton County, Ohio.[27]

Possibly the busiest center for Covenanter antislavery activity in Ohio was the village of Northwood in Logan County (not to be confused with the Northwood in suburban Toledo). For many years, fugitive slaves found a safe hiding place in a cave on the farm of Isaac Patterson, approximately two miles west of the village. James Torrance shipped grain and feathers north to Sandusky and could

Members of Little Beaver, Pa., RPC participated in the Underground Railroad.

Pastors at Utica, Ohio, RPC, including Armour McFarland and John Calvin Boyd, were conductors on the Underground Railroad.

New Castle, Pa., RPC and other RP churches nearby had many members who helped escaping slaves.

readily hide runaways in his wagons. Joseph Aiken sheltered slaves in his house.[28] The church's college, Geneva College, was established in Northwood in 1848 and was immediately a hotbed of abolitionism. J. R. W. Sloane, president of the college and later a leading abolitionist preacher in New York, concealed fugitives in the attic of his home. His son, Professor William H. Sloane of Columbia University, later wrote, "The first conscious memory I have is of seeing slaves taken from our garret near midnight, and forwarded towards Sandusky. I also remember the formal, but rather friendly, visitation of the house by the sheriff's posse."[29]

A student of Southern birth wrote he had noticed that a number of Black people from his own locality in Virginia seemed to pass through town, traveling north. Another student from Virginia, when asked why he had not graduated at Geneva, replied, "because they are n*****-lovers."[30]

Both the faculty and the students of Geneva College participated in the railroad work. In 1857, when the Synod was meeting at the college, a wagon load of escapees was being taken from the Patterson cave to the port of Sandusky. Word was spread quietly among the members of Synod, who immediately paused for special prayer for their safety.

Students and other Covenanters smuggled fugitives from Northwood to Sandusky, some ninety miles, by dressing as hunters and concealing the Black slaves in covered wagons. On one occasion, they took thirteen fugitives in two wagons. "They were ostensibly a hunting party of 10 or 12 armed men....The two covered wagons were a 'sanctum sanctorum,' into which no mortal was allowed to peep....The word of command, 'Stand back,' was always respected by those who were unduly intent upon seeing the thirteen deer... brought from the woods of Logan and Hardin counties and being taken to Sandusky."[31]

With such strong abolitionists as the Johnstons, Milligan, J. R. W. Sloane, William Milroy, and J. L. McCartney in the leadership of the college, it was practically impossible for proslavery sentiments to exist.[32]

Indeed, Siebert's list of some 3,000 names of station masters and conductors of the Underground Railroad includes, in every Ohio county having significant Covenanter population, numerous names of members, many from families long known in the denomination. In Logan County, for example, he found Covenanters by the names of Patterson, Johnston, Milligan, Young, Fulton, Trumbull, Jameson, Ritchie, Boyd, Sloane, Day, Forsyth, George, and Elliott, all active in smuggling fugitives and all long-standing Reformed Presbyterian families.

In Muskingum County, Robert Speer of New Concord operated a well-known station west of town on the National Road (now US Route 40). Rev. W. G. Robb, a grandson of Robert Speer, told some tales of the family activities. Slaves were brought in a load of hay from a station twenty miles south and were kept in the hay mow at night. In the morning, Mr. Speer would come to the barn and say, "Well, how many are there for breakfast this morning? Stick your heads out so I can count you." Frightened black faces would slowly appear at the hay mow door. Speer would call, "Nobody gets a bite to eat that isn't counted."

Another report is of a time when a slave hunter appeared at the house when the family were finishing breakfast. Speer invited the guest to stay, which in that era naturally required participation in family worship—and after reading a chapter of Scripture, the family sang the entirety of Psalm 119, giving the fugitives adequate time to escape. A granddaughter of Robert Speer inherited a notebook or list in which Speer had written the names of the fugitives he harbored from 1842–1856; he stopped the list (but not the work) when he learned that some slaves did not give their real names. His tally shows a total of seventy-seven fugitives.[33]

Other Covenanters in the neighborhood who harbored fugitives included John Jamison and James Boyd, along with a number of Seceders (Associate Presbyterians) and even a New School Presbyterian family whose pastor was proslavery.

The contrast between Geneva College at Northwood and Muskingum College at New Concord could hardly have been sharper, largely because the Reformed Presbyterians controlled the former and the much larger Presbyterian church (now the Presbyterian Church in the USA) the latter. Reflecting the divisions in its denomination, the trustees of Muskingum College included both pro- and antislavery advocates, so the college could not speak with one voice on the issue, which of course angered all sides. The president of Muskingum from 1838–1848, Samuel Willson, was firmly proslavery, as was George Junkin, the most prominent Old School Presbyterian minister in Ohio and president of Miami University until 1844.[34] Junkin, incidentally, later became the father-in-law of Thomas J. ("Stonewall") Jackson. In

Professors and students at Geneva College in Northwood, Ohio, were active in the Underground Railroad. The college leadership fostered an atmosphere of antislavery sentimets.

Solomon Ford Kingston, born into a slave family, graduated from Geneva College and was later pastor at Selma, Ala., RPC.

The Geneva College baseball team in 1884–1885 included Solomon Ford Kingston (front row, second to left).

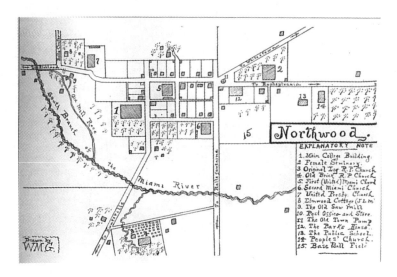

Map of Northwood drawn by W. M. Glasgow in The Geneva Book.

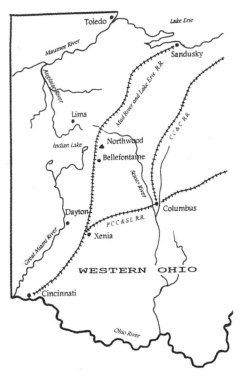

Geneva College was located in Northwood, Ohio. Students and professors often helped runaway slaves escape north to Sandusky, Ohio by masquerading as a hunting party.

1843, the Muskingum trustees prohibited the use of the college hall for "all abolitionists, colonizationalists, and political discussions."[35] When the Republican Party was formed in 1854, the community and even families were rent further among Democrats, Republicans, Free Soilers, and Know Nothings. But this was one battle that did not affect the Reformed Presbyterians, since they did not vote anyway, as part of their protest against the U.S. Constitution.

Indiana

Southern parts of both Indiana and Illinois had been heavily settled by proslavery people from the South, and it appears that whatever assistance was given to fugitives in both areas depended to a great degree on the Covenanters. In addition to David Stormont, another activist at Princeton, Indiana, was John Carithers. David S. Faris wrote in his diary for February 19, 1854: "At church. Mr. J. Little there. Bad news from Princeton. Mr. Carithers being found concealing a man of color."[36]

In Monroe County, the home of the Bethesda congregation near Bloomington, it was the Covenanters who carried on the work of the railroad. "Generally speaking," wrote Professor Henry Lester Smith, "the people of Monroe County were rather luke-warm in regard to escaping slaves....The small group of people that was actively engaged in aiding fugitives came originally from South Carolina. Some of them were influenced to move from South Carolina largely because of the slavery question." These people, of course, were Reformed Presbyterians. "The main motive actuating the majority of those who aided escaping slaves in this community then was a religious motive. That accounts for the persistency with which they carried on their work and for the risks they ran in performing what they considered their duty."[37]

The nearest station south of Bloomington was at Walnut Ridge, near Salem. Here Rev. J. J. McClurkin was active in the work, and Isaiah Reed transported fugitives to Bloomington. North of Bloomington, some Reformed Presbyterians lived near Morgantown, and James Kelso and John Cathcart operated a station there.

At Bloomington, the most active conductors were Thomas Smith, James Clark, Rev. James Faris, John Blair, Samuel Gordon, Samuel Curry, William Curry, Robert Ewing, John Russell, D. S. Irvin, W. C. Smith, Thomas N. Faris, Austin Seward, and John Hite. In his biography of his father, James Faris, D. S. Faris wrote,

Our house was a station on the U. G. R. R. Many poor, panting fugitives found their way to Canada on that line. James Clark, son-in-law of Dr. [Andrew] Todd, who lived on the main road, often brought them. His coarse base [sic] voice grew rather familiar. The call, 'A stranger here!' made in the dead of the night, was well understood. Safe quarters were found in the house, barn, fields or woods, according as they supposed there was danger of search. In one case…I never knew where the negro was secreted; but the hunters rode through the surrounding woods, cracking whips and breaking brush, at a fearful rate, and made it a night to be remembered. The man, in spite of them, got safely through.[38]

In his diary for January 6, 1854, D. S. Faris wrote, "Father started up to Morgantown with a colored man." On February 15, he noted, "A runaway is reported to be near. Probably going on tonight. Helping such is our mite towards the abolition of slavery."[39]

After the war, Rev. David J. Shaw, pastor of Bloomington, wrote an account which is entertaining enough to be quoted at length:

One Sabbath morning Mr. T[homas] Smith…heard from James Clark that a colored man, on his way to the North, had been arrested by some roughs, who were preparing to take him quickly to the South. Fearing that the liberty, if not the life, of a man depended on prompt action, they went to the residence of Judge McDonald, took out writ of habeas corpus, and compelled his captors to come to court and show cause for holding him in custody. The roughs, eager for their prey, employed a lawyer, but the friends of freedom did the same, and the Judge promptly gave the colored man his freedom. But an excited crowd had now gathered, and threatened to mob Messrs. Smith and Clark; one fellow, with horrid oaths, swore he would shoot every Abolitionist. The colored man was again taken, with the pretense that they were his friends, and was for a time deceived by the roughs, until he saw that they were going South; then by a cunning device he got into a corn field, and passing through perils of waters and perils of robbers, at every corner by day and night, at last, almost perished with hunger and watching, he got back among the Covenanters of Bloomington. After a few days' rest, he was conducted to a Quaker settlement many miles farther North. Joseph Hartin, one of the guides, when returning alone, was accosted by one or two men on horse back, who were patrolling the road to catch runaways, and asked if he knew any Abolitionists in these parts. He answered, innocently, "Who are they: Whigs or Democrats?" With a curse the other said, "He is an ignorant Irishman, and knows nothing," and so they let him pass.[40]

Illinois

Siebert found relatively few railroad routes in Illinois, but the routes that did operate were focused in Covenanter communities: the Eden or Bethel congregation near Sparta; Hill Prairie, also at Sparta; Elkhorn congregation near Oakdale; Church Hill near Coulterville; and societies at Nashville and Centralia. In these communities, Covenanter families who took part were Hayes, Moore, Milligan, Todd, McClurkin, Hood, Ramsey, Wylie, and Wilson.[41] Rev. Andrew C. Todd was said to have sheltered as many as seventeen fugitives at once.[42] The depth of commitment of these Covenanters is reflected in the fact that, when President Lincoln issued the first call for volunteers to put down the Rebellion in 1861, thirty-one men of Elkhorn congregation, with pastor A. C. Todd in the lead, immediately formed a company and enlisted. Because the Illinois quota was filled so quickly, the men had to cross to St. Louis, where they were mustered in as Company F, 10th Missouri Volunteer Infantry.

Not all rescues in southern Illinois had happy endings, though none seem to have been as tragic as the Seth Conklin case in Indiana. William Hayes was a Covenanter from Bethel congregation at Eden, having moved there from Galway congregation in Saratoga County, New York. He found in southern Illinois a culture that favored or ignored slavery, although by the terms of the Northwest Ordinance of 1787, the state was to be free of it. Many settlers had come from the South, and if they already owned slaves they were allowed to keep them, particularly if they had immigrated before Illinois became a state in 1818. This was possible because Territorial Governor Arthur St. Clair had ruled that the ordinance was intended only to prevent introducing *new* slaves. Those brought into the territory were listed as "indentured servants."

In 1819, the legislature passed a state "Black Code," and in 1824 the voters of Illinois were asked to approve a new state constitution which, in violation of the Northwest Ordinance, would permit slavery. Randolph County, the home of most of the Covenanter settlements, was one of only a handful of counties that voted in favor of permitting slavery; since they were heavily outvoted, antislavery people there did not find the county a congenial home.

Covenanter William Hayes lived approximately six miles from Andrew Borders, an enslaver who was notorious for mistreating his slaves. One of Borders's slaves, a thirty-one-year-old woman known as Sukey (Susan), bore with it until Borders threatened to sell her three small children "down south." On August 31, 1842, she took her children and ran away, finding her way to the Hayes home. Also with the family was Hannah, the teenage daughter of Sarah, another slave who had previously escaped from the Borders household. Hayes managed to get them on a riverboat, and eventually they landed near Knoxville. In northern Illinois, Hannah, Sukey, and her children were arrested by a justice of the peace and put in the Knox County jail, in accordance with the Fugitive Slave Act. Hayes became involved in a long and costly legal battle to secure the freedom of the five. In Knox County, Borders and his son James were arrested, convicted, and fined for false imprisonment. In the process, Sukey got to Galesburg and found work, but money talks; Borders, with the connivance of the sheriff, spirited the children away. Sukey never saw them again. Back in Randolph County, a vengeful Borders filed a civil suit against William Hayes for "enticing" his property to run away. Because Borders was a major land owner in the county and had cultivated a network of the well-connected, Hayes, as might have been predicted, was convicted and, when he appealed to the Illinois Supreme Court, the decision of the trial court was upheld. Hayes never recovered financially, but nor did he retreat from his antislavery convictions.[43]

Covenanters have historically lived within the laws of their country, so long as those laws did not try to usurp God's law. But, as they had disobeyed ungodly laws in Scotland and Ireland and had joined the rebellion against English tyranny in the colonies, so they did not hesitate to break iniquitous American laws such as the Fugitive Slave Act in order to be obedient to what they believed God's word required. Obedience to God was disobedience to the civil authority. By their involvement in the Underground Railroad, the Covenanters demonstrated not merely the sincerity of their hearts, but their commitment to action. Unlike those castigated by Thoreau, they emphatically did *not* do nothing but "talk" about slavery.

8

Ichabod

The War-clouds Gather

In November 1850, David S. Faris, a Reformed Presbyterian undergraduate at Indiana University, wrote an essay on the recently adopted Fugitive Slave Act, which in retrospect seems almost prescient:

> Alas, patriotic Spirit, thou hast deserted our firesides, thou hast given place to cowardice, and foolishness, in the breasts of many of our countrymen. But although the love of many has waxed cold, and the last spark of liberty has long since been quenched in the bosom of great numbers, by the miserable desire of pleasing Southern nabobs, yet there are many in the North, who are willing to resist this act of abomination, with their lives in their hands to the last extreme—yes, to death.[1]

The Militant South

Simultaneously with the efforts of the Underground Railroad, and despite the fact that the loss of slaves by that route was nowhere near the hemorrhage feared by slave owners, the South renewed its efforts to revive the slave trade from Africa, by either revoking the Constitution's prohibition or working around it by indirect action.

The laws against that trade had not been zealously enforced. For example, from 1804 to 1824, the collector of customs at Bristol, Rhode Island, was Charles Collins, who had been a slave captain, was still part-owner of two slave ships, and was additionally the brother-in-law of James de Wolf, a wealthy slave captain and later a United States senator. Collins, need it be said, was the proverbial fox guarding the henhouse. Moreover, the United States would not permit Britain to search ships flying the American flag (which had been one of the causes of the War of 1812), and so the American flag flew over slave ships, only some of which were actually registered in this country. In

1842, the two countries agreed to create a joint naval patrol off the coast of Africa, but the United States did not maintain its side of the bargain, and the joint operation did not work successfully.[2]

Moses Roney, editor of *The Reformed Presbyterian* magazine, published an essay in August 1837 on "Increase of the African Slave Trade," based on figures reported to the British Parliament. They had reported on January 1, 1836, that "considerable sums of money" had been deposited in mercantile houses in Cuba by American citizens

> for the purchase of negroes stolen, and brought direct from their native land...Never since the establishment of this mixed commission, has the slave trade of the Havana reached such a disgraceful pitch as during the year 1835. By the list we enclose it will be seen that FIFTY slave vessels have safely arrived in this port during the year just expired....There must have been landed upward of 15,000 negroes....In the spring of last year an American agent from Texas purchased in the Havana 250 newly imported Africans at 270 dollars a head. This perhaps would have been scarcely worth mentioning to your lordships, had we not learned that within the last six weeks considerable sums of money have been deposited by American citizens in certain mercantile houses here, for the purpose of making additional purchases of Negroes for Texas....[A] great impulse is given to the illicit traffic of the Havana.[3]

For a time, the South was falling behind in the national race, despite their advantage by the three-fifths rule. The South gained some members, but the Northwest gained more. It was time for the South to act if it were going to remain in power. The annexation of Texas, therefore, became an urgent necessity. A new political coalition emerged so that the South could resume control of the nation's direction. Clearly, if the South were permitted to continue controlling the country, that meant control by slave owners.

> From local magistrate to chief executive the Southern community was governed by the owners of slaves, and the great men whom they chose to speak for the South in Congress or to advise the President and his Cabinet or to sit upon the benches of the federal courts were invariably masters of plantations, trained from early youth to the exercise of authority and accustomed to receive the homage of their neighbors.[4]

From the 1830s, Southerners no longer admitted that slavery was evil or even undesirable. Pressure from abolitionists had led Southern society to circle the wagons and tighten the perimeters. The South became "the solid South;" in fact, the dominant interest-group in the country as a whole. Professional people were dependent on the plantation owners for their salary. Small farmers and mountain people sold their products to the plantation towns. Even the poor white people, whose standard of living was no better than the slaves but who still looked down on enslaved people as inferiors, had largely adopted the same attitude on social issues as had their wealthy neighbors.

The churches, too, had become the allies of the existing economic and social order and had begun to search the Scriptures for a justification of slavery. Both proslavery and antislavery causes developed biblical arguments for their point of view and then hunkered down to protect them.[5]

Because most of the national denominations wanted to preserve their peace and unity, their early pronouncements against slavery (which had never carried compulsion or sanctions anyway) were expunged from their Disciplines. In most cases, they did not actually advocate slavery, but the Methodists, Presbyterians, and others banned discussion of the issue and censured members who spoke out in favor of abolition. In Massachusetts at least, even the Quakers quashed their abolitionists and shut the doors of their meeting houses to antislavery speakers.[6]

Beginning in 1844 and 1845, the Northern churches attempted to correct this tendency. Both the Baptists and Methodists divided into Northern and Southern denominations, but the Presbyterians and Episcopalians continued as before. It is true that in 1837 the Presbyterian Church had divided into Old School and New School branches, and while there were genuine and serious theological issues between the groups, this division was, in part, slavery-related. However, even though the Old School was dominated by those who waffled inconsistently, including Charles Hodge and other faculty of Princeton Seminary, and the New School was influenced by antislavery people, both branches continued to include people on all sides of the slavery question.

Reformed Presbyterians were not unaware of what was happening in the larger Presbyterian world. A petition came before the Synod in 1849 asking "particularly that a remonstrance may be addressed to the principal slave-holding churches." A committee of three was appointed to draft such a remonstrance.[7] These remarks were directed especially at the Presbyterian bodies.

In the New School Presbyterian group, already in 1847, the Ripley Presbytery in Ohio had been formed out of the Chillicothe Presbytery of the New School General Assembly over the issue of slavery, and Judge Stephen C. Stevens of Indiana had called all antislavery Presbyterians to meet in Cincinnati to form an antislavery church. He had concluded that "there is no prospect of prevailing upon the [New School] Assembly to exclude slave-holders," so that more decisive steps were called for.[8] The result was the formation of the Free Presbyterian Church, which originated in 1846 when Rev. John Rankin was forced out of his congregation in Ripley, Ohio, and grew eventually to seventy-two congregations in seven presbyteries.[9]

As the South solidified its position, the North was also developing a sectional unity, especially in regard to the threatened expansion of slavery. The North was worried by the prospect of the annexation of Texas, both because slavery was legal there and because slaves were smuggled from there into Louisiana and Arkansas. Some in the South proposed dividing the huge tract into five states. Some in the East threatened secession if Texas were annexed. Moreover, many in the North were angered when, in 1836, the House of Representatives adopted its "gag rule"—to lay upon the table without debate all petitions that dealt with slavery. John Quincy Adams, not personally in favor of abolitionism, was the principal congressman who labored against that rule until it was abolished in 1844.

In 1847 Charles Sumner, Horace Greeley, William H. Seward, and Salmon P. Chase led the effort to ensure that slavery would not profit from the war with Mexico. The House of Representatives adopted the "Wilmot Proviso," which would prohibit slavery in any territory acquired as a result of that war, but it was defeated in the slave-owner-controlled Senate. This initiated a political struggle against slavery. Congress had reached an impasse. When California asked for admission as a non-slave state, the South called a convention to meet at Nashville in June 1850, to prepare an ultimatum to Congress. The South would secede if the new Southwest were not preserved as slave territory.

The Synod of the Reformed Presbyterian Church in 1847 had also condemned the Mexican War as "an unjust and bloody war against a neighboring republic, with the evident intention of enlarging the slaveholding power of the United States."[10] In its "Causes of Fasting," the Synod of 1849 resolved that

The sin of slavery is a subject to us of the deepest sorrow and humiliation. The captive yet mourns in his chains, and a mighty nation fastens them upon him. Man, by national authority and under national protection, trades in the bodies and souls of men: thus making merchandise of the image of God; and the manstealer is exalted to the high place of power; and the area of slavery is sought to be extended. In the guilt of our nation we are partakers. Woe unto us that we have sinned.[11]

Given their views on slavery, it is unsurprising to find them opposed to Henry Clay, "the Great Compromiser," and his compromise of 1850. They could see in that compromise only defeat for the Abolition Movement and victory for the Slave Power.

The Compromise of 1850

The compromise proposed by Henry Clay in order to break the impasse in Congress and avoid the threat of civil war was embedded in five Acts:

1. California was admitted to the Union with a constitution banning slavery;
2. Deseret (Utah) and New Mexico were allowed to form territorial governments and the state question of slavery was left to popular sovereignty;
3. Texas was paid $10 million to settle her claims against New Mexico and to pay its debts for the Mexican War;
4. The slave trade (but not slavery) was abolished in the District of Columbia;
5. A new Fugitive Slave Law greatly strengthened the rights of slave owners to retrieve fugitives who escaped to the North.

John C. Calhoun led the extremists of the South in opposition to the compromise. He demanded the admission of California as a slave state and the opening of New Mexico territory for slavery. He would have accepted an extension of the line to the Pacific prescribed in the Missouri Compromise. If he could not get that, he intended to propose an amendment to the federal Constitution to create a dual presidency in which each section would always have a veto over the legislation of Congress.[12] Naturally enough, the abolitionists objected both to Clay's compromise and Calhoun's response. But Daniel Webster, who thought the abolitionists too radical, made his famous speech of March 7, and won the day for Clay and compromise. Webster had never been strong on democracy, and in his old age, sympathized even more with the property interests of the South. To the conservatives of the North he was now "the Godlike Webster," but to the radical abolitionists his name was "Ichabod" (literally, "no glory"), as the Quaker abolitionist John Greenleaf Whittier dubbed him in his poem by that title.

> So fallen! so lost! the light withdrawn
> Which once he wore!
> The glory from his gray hairs gone
> Forevermore!
>
> Revile him not,—the Tempter hath
> A snare for all; And pitying tears,
> not scorn and wrath,
> Befit his fall!
>
> O, dumb be passion's stormy rage,
> When he who might
> Have lighted up and led his age,
> Falls back in night.
>
> Scorn! would the angels laugh, to mark
> A bright soul driven,
> Fiend-goaded, down the endless dark,
> From hope and heaven!
>
> Let not the land once proud of him
> Insult him now,
> Nor brand with deeper shame his dim,
> Dishonored brow.
>
> But let its humbled sons, instead,
> From sea to lake,
> A long lament, as for the dead,
> In sadness make.
>
> Of all we loved and honored, naught
> Save power remains,—

A fallen angel's pride of thought,
Still strong in chains.

All else is gone; from those great eyes
The soul has fled:
When faith is lost, when honor dies,
The man is dead!

Then, pay the reverence of old days
To his dead fame;
Walk backward, with averted gaze,
And hide the shame!

As is true of much of Whittier's poetry, "Ichabod" was drenched in biblical and Miltonian allusions that would have been clear to Whittier's contemporaries. The title was taken from 1 Samuel 4:21, where it was the name given to the posthumous son of Phinehas and grandson of Eli, after the ark of the covenant had been captured in battle by the Philistines. "The glory is departed from Israel." The image throughout the poem was of a soul who has fallen from heaven to hell ("so fallen! so lost!"). The mood was mournful—"a long lament, as for the dead, in sadness make"—because his soul truly was dead. Don't take pleasure at his fall, said the poet; anyone might fall into a trap of Satan ("the Tempter"). Angels would never laugh to see a soul, hounded by demons, driven "down the endless dark" to hell. Even though Webster defiantly lived on, his soul was dead. Rather than reveling at his shame, let the reader join in hiding it, just as Noah's sons Shem and Japheth walked backward with their faces turned away so that they could cover their drunken, naked father without looking at him (Genesis 9:23). Whittier was a distant cousin of Webster and had been a friend, but in this poem he encapsulated the response of the abolitionists to Webster's betrayal.

During the debate on the compromise, William H. Seward gave a now-famous speech in which he called the fugitive slave bill "unjust, unconstitutional, and immoral."

Has any government ever succeeded in changing the moral convictions of its subjects by force? But these convictions imply no disloyalty. We reverence the Constitution, although we perceive this defect....Your constitution and laws convert hospitality to the refugee from the most degrading oppression on earth into a crime...

I know that there are laws of various sorts which regulate the conduct of men. There are constitutions and statutes, codes merchantile [sic] and codes civil; but when we are legislating for States, especially when we are founding States, *all these laws must be brought to the standard of the laws of God, and must be tried by that standard, and must stand or fall by it.*...The Constitution regulates our stewardship; the Constitution devotes the [national] domain to union, to justice, to defense, to welfare, and to liberty. But *there is a higher law than the Constitution*, which regulates our authority over the domain, and devotes it to the same noble purposes. The territory is a part—no inconsiderable part—of the common heritage of mankind, bestowed upon them by the Creator of the universe. We are his stewards, and must so discharge our trust as to secure, in the highest attainable degree, their happiness...[13]

This was Seward's first speech in the Senate—in fact, one of the most significant maiden speeches in the history of the Senate—and immediately placed him in the forefront of antislavery public figures.

In commenting on the compromise measure, J. M. Willson, in the April 1850 issue of *The Covenanter*, wrote,

Slavery, if the signs of the times do not deceive us, has wrought pretty successfully upon the North already. Still, whatever the results of the discussion now going on, as it regards the institution of slavery, one effect will, certainly, be wrought—the pro-slavery element of the Constitution will be brought out in a clearer light than ever. The whole country will be compelled to see and acknowledge that this instrument contains guarantees and compromises with the accursed thing; and not a few, we hope, will be driven to the conclusion that to swear to support such compromises is a flagrant offense against Christian morality.[14]

Seward, when asked in the Senate why he swore to uphold the Constitution, since he had said, "The Law of Nations disavows such compacts—the Law of Nature, written in the hearts and consciences of freemen, repudiates them," had nothing to say. Willson was pleased that a prominent statesman had spoken for the supreme authority of God's law. Willson concluded,

Policy may prevail for the time. Ungodly politicians sent to Washington by the votes of Christians, may betray the interests of liberty for gain and for office—but truth will be circulated. There are still a few to stand up for the right, unterrified by Southern threats, and unseduced by the bribes of a timid and truckling administration.[15]

The attitude of the Covenanters to the Compromise of 1850 was also expressed in a paper on slavery written by David S. Faris in November 1850, when he was an undergraduate at Indiana University. He deals with various aspects of the slavery issue, in the course of which he spoke of the recent compromise:

It may be said with reference to this, that it does not ask more than is guaranteed to the South by the Constitution. Very well, but what inserted such a base, wicked and abominable clause in the so-called sacred document? Slave power, or rather Southern tyranny. Therefore, the constitutionality of the act, does not ameliorate, but rather adds to the wickedness of the indescribably tyrannical law, enacted during the session of the late Congress, for the purpose of recovering fugitive slaves. This law is unspeakably more insulting and violating to the conscience of free men than any act of the British Parliament antecedent to, or during the time of, the Revolution. Who claiming the name of an American will calmly and passively submit to such an arbitrary, villainous law? What descendant of our brave and worthy forefathers, can suffer the glorious deeds of his ancestors to be tarnished by disgracing the country and the nation which they founded, by such a diabolical act? It is enough to make the very blood run cold, to think that the North must submit to have their liberties and rights disrespected and trampled underfoot. To think, that one concession to the South, only makes them look for another; much more important that one act of submission to their power is expected to be followed [by one] more degrading, so to speak, than slavery itself. Alas, patriotic Spirit, thou hast deserted our firesides, thou hast given place to cowardice, and foolishness, in the breasts of many of our countrymen. But although the love of many has waxed cold, and the last spark of liberty has long since been quenched in the bosom of great numbers, by the miserable desire of pleasing Southern nabobs, yet there are many in the North, who are willing to resist this act of abomination, with their lives in their hands to the last extreme—yes, to death. Many are willing to exclaim in the affecting words of the celebrated Patrick Henry, 'I know not what course others may take, but as for me, give me liberty, or give me death.'[16]

Although this was a piece of rhetoric, it revealed what a Reformed Presbyterian young man of twenty heard around the dinner table or in the barn or after prayer meetings. David S. Faris was the second living son of James Faris, who, thirty years before, had been the friend of John C. Calhoun. The two older men had grown apart through the years and now stood at opposite ends of the spectrum with regard to slavery. In concluding his discussion of the Fugitive Slave Law, the younger Faris proclaimed that he would "pay no more attention to that most infamous law" than he would "if it had emanated immediately from Satan, or Beelzebub himself."

In another paper, dated November 4, 1850, titled "The Spirit of the Times," Faris said that a long period of peace had been given to the nation, but that with "all species of crimes" being perpetrated by the ungrateful citizens, that calm would doubtless be succeeded by terrible divine judgments. "Nor can we expect to escape the storm which is collecting to break forth." The North as well as the South would suffer, for both trampling on the inalienable rights of man and rebelling against the King of Nations.[17]

The ensuing Synod in May 1851 made a strong statement about the Fugitive Slave Law. In part, the Synod wrote:

Resolved, That this Synod reiterates its uncompromising opposition to the institution of slavery....That the fugitive slave law is essentially tyrannical; not only securing the enslavement of those who are in fact free, but in forbidding freemen to exercise the sympathies of Christian compassion and commanding them to assist in returning men to cruel bondage.

It brings deserved infamy upon our land, dishonors God, and is expressly contrary to the plainest precepts of his law—'Thou shalt not deliver unto his master the servant which is escaped from his master unto thee.' [Deuteronomy 23:15], 'Bewray [betray] not him that wandereth.' [Isaiah 16:3], 'Relieve the oppressed.' [Isaiah 1:17].

And it is the duty of all not only to refuse compliance with its provisions, but to show others its hideous enormity...

That it is the duty of the ministers of Christ to teach clearly that magistrates in Christian lands should yield to the authority of God's law, and that any law which is in opposition to the precepts of the Bible does not bind the conscience, and ought to be resisted by every means consistent with religion; for we must obey God rather than man.[18]

The Reformed Presbyterians in Scotland and Ireland followed closely the struggle against slavery in America, and their periodicals were free in giving advice to the American government and Reformed Presbyterians. The synods of the three countries maintained regular correspondence. In December 1850, the editor of the Irish RP magazine called the new American law "infamous." "Our hope, however, is that by this iniquitous measure, the doom of slavery in America will be sealed. A spirit will, we trust, be evoked which will not rest till the last chain of the enslaved will be shivered to pieces. We rejoice too, that the testimony of our fathers against slavery begins to be more generally appreciated in America."[19] A yearly correspondence between the synods of Scotland, Ireland, and America provided mutual encouragement and helped to get them ready for whatever the dark clouds might pour out upon the nation.

"Peace in Our Time?"

Franklin Pierce, described by William E. Dodd as "a popular but colorless young New Englander, …a colonel under [Winfield] Scott in the war with Mexico," a proslavery leader from New Hampshire, was elected president in 1852 by a landslide on a platform of compromise. He would enforce the laws and preserve the union. Twenty-seven states had given him their electoral votes (253–42); he lost only New Hampshire, Massachusetts, Kentucky, and Tennessee, and won 86 percent of the popular vote. It seemed that peace and unity were now to prevail in the nation. The country was tired of agitation and longed for prosperity. People were getting accustomed to the compromise, and opposition to the Fugitive Slave Law seemed to be fading.

But in 1852, Harriet Beecher Stowe published her novel *Uncle Tom's Cabin*. It caused an immediate stir; in its first year, 300,000 copies were sold in the United States and 1,000,000 in Britain, and the book went on to become the largest-selling novel of the nineteenth century. Near the beginning of the Civil War, Stowe met President Lincoln, who is reported to have said, "So this is the little lady who wrote the book that made this big war." Naturally, the reaction in the South was as vigorously opposed to the novel as that in the North (and in Britain and Ireland) was in favor. Nevertheless, it was expected that there would be no major disruption in the political realm for fifteen or twenty years at least.[20] The Compromise of 1850 had secured "peace in our time" (in the later infamous phrase).

The decades from the 1820s to 1850s were a period of rapid expansion as the Industrial Revolution led to the Agricultural Revolution; both of these affected the North more than the South. Railroads multiplied rapidly, New York City became the principal export center for both North and South, and Southerners became increasingly anxious that they were not keeping up. For example, the South had an investment $1 billion greater than that of the North, but their income was only about one third as much. Leaders of the South sought every opportunity to add new slave territory, including the private seizure of Nicaragua by William Walker and a proposal to purchase Cuba. Southern delegates in Congress attempted to repeal the law against the slave trade so that the South might have labor enough to compete with the influx of immigrants into the East and Northwest. There was a determined effort to solidify the South, including the Border States.[21]

The Impending Crisis

Just two years into Pierce's term, the question of a railroad connection with the Pacific was behind an event that was to split the country wide open. Secretary of War Jefferson Davis, speaking for the South, wanted a railroad to California through the Southwest, with its eastern terminus at St Louis, Memphis, or New Orleans, while Stephen Douglas of Illinois wanted a northern route from Chicago through Nebraska Territory. Douglas worked out a compromise plan with the proslavery element of Missouri, who wanted Kansas for the expansion of slavery. The Nebraska Territory was to be divided into two sections, the Missouri Compromise of 1820 was to be repealed, with each section deciding for itself to be slave or free territory. This plan Douglas called "popular sovereignty," but others dubbed it "squatter sovereignty."

Douglas's compromise was embodied in the Kansas–Nebraska Bill, which, after months of acrid debate in both Senate and House was signed by the president on May 30, 1854. The chief interest of the Southern voices was to open the Northwest to the possibility of slavery extension. The chief interest of Douglas was to extend the rail system of the North from Chicago to California. There were those in Congress who felt that the bill superseded the Missouri Compromise, but Archibald Dixon of Kentucky in the Senate and Philip Phillips of Alabama in the House insisted on explicit repeal of the 36°30' clause (which prohibited slavery north of that latitude). Accepting that repeal was one of Douglas's worst mistakes in a long and sorry career. It earned the opposition of such Southern luminaries as Senators Sam Houston and Thomas Hart Benton, and among the public it stirred immediate and vigorous anger from the abolitionists and the Free-Soil Democrats. Douglas, dubbed a second Benedict Arnold, was burned in effigy in many places. Chase, Sumner, Seward, and even moderates such as Edward Everett denounced Douglas for selling "the birthright of the free states for a mess of pottage."[22]

On March 4, the day the bill passed the Senate, D. S. Faris wrote in his diary, "Read the National Era. Great excitement regarding the repeal of the Missouri Compromise."[23] But the editor of *The Covenanter* expected no real change in the North regarding slavery. While the bill was still pending, he wrote that the Northerners, in general, did not truly *hate* slavery.

> We see them taking slaveholders to their homes, their pulpits, their communion-tables, their hearts. They yield to—often promote—the schemes of slave-holders. They vote for slave-holders for the highest offices, knowing that they will employ their official influences for the support of slavery. They will not listen to a word against the system. They will patronize no paper that opposes it. If ministers, they neither preach nor pray against it....Still more; they despise the coloured man *at home*. If he will go to Liberia, he is a decent man....In Africa, he is 'Mr.' or even 'his excellency;' but if he stays in America, where he was born, and some generations of his fathers before him, he is a 'n*****!'
>
> And yet, all this time—smiling upon slaveholders, and frowning awfully upon abolitionists and the enslaved—these people *say* that they dislike slavery; that it is a great moral and social evil; that the Gospel is against it, and will eradicate it. Are they sincere? No. Instead of hating slavery, they hate the slave. Instead of hating slavery, they do cordially hate the doctrine that the slave has, before God, the same rights that they have. Instead of hating slavery, they would hold slaves, and exercise all the functions of slaveholders

themselves, if the circumstances were different. The conclusion is this, that the antislavery professions of the North—we mean the majority—are a mere sham; a concession to the opinion of the world; perhaps to conscience; but hollow, mere words; backed by no abhorrence of the system, or none that will not readily give way to the attractions of place, power, gain, or fashion.

Nor will it avail to say that just now the North is rising, against the Nebraska bill. So it arose against the annexation of Texas, the Mexican War, the compromise of 1850. But what came of it? Nothing. And should the bill pass, we shall likely see the same huge results—Nothing![24]

Whatever might have been the North's true feelings about slavery, it was from this time caught in the storm that would finally eradicate American slavery. The conscience of the North was being awakened, but engaging in a battle required economic and political factors as well. The Covenanters, believing that any type of compromise with slavery was a sin, perhaps underestimated the force of antislavery sentiment. The anger of the Northerners might be ephemeral, but it was not entirely false. There were some sincere antislavery men, such as Seward, who nevertheless endorsed the idea of popular sovereignty for practical reasons, seeking thereby to gain an advantage for the antislavery cause.

Passage of the Kansas–Nebraska Bill signaled the beginning of the battle for Kansas. Eastern antislavery societies raised money to send antislavery settlers into the territory, and the South, especially Missouri, did the same thing to promote the proslavery cause. Most of the early settlers turned out to be antislavery. The border ruffians from Missouri rode across the border to vote, on the theory that "residing" in Kansas for even five minutes made them legal voters, and then went home again. An investigative committee of the House of Representatives discovered massive fraud. For example, in the election of March 30, 1855, for the Territorial Legislature, in the First District (Lawrence), an official census just days before the election counted 369 legal voters, but poll-lists showed that 1,034 ballots were cast. The Eleventh District, including Maryville, had a total of 36 inhabitants; seven legal votes were cast and 321 illegal.[25]

The town of Atchison, Kansas, was established in 1854 by proslavery men from Missouri at the encouragement of their proslavery Senator, David Rice Atchison; and very shortly their newspaper boasted, "We will lynch and hang, tar and feather and drown, every white-livered abolitionist who dares to pollute our soil."[26] William Phillips, a lawyer in Leavenworth, protested the illegal voting of Missourians and for this was shaved, tarred and feathered, and sold as a slave to a Black man in Missouri. Free immigrants were prevented from entering Kansas through Missouri. Some of them went the long way around through Iowa and Nebraska, but their firearms were confiscated by federal authorities—on what ground is unclear. The Territory had two capitals: Topeka for the Free-state government, and Lecompton for the proslavery faction. The town of Lawrence, settled by antislavery people, was shelled by artillery, looted, and partially burned on May 21, 1856. Civil war was carried on for some months, with both sides committing atrocities.[27] "Bleeding Kansas" resulted in bleeding as far away as Washington, D.C., where Senator Charles Sumner was beaten to unconsciousness in the U.S. Senate chamber by Representative Preston Brooks of South Carolina—beaten so badly that he required three years of therapy.[28]

A few Reformed Presbyterians, primarily from southern Illinois, were among the antislavery settlers of Kansas. These families settled near Olathe, on the Santa Fe Trail, and survived bands of border ruffians who rode through the country seeking and killing antislavery men. (Both sides left women and children alone.) Covenanters hid in the fields, in root cellars, and in haystacks to avoid death. Billy Cook, age sixteen, rode with a Jayhawker or antislavery band because it was too dangerous for him to stay home.[29]

This bitter warfare attracted the attention of the press across the nation. The same year, 1854, the Republican Party was established, mostly by dissatisfied or disillusioned members of the Whig party and Free-Soil Democrats. In 1856, the fledgling party ran John C. Frémont as its candidate for president, and while he did not win, he made a very respectable showing. Not until the war began did the party truly solidify.

Another political party was organized in 1855, the Radical Abolition party. This party never elected a candidate to office and in fact disappeared in five years. Its leading lights included Gerrit Smith, Frederick Douglass, and John Brown, and its major contribution to the antislavery debate was to embrace violence as a legitimate political tool. In his major speech at the organizing convention, Brown quoted Hebrews 9:22—"without the shedding of blood there is no remission of sins"—clearly wrenching the phrase from its biblical context. He appealed for both money and arms to take to Kansas, where his sons were engaged in the partisan warfare. By the time the party's nominating convention met in 1856, border ruffians had shelled, looted, and burned Lawrence, Kansas, and Preston Brooks had brutally caned Senator Sumner. To the Radical Abolitionists, proslavery forces were waging violent war against Black people and abolitionists, and the only way to meet such violence was with violence. Moreover, John Brown explicitly defined slavery itself as a state of war.[30]

Another shock soon horrified the people of the North when in 1857 the Supreme Court handed down its decision in the case of *Dred Scott v. Sandford*.[31] Scott, born a slave in Virginia, had been taken to St. Louis by his enslavers and while there, was sold to U.S. Army Major John Emerson. As Emerson was transferred to other posts, he took Scott with him—to Illinois, to Wisconsin Territory (Fort Snelling, now Minnesota), back to Missouri, then to Louisiana, then back to Fort Snelling. Scott sued for his freedom, on the grounds that residence in free territory gave him the status of a freeman. He won, but lost on appeal in the Missouri Supreme Court. He then filed suit in federal court, lost, and appealed to the U.S. Supreme Court. That court, with Chief Justice Roger B. Taney delivering their decision, rendered what legal scholars long considered the most notorious decision of its history.

Taney, writing the opinion for the majority, stated that the words of the Constitution, "the people of the United States of America," did not include Black people.

> Neither the Declaration of Independence nor the Constitution intended that people who had been imported as slaves, nor their descendants, should ever be included in the general words, 'we the people.' They had for more than a century before been regarded as beings of an inferior order, and altogether unfit to associate with the white race, either in social or political relations; and so far inferior, that they had no rights which the white man was bound to respect; and that the negro might justly and lawfully be reduced to slavery for his benefit. He was bought and sold, and treated as an ordinary article of merchandise and traffic, whenever a profit could be made from it....A negro of the African race was regarded by them as an article of property, and held, and bought and sold as such, in every one of the thirteen colonies which united

in the Declaration of Independence, and afterwards formed the Constitution of the United States...[32]

Dred Scott, therefore, had no right to sue in United States courts.

Actually, the court ruled on three issues. On the second, Taney's opinion for the court held that Scott had not become a free man by virtue of living in Wisconsin Territory because the clause in the Missouri Compromise excluding slavery was unconstitutional—it exceeded the authority of Congress by depriving slave owners of their property rights. Third and finally, Scott had not become free by virtue of living in Illinois, because once he returned to Missouri the law of that state governed his status. On the last of these, the seven majority justices concurred, and if the court had settled only that point, it is likely that the case would not be remembered today. What seized public attention were the first two points: the Supreme Court had held that Black people were not and could never be citizens, and Congress could not interfere with slaveholding in the territories.

On the second point, Taney argued that, while Congress has the right to acquire and administer new territories, it can do so only subject to the limitations on government power imposed by the Constitution. This, he said, includes property rights under the Due Process clause of the Fifth Amendment. "If a man owns property in a state, and moves it with himself to a territory, he still retains ownership of that property unless there is a Due Process taking." Taney conveniently overlooked the fact that a slave was not "ordinary property" but a special class. It was a somewhat quirky reading of the law, designed to underpin the Southern position, and therefore can justly be termed tendentious, although not altogether indefensible. At the time, it was a disaster to the opponents of slavery, because it meant that there was no legal way to prevent or even slow the spread of slavery throughout the nation.

The first point of *Dred Scott v. Sandford,* that Black people were not and could never be citizens of the United States, was the point that most aroused the fury of the abolitionists and the revulsion of later generations of Americans. To reach this conclusion, Taney drew a distinction between "the rights of citizenship which a state may confer within its own limits, and the rights of citizenship as a member of the Union." National citizenship is federal in origin, and Taney argued that both legislation and practice showed that Black people had "no rights which the white man was bound to respect." Thus, "Dred Scott was not a citizen within the meaning of the Constitution of the United States, and not entitled as such to sue in its courts."[33] It is true that a number of states had laws restricting free Black men—prohibiting them from voting, for example, or from carrying guns or knives, or from interracial marriage; or setting stronger penalties for felonies or misdemeanors committed by Black people than for white people guilty of the same infractions. Those state laws, together with Justice Taney's opinion in *Dred Scott,* gave the lie to the Declaration of Independence's fundamental affirmation "that all men are created equal; that they are endowed by their Creator with certain unalienable rights; that among these are life, liberty, and the pursuit of happiness."[34]

This decision was too much, even for strong Reformed Presbyterian taste. The church had always affirmed that the Constitution compromised with slavery in three ways: (1) by permitting the slave trade to continue for twenty years before it could be prohibited; (2) by requiring the return of fugitive slaves; and (3) by the three-fifths clause, which augmented the congressional and electoral representation of slave states by three-fifths of the slave population. Some Covenanters had even anticipated the Taney court in saying that slaves were not included in "we the people."[35] J. M. Willson, writing in *The Covenanter,* castigated the *Dred Scott* decision vigorously:

> These are astounding doctrines. The country has heard them with astonishment, and all the friends of liberty with dismay. That the Constitution recognizes slavery in the States, where it exists, we do firmly believe. That it contains provisions most iniquitous, as in the article regarding the return of fugitives, and the three-fifths principle, we have ever maintained; but in this decision we do as firmly believe there has been reached a deeper depth of iniquity. Can anything be more monstrous than the assertion—and it must now be regarded as part of the established law of the land—that a man who has in his veins a drop of negro blood, is no citizen—not even so much of a citizen as to be entitled to sue in the courts of the general government? That such a man is an outlaw? That he has no opportunity of redress for any wrong inflicted upon him in any case in which suit must be brought, if at all, in a United States' Court?…It seems to us that the cup of the nation's iniquity must be nearly full. Even foreigners may sue in the courts of the federal government; but a man of colour—born upon the soil—cannot. He may have shed his blood on the field of battle, as many of them have done—his father may have done so before him—still he is an

outlaw. Six hundred thousand human beings not only disfranchised [sic], but put out of the pale of law, so far as the Supreme Court of the country can do it, by one fell swoop! Before the iniquity of this act, common sins become mere peccadillos. Are we a nation of Algerians—of pirates? Most certainly we are if this be law.

We do not hesitate to say that this decision is far worse than the Constitution itself—bad as that is. It does deep dishonour to the generation which fought the war of the Revolution under the motto 'All men are born free and equal.' It has fixed the brand of indelible disgrace upon the country, and will send down the names of the perpetrators of the deed to infamy in coming ages. Still, we are free to say that the guilt rests upon the Constitution in part. Slavery has a place there. It was *allowed* a place there. The country has shut its eyes upon that fact. It would not see. It *would* laud the Constitution as a perfect instrument, while, all the time, it was sapping, by its omissions, and by its pro-slavery clauses, the very 'foundations'— the fear of God and regard for human rights....So long as the Constitution binds the free States, so long this iniquity will have no end. The free States off, the slaves would see to the rest. We do not despair. As things become worse, they are the more rapidly hastening to a turn for the better. It is darkest just before day.[36]

The dawn of that new day was nearer than the abolitionists dared to hope. In the West, a man appeared who was to become the most familiar figure in American history. He stood before the state convention of the newly formed Republican Party as their candidate for the junior senator from Illinois. Not an abolitionist in the strict sense of the word, Abraham Lincoln saw the issue clearly and spoke with great sincerity:

If we could first know where we are, and whither we are tending, we could then better judge what to do, and how to do it.

We are now far into the fifth year, since a policy was initiated, with the avowed object, and confident promise, of putting an end to slavery agitation.

Under the operation of that policy, that agitation has not only, not ceased, but has constantly augmented.

In my opinion, it will not cease, until a crisis shall have been reached, and passed.

'A house divided against itself cannot stand.'

> I believe this government cannot endure, permanently half slave and half free.
>
> I do not expect the Union to be dissolved—I do not expect the house to fall—but I do expect it will cease to be divided.
>
> It will become all one thing, or all the other.
>
> Either the opponents of slavery, will arrest the further spread of it, and place it where the public mind shall rest in the belief that it is in the course of ultimate extinction; or its advocates will push it forward, till it shall become alike lawful in all the states, old as well as new—North as well as South.[37]

Lincoln did not, at that point, advocate immediate and uncompensated emancipation of slaves, but simply the confinement of slavery to the old South so that it would naturally wither and die. But he saw in the Kansas–Nebraska Bill and the *Dred Scott* decision an attempt to make the whole nation a slave nation. This was the man of the hour. "The result is not doubtful. We shall not fail—if we stand firm, we shall not fail. Wise councils may accelerate or mistakes delay it, but, sooner or later the victory is sure to come."[38]

On the night of October 16, 1859, another event occurred to further solidify the division in the nation. John Brown, who had already won national fame by his stand against the border ruffians in Kansas, and for leading Black fugitives to Canada, struck a blow for the freedom of enslaved people by seizing the federal arsenal at Harper's Ferry, Virginia (since 1865 West Virginia). The incident led to his own execution and to a heightened tension throughout the nation. In the North, eminent men proclaimed him a hero; Ralph Waldo Emerson likened his gallows to the cross of Christ. Lt. Col. Robert E. Lee, who commanded the detachment of Marines and local militia who captured Brown and his party, claimed in his official report on October 19 that Brown's purpose was to "incite the negroes to join in the insurrection," although how he knew that aim at that time is unclear.[39]

The day after his conviction, Brown was brought to Court to hear his sentence and was surprised to be asked why sentence of death should not be pronounced. Brown was expecting some continuation or time for appeal, but rose and "in a singularly mild and gentle manner" denied that he had intended "murder, or treason, or the destruction of property, or to excite or incite slaves to rebellion, or to make insurrection." His aim was to lead slaves to Canada as he had done in Missouri the previous winter, only on a larger scale.[40] Brown's letters written from prison show that he was not insane, as many have since claimed.

A. M. Milligan, pastor of the New Alexandria Reformed Presbyterian Church in Pennsylvania, wrote to Brown on November 24, 1859, in a pastoral vein, saying that "there are some orthodox and earnest Christians who regard you as a martyr to civil liberty." He added,

> If you have made all the sacrifice for Christ's and his cause's sake, you have the promise of a hundredfold more in the present life, and in the world to come life everlasting....You have been called before judges, and it has been 'given you what to say and how to speak;' and I pray that when you are called 'to witness a good confession before many witnesses,' there may be given you dying words that will scathe and burn in the heart of this great and mighty nation, until their oppression of men and treason against God shall be clean purged out.[41]

Brown replied to Milligan on November 29, 1859, among his last letters:

> My dear Covenanter Friend:—Notwithstanding I now get daily more than three times the number of kind letters I can possibly answer, I cannot deny myself the satisfaction of saying a few words to a stranger, whose feelings and whose judgment so nearly coincide with my own. No letter of a great number I have got to cheer, encourage, and advise me, has given more heart warming satisfaction or better counsel than your own. I hope to profit by it, and I am greatly obliged for your visit to my prison. It really seemed to impart new strength to my soul, notwithstanding I was very cheerful before. I trust, dear brother, that God, in infinite grace and mercy, for Christ's sake, will 'neither leave me nor forsake me,' till I have shown His power to this generation, and his strength to every one that is to come.' I would most gladly commune further as we journey on; but I am so near the close of mine that I must break off, however reluctant.
>
> Farewell, my faithful brother in Christ Jesus! Farewell!
>
> Your friend,
JOHN BROWN[42]

It is difficult—and fallacious—to assess the actions of the past by the standards of the present. Despite Brown's appreciation, careful reading shows that Milligan did not explicitly endorse Brown's use of extra-judicial violence. "There are some who regard you as a martyr" implies but does not state that Milligan shared that view. (See, for an example of identifying Brown as a martyr, the title of the Sanborn biography in note 42 above.) It is clear, of course, that the two men shared the same beliefs about slavery and the same desire to see it eradicated, but Milligan did not dwell on their differences. Instead, he offered sympathy and support for Brown's words of defense; he offered the kind of consolation that a minister or chaplain might give, "If you have made all the sacrifice for Christ's and his cause's sake…" He prays that Brown's dying testimony will move the nation toward abolishing slavery. Brown knew the position of the Reformed Presbyterians, including Milligan, on slavery, and he was grateful for words of encouragement from a fellow Christian.

9

An Inalienable Right

The Civil War and Emancipation

A young Reformed Presbyterian soldier ran with his comrades across the fields in hot pursuit of the retreating Confederates. Through a heavy May rain, his unit, Company F of the 10th Missouri Volunteer Infantry, led the attack. After months of tedious efforts to capture Vicksburg, General Grant had directed part of his vast Army of the Tennessee to capture Jackson, the capital of Mississippi, and thus prevent Confederate General Joseph Johnston from reinforcing Vicksburg. Now, within three miles of Jackson, the 10th Missouri was leading the assault on Jackson's defenders, facing the 24th South Carolina regiment. In the running battle, Andrew Todd Kennedy was shot in the left foot and unable to continue. He was one of his regiment's eighty-five casualties that day.

Kennedy was taken in an ambulance to a temporary hospital in the Jackson City Hall. Less than twenty-four hours later, the Confederates recaptured the city, and the retreating Union force abandoned their wounded. So began his experience as a prisoner of war, which lasted fifty-nine days, until he was paroled on July 6 (just two days after the Union victories at Vicksburg and Gettysburg). It was later found that the musket ball had fractured the metatarsal bones of the first, second, third, and fourth toes, and the subsequent gangrene destroyed a great deal of tissue.[1]

Covenanters who fought in the Civil War had the same variety of experiences as other soldiers, North and South. Some came through the war physically unscathed, some with physical or psychological wounds that lasted a lifetime, and others failed to come through at all. Kennedy was fortunate in getting medical attention while the gangrene could still be controlled and in being exchanged relatively quickly. Since all prisoner exchanges occurred at Richmond, Virginia, he spent several weeks in the notorious Libby Prison there. But he survived.

Why were young Reformed Presbyterians, who consistently protested against the evils of the U.S. Constitution, active in this massive war to save the Union? We must first examine the steps that led to the bloody Civil War, then at behaviors and attitudes of the Reformed Presbyterians regarding the war.

The Election of Lincoln

At its nominating convention in Chicago in May 1860, the Republican Party adopted a platform that attempted to make as many concessions to the South as possible and still hold its antislavery voter base. The platform planks most relevant to the slavery issue were, in brief:

2. The Federal Constitution, the rights of the States, and the Union of the States must and shall be preserved.

3. We hold in abhorrence all schemes for disunion, come from whatever source they may.

4. The maintenance inviolate of the rights of each state, to order and control its own domestic institutions according to its own judgment exclusively, is essential.

7. The new dogma that the Constitution, of its own force, carries Slavery into any or all of the Territories of the United States, is a dangerous political heresy, at variance with the explicit provisions of that instrument itself, with contemporaneous exposition, and with legislative and judicial precedent; is revolutionary in its tendency, and subversive of the peace and harmony of the country.

8. The normal condition of all the territory of the United States is freedom.

9. The recent re-opening of the African Slave Trade [is] a crime against humanity and a burning shame to our country and age.

10. The recent vetoes by the federal governors of the legislative acts of Nebraska and Kansas prohibiting slavery illustrate the deception and fraud of "popular sovereignty."[2]

Another plank supported Henry Clay's proposal for a protective tariff. The whole is a carefully calculated and balanced political compromise. "[I]f the Southerners had kept cool they could have read between the lines of this declaration all the guarantees that they required, save alone on the subject of slavery in the new Territories, which the Republicans could not possibly yield and hold their followers together."[3] Voters had four options in the 1860 election: the Republican party nominated Abraham Lincoln on the third ballot, the Northern Democrats nominated the pro-Southern Stephen Douglas, the Southern Democrats nominated John C. Breckinridge, and the Constitutional Union Party (which was an assortment of former Whigs, Know Nothings, and other parties and splinter groups) nominated John Bell.

The Covenanters and Garrisonian abolitionists were again urged to vote in the election. Horace Greeley's letter to J. R. Thompson of September 2, 1860, illustrates the attitude of many Republicans: "Is your church one of those that *talks* against slavery but refuses to *vote* against it? If so, I must regard it as a barren figtree." Greeley clearly regarded the Republican platform as antislavery, but the Garrisonians and Reformed Presbyterians had another opinion. J. W. Shaw, pastor at Coldenham, New York, from 1844 to 1881 and a frequent contributor to *The Reformed Presbyterian,* wrote dismissively of Greeley's attitude in the issue of October 1860. What good does it do, he asks, to send a good man to Congress when, in the very nature of the political process, he will have to compromise and thus be unable to accomplish the measures needed? Besides, in order to take his seat in Congress he must swear to support the Constitution and laws that he was elected to oppose and change. The Slave Power would not permit such a representative; "he would be cared for as a madman, if not tried and hung as an insurrectionist."[4]

The Covenanters' unwillingness to compromise with slavery was, of course, shared by the Garrisonians, who went so far as to say in the *National Anti-Slavery Standard* of September 29, 1860, "we shall look upon Mr. Lincoln's election as a calamity to the anti-slavery cause." Reformed Presbyterians did not condemn Lincoln entirely, but condescendingly described his position as pitiable:

> He has never pretended to be anything but what he now stands for before the nation. He was taken by the Chicago Convention, instead of Mr. Seward, precisely because he represented just as little anti-slavery as could be without being none at all. But, for all this, we admit that, if elected, he will be the most respectable President we have had since John Quincy Adams. We incline to believe that he will not be more pro-slavery in his action than he can help, and that he had rather not be pro-slavery at all. But we opine that that gives him but a small claim on the vote of an Abolitionist.[5]

The South, on the other hand, looked upon the possibility of
Lincoln's election with alarm. They saw in it only another effort by
Northerners to destroy slavery. During the course of the campaign,
Douglas went barnstorming, a type of self-glorification that presidential candidates simply did not do at the time and which showed his
increasing desperation. He went into the South to persuade them that
secession would mean war and to urge them to preserve the Union.
By this time, however, the South paid little heed and gave most of its
electoral votes to Breckenridge.

Many in the South were ready to take action. Robert Barnwell
Rhett (1800–1876) and William Lowndes Yancey (1814–1863), two
of the most reckless Southern "fire-eaters," were ready to take the first
steps for breaking the Union as soon as news of Lincoln's election
should arrive. When the ballots were counted, Lincoln polled only
about 40 percent of the popular vote (only a half million more than
Douglas, his nearest rival in the popular vote), but won 180 electoral
votes out of 303 (Breckinridge had 72, Bell 39, and Douglas only 12).
Lincoln did not carry any Southern or Border States; in fact, he was
the first president ever elected without a single slave state.

Before Lincoln was inaugurated on March 4, 1861, seven
Southern states declared their secession from the Union. On April
12, Southern forces attacked and took Fort Sumter, which guarded
Charleston harbor. Thus was the Rubicon crossed. Lincoln called for
a volunteer army to put down the rebellion, and in response, four
additional Southern states seceded. The war was on. As with many
modern wars, the cause of the war was complex and controversial. To
many Northerners, the war's purpose was (as President Lincoln had
announced) to preserve the Union; to many Southerners, the purpose
was to defend their homeland against invaders and to preserve their
regional culture. To other Northerners, the purpose was to destroy the
slave system and free the slaves; to many Southerners, its purpose was
to preserve and extend the slave system, which they euphemistically
called "our southern institutions." To yet other Northerners, the
South's unwillingness to accept the election of Lincoln challenged
the authority of the Constitution; to yet other Southerners, the war
threatened states' rights, self-determination, and liberty.[6]

Covenanters and the Civil War

Reformed Presbyterians were not unanimous in their assessment
of the president's war aims, but most stoutly supported the war if it

would bring about an end to slavery. Did they believe that war was necessary to destroy slavery? Yes, as a last resort; and again we must assess this by the perspective of the time: yes, it seemed to be a last resort.

The editor of *The Reformed Presbyterian* seemed to express the view of the church in February 1860, in an essay titled "The Country's Dangers: Their Causes and Remedy." The country, he said, was in danger of losing its liberty, of civil war, and of punishment from God. The causes of these catastrophes were national forgetfulness of God, the sanction and support given in the Constitution to sin, and the failure of the religious part of the community to protest. The remedy, he said, was, "In the first place, *let slavery in all its odiousness be held up to be loathed and despised.* It is one of the things that cannot bear the light....It must not be let alone. It must be dragged to the light.... In the second place, *let the evils in the Constitution be removed, and let it exemplify the scriptural institution of civil government.* Until this is done, the favor and approval of God need not be expected."

Let the South, he continued, be told that "the partnership cannot continue without a readjustment of the terms." Those people who have continually assured the South that the abolitionists were "a few insignificant fanatics" have been encouraging the slaveholders to continue in their sin and emboldening the South to further aggression.

"In the third place," the editor said, "*let slavery be met and put down with its own weapons.* This is the alternative if the two preceding fail." Slavery was set up and maintained by force, demanded unconditional submission, and maintained itself by the sword. The Slave Power could not find fault with those who countered it with the same weapons.[7] For Reformed Presbyterians, then, the justification for a war to end slavery was established well before the war began.

When the Synod met in New York City, May 28, 1861, the war had just begun. Fort Sumter had been taken shortly before. Whether this was a defiant act of rebellion or the opening of a war for Southern independence was not clear at the time, but most people in both sections regarded it as a declaration of war. (Actually, from the Southern point of view, the hostile action that began the war was the election of Abraham Lincoln.) A solid South had created a solid North. Two hundred thousand volunteers offered their services to the new Confederacy; money poured into its treasury; men gathered for drill without the call of their officers; and women urged their menfolk to meet and conquer the foe. Although Robert E. Lee is the most prominent soldier to resign from the U.S. Army and fight for the South, 445 Civil War generals were West Point graduates; 294 fought for the Union and 151 for the Confederacy. At the opening of the Civil War, Confederate General P. G. T. Beauregard, a West Point graduate and former West Point superintendent, opened fire on Fort Sumter, which was under the command of Major Robert Anderson, a West Point graduate and Beauregard's artillery instructor. And in every major battle of the Civil War, a West Point graduate commanded one or both sides. President Lincoln called for 75,000 volunteers for three months' service to put down the rebellion, and Congress was called to meet in extra session on July 4 to devise ways to compel the South to return to the Union fold. Confederate victory in the First Battle of Bull Run (or First Manassas) on July 21 shocked the nation out of some of its overconfidence.

The Synod felt that some public explanation should be made about the position of the church. They believed the war to be an "iniquitous war...*in the interest of slavery,* against the United States." They acknowledged the "numerous excellencies of the civil institutions" of the land. Its codes of laws were just, in general. They were thankful for the privileges and protection it gave them. Despite all this, they were constrained,

> in conscience, to maintain, as we and our fathers have heretofore done, a state of dissent from the constitution of the United States, inasmuch as there is in this instrument no acknowledgment of the name of God, Most High and Eternal; no recognition of the supremacy of His law contained in the Scriptures of the Old and New Testaments; no profession of subjection to the Mediatorial authority of the Son of God, who is 'King of kings and Lord of lords;' while on the other hand this constitution contains certain 'compromises' in the interest of slavery and slaveholders.

The Synod issued four declarations to prevent any misunderstanding of their position:

1. ...we disclaim all allegiance to the government of any foreign nation.
2. ...we consider ourselves under obligations to live peaceably with all men, to advance the good of society, and to conform to its order in every thing consistent with righteousness.

3. ...we disown all sympathy, even the least, with the traitors styling themselves 'the Confederate States,' now in arms against these United States.
4. ...we will, as true patriots, defend this, our common country, against these and all like enemies.[8]

Reformed Presbyterians went into the war in substantial numbers. Reference has already been made to Rev. Andrew C. Todd, who served as captain of a company of volunteers that included thirty-one men from his own Elkhorn congregation, including his nephew Andrew Todd Kennedy. Illinois's quota of volunteers filled so quickly that Todd's company had to cross to St. Louis in order to be mustered in—as Co. F, 10th Missouri Volunteer Infantry.[9] Seventeen members of the Brookland congregation in Westmoreland County, Pennsylvania, fought in the war. One of these was Thomas Banks of the Middletown branch, later an elder in the congregation, who served as aide to General Phil Sheridan and was beside him on his famous ride.[10] Sixty-nine Geneva College students or alumni served, of whom only two (not Covenanters) were in the Confederate army. Of the sixty-seven, two became generals—Robert P. Kennedy (brevet brigadier general) and Benjamin P. Runkle (brevet major general); one was a surgeon, three chaplains, two majors, three captains, three lieutenants. Twelve Geneva graduates were killed in action.[11]

The commander of Pennsylvania Reserves (fourteen regiments) at the Battle of Gettysburg was the son of a former Reformed Presbyterian pastor.[12] David B. Willson, the son of James M. Willson and grandson of James Renwick Willson, was a contract surgeon for the army and saw service in the Vicksburg campaign. Members also served valiantly in the ranks, although only a few can be mentioned here as illustrative. William R. Dunn of the 76th Pennsylvania Infantry (Keystone Zouaves) had his trigger finger shot off at Petersburg. Hugh Walkinshaw, serving in the 39th Iowa under General Sherman, was captured at the Battle of Allatoona Pass in Georgia and incarcerated in Libby Prison in Richmond. Allen and Thomas C. Dunn, brothers, were in the 36th Iowa Infantry, captured at Marks Mill, Arkansas, and sent to Hempstead Prison in Texas. Robert died there, leaving three children and a pregnant wife at home, and Thomas escaped.

After the war, it proved impossible to construct a reliable list of the countless Covenanters who served in the ranks, many of them suffering death, injury, or imprisonment.

Many years after the war, Rev. David S. Faris wrote, "The Synod understood that…the all-controlling motive in the South was the right to hold slaves and take them everywhere. Reformed Presbyterians also believed that providentially the war was for the overthrow of the slave power, and for the freedom of the slaves."[13]

As chapter 5 has demonstrated, some Reformed Presbyterians demurred. Nathan R. Johnston wrote that "some Covenanters urged that, as it was a war only in defense of a Constitution and Union that we had always declared to be pro-slavery and atheistic, we could not now fight for them." As late as April 1865, Reformed Presbyterians argued whether Christians could defend or swear an oath of loyalty to an ungodly government such as the United States.[14] *The Reformed Presbyterian* carried essays warning Covenanters against enlisting in the military, although one author, who signed his name LIBERTAS, equivocated slightly because "it is not so bad to maintain what is not altogether right, as it is to overthrow it, and establish and maintain what is a greater wrong." In another issue, a communication reprinted from the *Belfast Covenanter* advised its American cousins to give their *moral* support to the Union cause, but not their *active* participation.[15]

Reformed Presbyterians were not alone in this moral confusion. As we have seen, controversy still surrounded the actual war aims of President Lincoln. He wrote to Horace Greeley in 1862, "My paramount object in this struggle is to save the Union, and is not either to save or to destroy slavery."[16] Yet, at that time, many Americans on both sides of the conflict believed that the fundamental cause of the war was slavery and its extinction the aim. President Lincoln said so very clearly in his Second Inaugural Address in 1864. Governor Sam Houston of Texas believed so. George C. Eggleston, a former Confederate, wrote in his *History of the Confederate War, Its Causes and Its Conduct,* that slavery was the basic cause: it was "clear from the beginning that in the last analysis, the war involved as its issue the maintenance of slavery, or the destruction of that system, root and branch."[17]

Lincoln, we must remember, was in a delicate situation. He had to keep Britain neutral while holding on to the Border States—Delaware, Maryland, Kentucky, and Missouri, slave states that had not seceded. Britain initially favored the North under the assumption that the struggle was for the freedom of the slaves, but the Border States would be driven into the arms of the Confederacy if Lincoln announced prematurely that emancipation was the object of the war.

Uniform of a private in the 76th Pennsylvania Regiment. A Reformed Presbyterian, William R. Dunn, served in this regiment, also known as the Keystone Zouaves. The Metropolitan Museum of Art photo, CC0, via Wikimedia Commons

Thomas Banks, later an elder in Brookland RPC, was General Phil Sheridan's Aide and with him on his ride to save the Battle of Cedar Creek. Painting by Thure de Tholstrup, 1886. Public domain.

The British sympathized with the plantation aristocracy of the South, on the theory that "Yankees" were noisy, boastful, and vulgar, while the aristocrats of the South were gentlemen. In addition, Lincoln had to unite the North, many of whose people held racist views and did not want to fight to free the Black slaves, but *would* fight to preserve the Union.[18] Britain wanted Southern cotton to feed its textile industry and cast covetous eyes on the Southern market for their manufactured goods. Britain resented the Union blockade of Southern ports, but without it, the Union would have had a much more difficult time choking off the *matériel* of the Confederacy. In short, it was strategic for Lincoln to keep people guessing about his intentions. Stephen Douglas, in a backhanded compliment, credited Lincoln with a "fertile genius in devising language to conceal his thoughts."[19] Initially, the issue of emancipation was not the only source of Northern discontent. Widespread disappointment with the conduct of the war, the continuing antipathy of the press against a president they called uncouth and illiterate, and the Democrats' hope of political gains, all played their parts in the elections of 1862.

But in the end, his policy was successful; the Border States remained outside the Confederacy, and Britain did not extend diplomatic recognition to the Confederacy or use its navy to break the Union blockade. The Federal armies were sufficiently committed to the war that, when the time was right—i.e., the North had a plausible if incomplete victory at Antietam in September 1862—Lincoln could use a preliminary Emancipation Proclamation as a strategic weapon, causing both the strength and the morale of Confederate armies to suffer without damaging the Union war effort. Moreover, he wrote his proclamation so that the Border States would not be infuriated and bolt to the Confederacy after all. To accomplish this, he proclaimed that "all persons held as slaves within any State or designated part of a State, the people whereof shall then be in rebellion against the United States, shall be then, thenceforward, and forever free." Obviously, this meant that no slave was actually emancipated by Lincoln's proclamation, because the Confederate States did not recognize his authority and the Border States were not in rebellion.

Nevertheless, his proclamation had a great psychological effect on the armies, the civilian populations, and the slaves in all of the states. His final proclamation of January 1, 1863, was what the abolitionists had been struggling toward for more than six decades, the fulfillment of the dream of millions of Black and white Americans since 1619, and the dream nurtured by Reformed Presbyterians since before 1800. The effect on the Union army can be measured by the fact that in the 1864 election, Lincoln got 80 percent of the soldiers' vote.[20] What we find in Lincoln, then, in the words of historian Richard Striner, is a great moral leader, "a fervent idealist with a remarkable gift for strategy."[21]

Among the antislavery forces in Great Britain were the European Covenanters. In *The Covenanter,* published in Ireland, they commended "our brethren, faithful Covenanters in America, who have all along stood aloof from any participation in the accursed system of Slavery—that their testimony has begun to tell upon the public mind....As far as we can see at present, the disruption of the Union will be the shortest and most effectual way for the abolition of American Slavery."[22]

This opinion proved to be correct, in that emancipation was a powerful weapon to prosecute and shorten the war.

The Covenanters Visit Lincoln

On two occasions during the war, representatives of the Reformed Presbyterian Church met with President Lincoln at the White House regarding public affairs. The first of these was announced in a special dispatch of the Pittsburgh *Gazette* on December 12, 1862. This came after Lincoln's preliminary Emancipation Proclamation and the disastrous midterm elections, and before his final proclamation. The Pittsburgh and New York Presbyteries sent Revs. A. M. Milligan and J. R. W. Sloane respectively to call on the president,

> to urge him to steadfastly adhere to his proclamation of freedom. They had an interview of over an hour, and came away highly gratified with the results of their conversation. Mr. Lincoln assured them that he believed emancipation was the only salvation of the country, and that there could be no peace till slavery was abolished, and that he meant to stand by his proclamation.[23]

The two ministers had first called upon the two Pennsylvania Senators, Charles Sumner and David Wilmot, both of whom were supportive. Congressman John A. Bingham of Ohio had arranged the appointment with Lincoln and went with them. After Milligan had read their prepared remarks, Bingham added that "It was fit, at any rate, that the old church of freedom should be heard by herself in this crisis of our nation."[24] Lincoln was gratified by their encouragement,

*New Alexandria, Pa.,
RPC was home to pastor
A. M. Milligan.*

*RP pastor Alexander McLeod
Milligan was a recipient of rotten
eggs and other abuse because of his
antislavery speeches and writings.*

*J. R. W. Sloane was a leading
Reformed Presbyterian in the
abolitionist movement. His sermons
against slavery were published in
newspapers such as the* New York
Times, *he called upon the president
to end slavery, and he often shared
a platform with William Lloyd
Garrison.*

and expressed unequivocally his belief that "he never could see slavery in any other light than as an evil—as only evil, and that continually." They left his office with "mutual [expressions of] pleasure at the interview" and "a warm pressure of the hand and cordial good wishes for each other's welfare."[25]

On March 30, 1863, the president issued a proclamation calling on the people of the United States to keep Thursday, April 30, "as a day of national humiliation, fasting, and prayer" and "to abstain on that day from their ordinary secular pursuits, and to unite...in keeping the day holy to the Lord." This proclamation was in response to a resolution of the Senate requesting such a day. The proclamation contains certain basic principles of Christian civil government as Lincoln saw them, with much of which Reformed Presbyterians would be hard-pressed to disagree.

> Whereas it is the duty of nations, as well as of men, to own their dependence upon the overruling power of God, to confess their sins and transgressions in humble sorrow, yet with assured hope that genuine repentance will lead to mercy and pardon; and to recognize the sublime truth announced in the Holy Scriptures, and proven by all history, that those nations only are blessed whose God is the Lord; And, insomuch as we know that by his divine law, nations, like individuals, are subjected to punishments and chastisements in this world, may we not justly fear that the awful calamity of civil war which now desolates the land may be but a punishment inflicted upon us for our presumptuous sins, to the needful end of our national reformation as a whole people?... [W]e have forgotten God...and we have vainly imagined, in the deceitfulness of our hearts, that all these blessings were produced by some superior wisdom and virtue of our own. Intoxicated with unbroken success, we have become too self-sufficient to feel the necessity of redeeming and preserving grace, too proud to pray to the God that made us. It behooves us, then, to humble ourselves before the offended Power, to confess our national sins, and to pray for clemency and forgiveness.[26]

Lincoln's sense of divine judgment for national sin was more fully stated, of course, in his magnificent Second Inaugural Address two years later. In his great conclusion of the address, he was to say,

Yet if God wills it that [the war] continue until all the wealth piled by the bondman's two hundred and fifty years of unrequited toil shall be sunk, and until every drop of blood drawn by the lash shall be paid by another drawn with the sword, as was said three thousand years ago, so still it must be said: "The judgments of the Lord are true and righteous altogether."

The Covenanters were heartened by the March 30 presidential proclamation. The Synod of 1863 said, "In all this we rejoice, and hail these [words] as evidence of a better mind on the part of the nation and its rulers, and as tokens that the Lord intends good to the land by the terrible afflictions he has brought upon it."[27]

The same Synod appointed a committee to visit the president a second time, now "on the subject of the nation's duty to acknowledge God, and his Christ and his law, and to do this in its constitution." The committee—Samuel O. Wylie, J. R. W. Sloane, and William Brown, a ruling elder from Second Philadelphia congregation— reported to the Synod of 1864 that they had presented the matter to the president and found the result of their mission to be "hopeful and encouraging." Dr. Sloane's son, Professor William Sloane of Columbia University, later wrote, "Referring to a conference with himself, by Dr. Sloane and Dr. Milligan, President Lincoln said, shortly before his assassination, 'I know these Covenanters well. They have made two demands of this nation—submission to God, and freedom for the slave. One of these demands has been granted during my first administration; and perhaps, during my second, they will obtain the other.'"[28]

Thomas Sproull wrote the same in 1865.[29] With reference to this, David M. Carson includes this note:

> In Gideon Welles's diary there is a brief note on Lincoln's reaction to this matter: 'December 3, Saturday. The President read his [State of the Union] message at a special Cabinet-meeting today, and general criticism took place....One paragraph proposing an Amendment to the Constitution recognizing the Deity in that instrument met with no favorable response from any one member of the Cabinet. The President, before reading it, expressed his own doubts in regard to it, but it had been urged by certain religionists.'[30]

These accounts need to be put in context. Lincoln's responses on both occasions, and to both proposals, were common during the war. Ministers of a variety of denominations— Methodist, Baptist, New School Presbyterian, Quaker, and others—met with the president to urge emancipation, to advise him on how to win the war, etc. Loath as he was to offend the clergy, he often spoke encouraging words but made no promises. On one occasion, he told a ministerial delegation, "I hope it will not be irreverent for me to say that if it is probable that God would reveal his will to others, on a point so connected with my duty, it might be supposed he would reveal it directly to me."[31]

Covenanter Work among Freedmen

Even before the war ended, the need to help the freed slaves was a major concern among the abolitionists. A number of benevolent societies, such as the American Missionary Association, had been formed, and education was one of their top priorities. Because of the scarcity of trained Black teachers, and because most Southern white teachers refused to teach Black students, these Northern associations recruited thousands of young teachers from the North. Reformed Presbyterians were among the earliest of many groups to establish schools, clean housing, and mission work among the newly emancipated Black slaves.

As the Union armies advanced, they were increasingly encumbered with "contraband"— slaves emancipated by Confederate military losses or by the flight of their owners. Destitution, cold, lack of necessities and of medical care, and general wretchedness prevailed. The contrabands were almost naked and had little food. Although it had no congregations remaining in the South, the Reformed Presbyterian Church recognized a responsibility to help these needy people. When the Board of Domestic Missions heard of the conditions at Port Royal, South Carolina, they asked Rev. Nathan R. Johnston (then in Vermont) to go there to investigate possibilities for establishing a work among the freedmen. Johnston traveled on a government ship in March 1862. Reaching Beaufort first, he found great need, but little cooperation from the military. Continuing on to Port Royal, Johnston set to work: on Sabbaths, he taught a class of soldiers at 9 a.m., preached in the Episcopal church at 11 a.m. to a mixed crowd of soldiers and Black congregants, and at 3 p.m. and again in the evening to congregations of Black people. He began a day school to teach reading, and a night class for those who worked during the day. He appealed to the church for donations of clothing, "chosen with an eye to the needs of a southern climate." He was assisted by two Christian soldiers. In these efforts, the Reformed Presbyterians became the first Presbyterian church to come to the aid of the freedmen.[32]

> These schools had only become fairly organized, when I was obliged to leave, committing them to other hands. Leaving these poor people, so long oppressed, and now so anxious to learn, and to whom I have preached the gospel of Christ—the gospel of freedom—was one of the severest trials of my life. This, probably, is the place to add, that while I labored among the contrabands of Port Royal for their educational and religious interests, I also labored much to relieve them from their great physical destitution. My otherwise unoccupied hours were employed in giving counsel to the fugitives and the friendless, in protecting them from the abuses, the cruelties and the brutality of the soldiers, in clothing the naked, and in visiting the sick.[33]

Wartime turmoil in the South forced Johnson to give up the work in Port Royal in October 1862. At the same time, Revs. Joshua Kennedy and Robert Shields started a work at Fernandina, Florida, and were later joined by Rev. T. M. Elder. Kennedy and Elder had to leave soon because of illness, but Kennedy worked among the freedmen at Fernandina and St. Augustine until a smallpox epidemic forced him to close the school in April 1864. Hardie H. Helper, a brother of Hinton R. Helper (author of *The Impending Crisis of the South*), was appointed general superintendent of that area and he and Kennedy became friends. In a letter of July 1864, Helper admonished Kennedy not to send down any "over-zealous and foolish women" to teach the Black children, but a "strong-minded" and "strong-armed" man. This letter caused negative reaction in the church, but Kennedy seemed to agree with him, saying, "he is correct in reference to the male instructor." Helper said that the most stringent civil laws must be enacted for Black freedmen, but many in the church felt that more gospel and gentleness would better succeed.[34] Success in Florida was ephemeral. During the same period, works were begun in Little Rock and Duvall's Bluff in Arkansas, but these too did not succeed.[35]

Rev. James Wallace was authorized in 1863 to explore opportunities for a freedmen's mission on the Mississippi, but found access closed because of military operations, so he went instead to Washington.

There, in Fairfax County, Virginia, he found about 300 Black residents and an abandoned Presbyterian church and parsonage, and began to work. Very shortly, this work was terminated by Southern raiders.

With the fall of Natchez to Grant's army on July 4, 1863, the Mississippi River was open to Union forces and, after exploring Little Rock and Vicksburg, Wallace settled on Natchez in January 1864, on the advice of Colonel John Eaton, general superintendent of freedmen for Mississippi and Tennessee. Eaton said that Natchez was the largest and neediest field in his department. On March 15, 1864, Wallace described the beauty of Natchez, built on a plateau overlooking the river, with a number of impressive mansions. There were, he reported, "four thousand freed-people, emancipated when the Federal army came here last July....These are living in small huts... in great destitution, and have suffered terribly during the winter for want of necessary clothing and shelter." He spoke well of the military authorities at Natchez and the arrangements they made for housing and schools. He was given the use of one of the Presbyterian churches of Natchez for services for the freedmen. In September, Rev. J. C. K. Faris, a son of Rev. James Faris of Bloomington, Indiana, became superintendent of the Reformed Presbyterian work at Natchez. He was joined by several other teachers, as well as his brothers Daniel and Isaiah. They had four schools in Natchez, with 230 students, and two schools on nearby plantations, with about 100 pupils. There were as many as nine teachers at once in these schools. This work was closed in October 1866, when the Southern white landowners returned, reclaimed their confiscated property, and made the "Yankee" teachers unwelcome.[36]

When James Wallace's 1863 venture in Fairfax County ended abruptly, the Board of Domestic Missions purchased property for work among the freedmen in Washington, D.C. The Board established a mission there in April 1864, with Rev. J. S. T. Milligan in charge, to build a facility for a school and housing for the newly freed people. J. O. Baylis, T. M. Elder, J. M. Armour, and J. M. Johnston served in succession as administrators. A large school building was erected in 1865 and a graded school system worked out to conform to the city plan. A report from the *Boston Weekly Journal* in September 1865 was reprinted in Scotland.

Work of the Reformed Presbyterians. The Reformed Presbyterians (those who uphold the tenets of the Covenanters or 'Hill-men' of the Scottish Reformation), resident in Washington, have been doing much to aid in the elevation of the coloured people in the National Capital. True as the needle to the pole has this denomination ever been to the gospel which inculcates the immeasurable iniquity of human bondage; and in the locality there, where those who are refugees from the land of whips and chains, are most numerously congregated, they have erected a large chapel and schoolroom, 32 by 64 feet, and sixteen tenement houses, containing two rooms each, for coloured people. These buildings are on land purchased by this denomination. Several teachers will be employed at the opening of the school in September.[37]

In addition to the development of affordable housing, this mission undertook another new initiative: an industrial school to teach manual skills to men and women and to help them find employment. The motivation for the housing project was the exorbitant rents being charged Black tenants; but even the "reasonable" rents were hard to collect. The housing had been built quickly and cheaply, and deteriorated rapidly. This work continued until 1870 when it, too, had to be given up

At least three reasons explain why the Reformed Presbyterian Church did not achieve long-lasting success in these missions, if success is to be measured by the establishment of congregations. First, "the church began its work in the first flush of romantic enthusiasm for the freedmen, whose plight as slaves they had been so long bewailing." Second, the missionaries were sure that the Black freedmen "would welcome fellowship with a church which had been so abolitionist in its sentiments," whereas of course the slaves, isolated from news and unable to read, had never heard of Reformed Presbyterians or their abolitionist ideals. Third, "Covenanter forms of worship and doctrine were in such contrast to those familiar to Negroes that they were difficult for Negroes to accept."[38]

The church, then, had to reassess its goals. Was its purpose to make Covenanters of the Black people and to organize congregations, or was it to meet needs—to *do good*?[39]

Thus, a more achievable goal was established: the education of Black leaders who in turn would be able to teach and preach. In 1866, at the instigation of the Synod, Geneva College began an effort for the education of free Black people. "Professor [James L.] McCartney made negotiations with State Superintendents of Southern schools for

J. M. Armour served as an administrator at the RP mission to freedmen in Washington D.C. The mission ultimately ended in 1870.

Knox Hall (right) was part of the Selma, Ala., RP Church building (not pictured). Beside Knox Hall was the teachers' residence (left). Photo from 1945. The Selma mission was started in 1874 and grew quickly. Selma RPC is the only lasting Reformed Presbyterian Church from the multiple missions to freedmen.

suitable young men and women of color to induce them to come North and receive a practical Christian education at Northwood." This project was described in the St Louis *Missouri Democrat* as "a very praiseworthy undertaking." It spoke of Northwood as "possessing the peculiar advantages of easy access by several leading railroads, of being composed of a moral and religious community, and an isolation that protects it from influences that habits, manners, and prejudices have widely engendered." The Board of the College wrote, "[O]ppression, long and systematic, has degraded the race but has not destroyed them. The germ of moral and intellectual life has survived the fiery ordeal to a degree altogether surprising. They can be built up and made a prosperous people, but their education must necessarily be a slow process, and should be conducted with system and comprehensive views."[40]

Among the Black students at Geneva College in those immediate postwar days were John Franklin Quarels of Macon, Georgia, who became a lawyer, politician, and a U.S. Consul in Spain; Daniel Webster Boxley of Rolla, Missouri, who became an educator and rancher; Mary Anna Ramsey of Natchez, Mississippi, who became a teacher; Welby Williams of Natchez, who became a teacher and merchant; and Benjamin Franklin Peppers of Macon, Georgia, who became a lawyer at Northwood and later a postmaster and preacher. Each student was required to work two hours every day and a half day on Saturday, so as not to interfere with their studies.[41]

In March 1874, Lewis Johnston, a Black student from the seminary who had been licensed to preach, selected Selma, Alabama, as the site for a new mission. Johnston moved quickly. By May, Knox Academy began operations with fourteen pupils. Ten years later, Knox reported 530 pupils and a Black congregation with 38 members. By 1910, the school enrolled 601 and the congregation numbered 82, with 165 in the Sabbath School and 25 in the youth group. In 1930, there were 553 students, 125 of whom were in the high school. During the Great Depression, many schools were forced to close; one university in Selma closed and another church school ran on a part-time schedule, but Knox Academy continued to run full-time with 401 students in 1932 and 352 in 1933. In 1934, the Selma Board of Education had warned that they could not pay salaries after the first of the year, but the Black community took on the responsibility of financing the first eight grades of Knox Academy. They were still carrying on the school in 1936 with 325 students. By 1937, the city of Selma was providing education for Black children, and the Synod sold the buildings to the city Board of Education.[42]

For many years, the Black faculty at Knox was supplemented by a number of white graduates of Geneva College, primarily Reformed Presbyterians, who taught there, usually for terms of two to five years, continuing the pattern established in many "freedmen's missions" after the Civil War.

The influence of Knox Academy in the South was substantial. Many of its graduates went on to historically Black colleges and universities and some to Geneva College. The teachers at Knox established the only public library for Black people in Selma. The congregation continues today, and until recent years, a kindergarten was conducted in a building beside the church. Rev. Claude Brown, a son of the congregation and the pastor from 1942 until his death in 1975, was heavily involved in civic activities in the African-American community of Selma, including teaching classes for ministers in theology, sermon construction, and church planning. He was known and respected in the white community of Selma as well. One of the members, W. J. Anderson, owned and operated the private Burwell Hospital at a time when African-Americans were not permitted access to white medical facilities.[43]

Summary

How much attention should be paid to a marginalized group of uncompromising dissenters in the history of a nation in which people have traditionally been taught to get along together by compromise? Their principles were mined from the rich veins of Scripture, forged in the crucible of persecution, and shaped in the smithy of the American frontier. Though few in number, the Reformed Presbyterians had a significant impact on the antislavery movement. They were apparently the first denomination to make and enforce consistently an absolute prohibition against slave ownership by members and were among the first to reject colonization schemes and demand immediate emancipation. Their leading ministers were among the founders and leaders of antislavery societies. They were brothers-in-arms of Garrison and other abolition leaders and speakers, and preached and published often against slavery. The Reformed Presbyterian Theological Seminary had a racially integrated student body as early as the mid-1840s. The church's members and institutions were active in the Underground Railroad. The church was the first Presbyterian group to establish a mission among the freedmen of the South, in the second year of the war. In short, they wielded an influence well beyond what might be expected from so small a number. Moreover, because they did not participate in voting or political parties, they were non-political, and until the outbreak of the Civil War, they prosecuted their campaign only through moral suasion and civil disobedience, not through violence or politics. At a time when the majority of people in the United States believed neither that "all men are created equal" nor in "liberty and justice for all," the Reformed Presbyterians were a voice of conscience. Their attitude of uncompromising protest against oppression of any kind was a great service to the nation and to its Black and white citizens.

Knox Academy in 1928,
of what might have been a
graduation.

The Knox Academy
Band in 1911

Knox Academy students in 1904. Photo from the Reformed Presbyterian Standard.

Knox Academy Kindergarden with Pastor Claude Brown (center) in 1945.

Appendix: Covenanter Congregations Existing in the United States 1800–1865

*m = merged with one or more congregations, so the organization
continues, although not separable under that name. For
example, First and Third Philadelphia merged in 1952 as
United Philadelphia and in 1966 became Broomall; Second
Philadelphia in 1973 became Elkins Park.*

*N = change of name but the organization is unchanged. Data
taken from J. S. Tibby, compiler,* CovenanterRecord: list of
congregations with their historical record *(MS, 1902) and
from Owen F. Thompson,* Sketches of the Ministers of the
Reformed Presbyterian Church of North America from 1888
to 1930 *(Blanchard, Iowa, 1930).*

Congregations with a single date (establishment) are still in existence.

*This is not a history of congregations, but a list to demonstrate the small
size of the denomination. Some congregations were in or near villages
that may no longer exist or that may not appear on modern maps.
Many congregations became disorganized for a period of time and were
later reorganized; this list ignores those lapses. Congregations frequently
changed their names or merged with others; these are generally
noted, but in some cases, these changes are difficult to disentangle.
Congregations founded in 1865, but after Lee's surrender on April 9,
are not included.*

1. Conococheague, Franklin Co., Pennsylvania 1742–1898
2. First Philadelphia 1751m

3. Coldenham, Orange Co., New York 1753
    Walkill, 1759; N 1807
4. West Hebron, Washington Co., New York 1769–1923
    Argyle 1769; N 1857?
5. Rocky Creek, Chester District, South Carolina..........1772–1830
6. Big Rocky Creek, Flint Hill, Fairfield Co., South Carolina ....
                                                                    1783–1828
7. Little Rocky Creek, Chester District, South Carolina 1792–1831
8. Beaver Dam, Chester District, South Carolina...........1791–1830
9. Duanesburgh, New York..1793–1833
    Curriesbush and Princetown 1793; N 1807
10. Galway and Broad Albin, Saratoga Co., New York.....1793–1841
    Galloway, Balston Spa, Saratoga Co., N 1804
11. Monongehela, Pennsylvania 1793–1918
12. Princeton, Indiana 1813–1943
13. Schenectady, New York..1792–1833
14. Baltimore, Maryland 1797–1905
15. Kortright, Delaware Co., New York 1796–1909
    Harpersfield 1796; N 1808
16. Ashland, Boyd Co., Kentucky 1797–1804
17. Miller's Run, Washington Co., Pennsylvania..............1797–1944
    Chartiers 1797; N Canonsburg 1806; N 1835
18. First New York City 1797m
19. Ryegate, Caledonia Co., Vermont.............................1798–1916
20. Elkton, Todd Co., Kentucky 1799–1819
21. Pittsburgh, Pennsylvania 1800m
    Pittsburgh and Allegheny 1833; Allegheny from 1865
22. Blue Lick, Washington, Mason Co., Kentucky...........1801–1814
23. Duck River, Hickman Co., Tennessee 1805–1819
24. Garrison, Fayette Co., Indiana 1805–1884
25. Beech Woods, Preble Co., Ohio................................1809–1884
    Merged with Garrison 1853
26. Pine Creek and Union, Glade Mills, Butler Co., Pennsylvania .....
                                                                    1806–1925
27. Rose Point, Lawrence Co., Pennsylvania 1806
    Shenango and Neshannock 1806; N Slippery Rock; N Rose
    Point 1927
28. Little Beaver, New Galilee, Lawrence Co., Pennsylvania ....
                                                                    1807–1942

29. White Lake, Sullivan Co., New York.................................1808
30. Cedarville, Green Co., Ohio 1812–1923
    Massie's Creek 1812; N Xenia 1850–1863
31. Xenia, Ohio 1810–1841
32. Brush Creek, Locust Grove, Adams Co., Ohio.........1812–1895
    Chillicothe 1815; N 1829
33. Hephzibah (Elk River), Lincoln Co., Tennessee........1812–1833
34. Greensburg, Pennsylvania 1813–1867
35. Utica, Ohio 1813–1949
    Licking Creek 1813; N 1823
36. Youngstown, Ohio....................................1814–1970
    Austintown 1803; N Poland and North Jackson 1814; N
    Youngstown 1885
37. Bovina, Delaware Co., New York ....1816–1943 m
38. Albany, New York 1815–1853
39. Craftsbury, Orleans Co., Vermont....................1816–1911
40. Cincinnati, Ohio.....................................1816–1958
41. Camp Run, Wurtemburg, Lawrence Co., Pennsylvania...............
                                                          1818–1849
42. Bethesda, Hazelwood, Chester District, South Carolina ....
                                                          1816–1833
43. New Milford, Susquehanna Co., Pennsylvania...........1817–1838
44. Broad Albin, Fulton Co., New York.........................1818–1838
45. Topsham, Orange Co., Vermont............................1818–1896
46. Paterson, New Jersey 1821–1833
47. New Concord, Ohio..................................1821–1961
    Salt Creek 1821; N 1871
48. Bethel, Sparta, Randolph Co., Illinois 1819m
49. Bethesda (Bloomington), Indiana 1821
50. Brookland, Westmoreland Co., Pennsylvania.............1822–1933
    Thompson's Run and Puckety 1823; N 1835
51. Walnut Ridge, Washington Co., Indiana 1821–1861
52. New Alexandria, Pennsylvania.........................1819–2004
53. Jonathan's Creek, White Cottage, Muskingum Co., Ohio............
                                                          1820–1963
54. Greenfield, Harrison Co., Ohio.........................1822–1851
55. Londonderry, Guernsey Co., Ohio.........................1822–1912
56. Sterling, Cayuga Co., New York.........................1823–1901
    Clyde and Galen 1823; N 1830

57. York, Livingston Co., New York 1823–1944
    Caledonia 1825; N 1830
58. Argyle, Salem, Washington Co., New York 1823–1857
59. First Newburgh, New York 1824m
60. Clarksburg, Indiana Co., Pennsylvania 1824–1918
    Black Legs 1824; N 1843
61. Lisbon, St Lawrence Co., New York............................... 1832
62. Lansingburgh, Rensselaer Co., New York.................. 1828–1842
63. Troy, New York 1828–1849
64. Walnut Creek, Pickerington, Fairfield Co., Ohio 1829–1854
65. Second New York City... 1830 m
66. Black Warrior, Boligee, Greene Co., Alabama........... 1830–1833
67. Milton, Northumberland Co., Pennsylvania 1830–1833
68. Rochester, New York 1834–1895
69. Muskingum and Tomica, Dresden, Muskingum Co., Ohio..........
                                            1831–1908
70. First Miami, Logan Co., Ohio............................ 1831–1877m
71. Ballibay, Camptown, Bradford Co., Pennsylvania 1832–1837
72. Wilmington, Delaware 1832–1833
73. Allegheny, Pennsylvania 1833m
    See Pittsburgh 1800
74. Southfield, Michigan... 1834
75. Oakdale, Illinois.. 1834–2010
    Elkhorn 1834; N 1895
76. Old Bethel, Houston, Randolph Co., Illinois 1831m
77. New Hartford, Oneida Co., New York..................... 1837–1843
78. Utica, New York 1837–1841
79. Loudonville, Ashland Co., Ohio 1838–1845
80. Bloomfield, Pontiac, Michigan 1840–1855
81. Buffalo, New York 1848–1855
82. Cedar Lake, Ray, Steuben Co., Indiana 1841–1927
83. Second Philadelphia, Pennsylvania........................... 1842m
84. Sandusky, Crestline, Crawford Co., Ohio 1843–1876
85. St Louis, Missouri.. 1846–1918
86. Sharon, Des Moines Co., Iowa 1846
    Lind Grove and Cedar 1846; N 1854
87. Rehoboth, Indiana Co., Pennsylvania...................... 1847–1971
    Warsaw and Montgomery 1847; N 1855
88. Salt Fork, Sugar Tree, Guernsey Co., Ohio 1847–1869

89. Third New York City 1848m
90. Wilkinsburg, Pennsylvania.. 1848–1981
91. Vernon, Waukesha Co., Wisconsin 1848–1940
      Waukesha 1848; N 1850
92. Syracuse, New York...1849
93. Third Philadelphia, Pennsylvania 1850m
94. Second Miami, Logan Co., Ohio......................... 1851–1877m
95. Macedon, Mercer Co., Ohio 1852–1888
96. Springfield, Balm, Mercer Co., Pennsylvania............ 1852–1894
97. Lake Eliza, Lake Co., Indiana................................. 1852–1886
98. Fourth Philadelphia, Pennsylvania 1853–1859
99. Rushsylvania, Logan Co., Ohio 1853–1888
100. Detroit and Novi, Michigan 1854–1871
      Detroit disorganized 1913
101. First Boston, Massachusetts..................................... 1854–1953
102. Brownsville, Monroe Co., Ohio 1854–1879
103. Church Hill, Coulterville, Illinois............................ 1854–1923
104. Rehoboth, Louisa Co., Iowa................................... 1854–1930
105. Second Newburgh, New York 1854–1919
106. Clarinda, Iowa 1855
107. Hopkinton, Delaware Co., Iowa 1856–1992
      Maquoketa 1856; N 1879
108. Lind Grove, Mediapolis, Des Moines Co., Iowa 1856–1896
109. Brooklyn, New York 1857–1921
110. Houlton, Aroostook Co., Maine 1859–1897
111. Oil Creek, Titusville, Pennsylvania 1860–1917
112. Middle Wheeling, Roney's Point, Ohio Co., West Virginia........
                                                                                      1842–1897
113. Salem, Stanton, Jefferson Co., Pennsylvania 1860–1905
114. Walton, New York 1861
115. Grove Hill, Bremer Co., Iowa................................ 1861–1868
116. Staunton, Macoupin Co., Illinois 1863–1911
117. Washington, Iowa...1863
118. Davenport, Iowa.. 1864–1869

Notes

Chapter 1, Introduction

1   Jane Grey (Cannon) Swisshelm, *Half a Century*, 3rd ed. (Chicago: Jansen, McClurg & Co., 1880), 65. Swisshelm (1815–1884) was a Reformed Presbyterian woman from Wilkinsburg, near Pittsburgh, Pennsylvania, living temporarily in Louisville, Kentucky. Her record of the Kentuckian's actual words was, "A good cook, good washah and ironer, fust rate housekeepah! I'll let you have ah for two hundred dollars a year. But I'll tell you honest, you'll have to hosswhip her youahseff about twice a week; that wife ah yoahs could nevah do anythin with ah."

2   James Davison Hunter, *To Change the World: the Irony, Tragedy, and Possibility of Christianity in the Late Modern World* (Oxford: Oxford University Press, 2010), 38.

3   Max Weber, *The Sociology of Religion*, 4th ed., rev. by Johannes Winckelmann, tr. Ephraim Fischoff (Boston: Beacon Press, 1993), 178–179.

4   Weber, 166–168.

5   Weber, 175–176.

6   Marissa D. King and Heather A. Haveman, "Antislavery in America: The Press, the Pulpit, and the Rise of Antislavery Societies," *Administrative Science Quarterly* 53 (2008), 500–502. The authors use the terms "this-worldly" and "other-worldly" instead of "ascetic" and "mystical."

7   To be fair, this came about perhaps as a reaction against the heterodox "social gospel" movement of the early twentieth century.

8   *Minutes of Synod* 1836, 16–19.

Chapter 2, My Kith and Kin Had Died at the Stake

1   Daniel Ritchie, "Radical Orthodoxy: Irish Covenanters and American Slavery, circa 1830–1865," *Church History* 82/4 (2013), 813.

2   "The Coming of the Lord: the Northern Protestant clergy and the civil war crisis," in Randall M. Miller, et al., eds., *Religion and the American Civil War* (New York: Oxford University Press, 1998), 120.

3   Neatly encapsulated in the question, "Shall the planting South or the industrial and farming North govern the nation?" Charles A. Beard and Mary R.

Beard, *The Making of American Civilization* (New York: Macmillan, 1937), 453.
4   Timothy L. Smith, *Revivalism and Social Reform: American Protestantism on the Eve of the Civil War* (Abingdon, 1957; rpt Gloucester, MA: Peter Smith, 1976), 179.
5   Smith, 180.
6   There was clearly a bifurcation between the two camps. Whether these denominations were fair to Garrison is another question entirely. Leading Reformed Presbyterian ministers such as J. R. W. Sloane and Nathan R. Johnston retained confidence in and friendship with Garrison as a fellow Christian. As the larger denominations attempted to preserve their national unity by suppressing antislavery discussion, they increasingly demonized Garrison and the other abolitionists as unchristian, heretical, and uncharitable.
7   Cf. James G. Birney, *The American Churches, the Bulwark of American Slavery*, 3rd ed. (Newburyport, MA: 1842), *passim*.
8   Birney, 48.
9   Ritchie, 846.
10   John Knox, *The History of the Reformation of the Church of Scotland* (Paisley: Printed by John Neilson for David Gardner, 1791), II, 325–341. [Emphasis added.]
11   Knox, II, 19–30.
12   David Ray Wilcox, "The Reformed Presbyterian Church of North America and the Anti-Slavery Movement" (Thesis, M.A., Greeley: Northern Colorado University, 1948), 5–6. "Around 800 documents are still extant recording agreements made by members of the Scottish nobility and gentry from around 1450 to 1603..." Clare Jackson, *Restoration Scotland, 1660–1690: Royalist Politics, Religion and Ideas* (Woodbridge: Boydell, 2003), 67.
13   See Thomas Houston, *The Fellowship Prayer Meeting* (Glasgow: R. S. Brown, 1856), 75–76.
14   Macinnes, "The Scottish Constitutions, 1638–51: The Rise and Fall of Oligarchic Centralism," in John Morrill, ed., *The Scottish National Covenant in its British Context* (Edinburgh: Edinburgh University Press, 1990), 106–133.
15   John Howie of Lochgoin, *The Scots Worthies* (1775; Edinburgh: The Banner of Truth Trust, 1902), 626. The numbers he cites were published in 1690 (shortly after the Revolution) in *A Short memorial of the Suffering and Grievances of the Presbyterians in Scotland*. J. D. Douglas, *Light in the North* (Grand Rapids, MI: Eerdmans, 1964), 142–143. See also Wilcox, 8–9.
16   Praying for the salvation of the Jews is today considered offensive by Jews and some Christians, but compared to the prohibition or active persecution of Jews elsewhere at the time, this was a comparatively enlightened position.
17   Wilcox, 8–9. See also Chris Villi, "The Historical Impact of Covenanter Societies" (unpublished, 2011).
18   In Robert Wodrow, *The History of the Sufferings of the Church of Scotland from the Restoration to the Revolution* (Glasgow: Blackie & Son, 1836), III ch 4: 207–211, at 210. Available, *inter alia*, at http://www.freechurch.org/resources/confessions/confessions.htm (accessed May 26, 2009). Excerpt in Gordon Donaldson, *Scottish Historical Documents* (Glasgow: Neil Wilson, 1974), 240–241.

19   The Queen still annually appoints a Lord High Commissioner to the General Assembly; in 2021, Prince William, Duke of Cambridge and Earl of Strathearn. The Commissioner addresses the Assembly at opening and closing, and reports to the Queen, but no longer has the power he had after 1689. During the Assembly, the Commissioner lives in the Palace of Holyroodhouse.

20   Johannes G. Vos, *The Scottish Covenanters: Their Origins, History, and Distinctive Doctrines* (Tsi-tsi Har, Manchuria: The Author, 1940), 135–136.

21   Jane Grey Swisshelm, *Half a Century* (Chicago: Jansen, McClurg, 1880), 43–44; Vos, 329. Her knowledge of Scottish battle tactics was not astute.

22   John H. Thomas, *A Cloud of Witnesses, for the Royal Prerogatives of Jesus Christ*, 15th ed. (Pittsburgh: Eichbaum and Johnston, 1824), 348.

23   Oliver Perry Temple, *The Covenanter, The Cavalier, and The Puritan* (Cincinnati: Robert Clarke, 1897), 94–96. The term Scots-Irish (or its obsolete form "Scotch-Irish") refers to Protestant families who migrated from Scotland to the "Ulster Plantation" of Northern Ireland and, usually after a generation or several, to America (including Canada). They are therefore primarily Scottish in ethnicity but arrived from Ireland.

24   The earliest description of how such a meeting should be organized came in a letter by John Knox in October 1557. John Black Johnston, *The Prayer-Meeting, and its History, as identified with the life and power of godliness, and the revival of religion* (Pittsburgh: United Presbyterian Board of Publication, 1870), 139–140. Knox's list is an obvious model for the directions published by Reformed Presbyterians as *A Short Directory for Religious Societies* (Newburgh, NY: Dennis Cole, 1806). First published in 1772 in Scotland.

25   Reid W. Stewart, ed., *The Minutes of the Correspondent, May 1780 to February, 1809 (Being the Oldest Minutes of any Presbyterian Group West of the Allegheny Mountains* (Apollo, PA: Presbyterian Historical Society of the Upper Ohio Valley, 1994), vii, xx–xxi.

26   W. M. Glasgow, *History of the Reformed Presbyterian Church in America* (Baltimore: Hill and Harvey, 1888), 244; cf. S. Helen Fields, ed., *Register of Marriages and Baptisms Performed by Rev. John Cuthbertson, 1751–1791* (Washington, DC, 1934; rpt 2001), x.

27   Frederick Jackson Turner, *The Frontier in American History* (New York: Henry Holt, 1921), 105.

28   Glasgow, 244.

29   *Renewal of the Covenants, National and Solumn League, a confession of sins, an engagement to duties, and a testimony* (Philadelphia: B. Franklin, 1744; rpt 1748; rpt Beaver Falls, Pennsylvania, 1895), 25, 31–32. "Protestation and Testimony of the witnessing remnant of the Anti-popish, Anti-prelatic, Anti-erastian, Anti-sectarian, true Presbyterian Church of Christ in Scotland, against the sinful incorporating union with England and their British Parliament, concluded and established May, 1707," in *Testimony-Bearing Exemplified* (Paisley, 1791; New York, 1834) 347–362. Craighead had been a Presbyterian, then was a Reformed Presbyterian for a time before returning to the Presbyterian Church. His career illustrates the fluid Presbyterianism of the frontier and the unifying power of anti-Royalist sentiments. The quotation is from Arthur Lynn Cross, *The Anglican Episcopate and the American Colonies* (New York: Longmans, Green,

1902), quoted in C. H. Van Tyne, "Influence of the Clergy and of Religious and Sectarian Forces on the American Revolution," *American Historical Review* 19 (October 1913), 46–47.

30   *Pennsylvania Gazette,* June 9, 1743. Alice M. Baldwin, "Sowers of Sedition," *The William and Mary Quarterly,* V/1 (January 1948), 64–66. Perhaps the royal government's attitude reflected continuing anxiety about the Jacobite Rebellion of 1715, knowing that many Scots still did not accept the Hanoverian dynasty, and nervously anticipating the rising that erupted in 1745. Had the governor known Scottish history a little better, he would have been certain that the Covenanters were singularly unlikely to support a return of the Stuart monarchs.

31   Baldwin, 67–68. Also in Wilcox, 27.

32   Originally the term "District" as used in the Carolina colony was applied to a loosely defined area for crown land-grants. When the colony was divided into North and South in 1729, North Carolina instituted counties, but South Carolina continued to use the term "District" until after the Revolutionary War, when they established counties. Bounty lands were granted as a reward to repay citizens for risks and hardships endured in the service of their country, often military service. Such grants had been standard practice in the British empire well before the American Revolution. It is not clear the purpose for which the bounty lands settled by Martin's colony were granted. They may have been granted simply in return for populating the area, which was backward and underpopulated in this period.

33   Glasgow, *History,* 379–392.

34   John Cuthbertson, *Diary, 1751–1791, passim.* The original is now in the Barbour Library, Pittsburgh Theological Seminary. Extracts have been published as *Register of Marriages and Baptisms Performed by Rev. John Cuthbertson, 1751–1791,* ed. S. Helen Fields (Lancaster, PA: Lancaster Press, 1934; rpt Bowie, MD: Heritage Books, 2001). A typescript copy of the complete diary is in the Archives of the Reformed Presbyterian Church of North America, Pittsburgh. See also Wilcox, 29–30. Cuthbertson does not specify the ethnicity of the groom; we have followed the "best available evidence" and considered this the implication of Cuthbertson's note.

35   Glasgow, *History,* 64, and Wilcox, 31–32. Cf. Hinton Rowan Helper, *The Impending Crisis of the South: How to Meet It* (New York: Burdick Brothers, 1857), 196–197.

36   Glasgow, *History,* 68.

37   Wilcox, 32.

38   *The Debates in the Federal Convention of 1787, Reported by James Madison, a delegate from the state of Virginia.* Ed. by Gaillard Hund and James Brown Scott (Oxford: Oxford University Press, 1920), Thursday June 28, 1787. Available at http://avalon.law.yale.edu/18th_century/debates_628.asp (accessed June 15, 2009).

39   Glasgow, *History,* 78; Wilcox, 33–34.

40   *Reformation Principles Exhibited by the Reformed Presbyterian Church in the United States of America* (New York, 1807), 136–137. Hereafter cited as *Reformed Presbyterian Testimony,* its usual title after 1833.

41   Expressed most clearly in Samuel Rutherford's *Lex, Rex* (1644), which in

turn built on the political theory of George Buchanan (1579). Whether that deficiency renders the Constitution non-Christian, anti-Christian, or still a product of Christianity remains a source of disagreement.

42   Merton L. Dillon, *The Abolitionists: The Growth of a Dissenting Minority* (Dekalb, Illinois: Northern Illinois University Press, 1974), 132.

43   Dillon, *The Abolitionists*, 190–191.

44   Richard E. Beringer et al., *The Elements of Confederate Defeat: Nationalism, War Aims, and Religion* (Athens: University of Georgia Press, 1988), 28.

Chapter 3, The Sum of All Villainies

1   Hugh Thomas, *The Slave Trade: The Story of the Atlantic Slave Trade: 1440–1870* (New York: Simon & Schuster, 1997), 25. Note that many of the secondary sources for the present chapter post-date Dr. Wilcox's work (1948), particularly the controversial data reported by Robert William Fogel and Stanley L. Engerman, in *Time on the Cross* (Boston, 1974) on slave life. Those data do nothing to justify or mitigate slavery, because the issue was (and remains) bondage vs. freedom. An exploration of what Reformed Presbyterians and other abolitionists were actually opposing is, however, important to a nuanced account of what they did.

2   See Kevin Bales, *Disposable People* (Berkeley: University of California Press, 1999), *passim*.

3   The first Africans taken involuntarily by Europeans were seized in 1443 at Capo Bianco (Mauritania) and taken to Portugal as slaves. Chrystal Ponti, "America's History of Slavery Began Long Before Jamestown," *History*, August 26, 2019. Bartolomé de Las Casas, in his *Historia de las Indies*, reported that the king of Portugal authorized each Spanish settler to import "about a dozen blacks from Castile if they would free their Indian slaves." Las Casas agreed, but later claimed that he did not know how Black people came to be enslaved in Iberia. He describes a raid by the Portugese in 1444 in which 216 Africans were captured. Addendum to Las Casas, *The Only Way*, ed. Helen Rand Parish, tr. Francis Patrick Sullivan, S. J. (New York: Paulist Press, 1992), 202–208.

4   The enslavement of native Americans at the beginnings of European exploration of North America is traced in Almon Wheeler Lauber's "Indian Slavery in Colonial Times within the Present Limits of the United States" (Diss. Ph.D., Columbia University, 1913), in *Studies in History, Economics and Public Law, Edited by the Faculty of Political Science of Columbia University*, 54/3, 1914. "The enslavement of the natives was practiced by the Indians themselves, the Spanish, the French, and the English" (7 [259], 352 [604]). Available online at Google Books. See also Rebecca Onion, "America's Other Original Sin," *Slate* January 18, 2016 (accessed online June 30, 2020).

5   See generally Thomas, *passim*.

6   Seymour Drescher, "British Way, French Way: Opinion Building and Revolution in the Second French Slave Emancipation," *American Historical Review* 96/3 (July 1991), 709.

7   Linda M. Heywood and John K. Thornton, *Central Africans, Atlantic Creoles, and the Foundation of the Americas 1585–1660* (Cambridge, UK:

Cambridge University Press, 2007), cited in Chrystal Ponti, *History*, August 26, 2019: "Significant numbers of them were brought in as early as 1526."

8   Lisa Rein, "Mystery of Va.'s First Slaves Is Unlocked 400 Years Later," *The Washington Post*, Sunday, September 3, 2006, p. A01. Linda M. Heywood and John K. Thornton, *Central Africans, Atlantic Creoles, and the foundation of the Americas, 1585–1660*, (Cambridge, UK: Cambridge University Press, 2007).

9   Richard Hofstadter estimates that, "If we leave out of account the substantial Puritan migration of 1630–40, not less than half, and perhaps considerably more, of all the white immigrants to the colonies were indentured servants, redemptioners, or convicts. Certainly a good many more than half of all persons who went to the colonies south of New England were servants in bondage to planters, farmers, speculators, and proprietors." "White Servitude," ch. 2 of *America at 1750* (New York: Alfred A. Knopf, 1970). Slavery was apparently first codified in the English colonies with the Virginia Slave Codes of 1706.

10   Thomas, 174. Black slaves accompanied Coronado and other *conquistadores* in Florida and New Mexico in the previous century, but they returned to New Spain with their masters.

11   Slavery had been widespread among Native Americans; slaves were acquired through conquest, gambling, barter with other tribes, and sale. The extent of the trade may be estimated from the fact that various tribes in the Southeast owned slaves from the northern Plains.

12   Bailey W. Diffie, *Latin American Civilization, Colonial Period* (Harrisburg, PA: Stackpole, 1945).

13   Robert William Fogel and Stanley L. Engerman, *Time on the Cross: The Economics of American Negro Slavery* (Boston: Little, Brown, 1974), 14. They also report that "the death rates among European troops in West Indian colonies exceeded that of slaves" (26).

14   Fogel and Engerman, *Time on the Cross*, 20–29.

15   Jubal Early, *The Heritage of the South* (Lynchburg, VA: Press of Brown-Morrison Co., 1915), 1–24.

16   Diffie, *Latin American Civilization*, 473; U.S. census data for 1800.

17   The first slave ship built in America seems to have been the *Desire*, 120 tons, built in Marblehead, Massachusetts, in 1636. George Francis Dow, *Slave Ships and Slaving* (n.pl.: Marine Research Society, 1927), 267.

18   Gradual emancipation usually meant that while adult slaves remained in existing servitude, the children born to slaves after a specified date were set free upon their eighteenth, twenty-first, or even twenty-eighth birthday (to work off the expense of their upbringing).

19   Early, *Heritage of the South*, 24–57.

20   U.S. census data, consulted at http://fisher.lib.virginia.edu/collections/stats/histcensus/php/newlong2.php (accessed June 2, 2009). Figures for 1790 for those of the above states that were not yet in the Union (Louisiana, Mississippi, Tennessee) are as published in *The Evangelical Witness* I (1822–1823), 132.

21   The percentage of slaves in the total population of the South in 1650 was 3 percent, and in 1860 ca. 44 percent; in the British Caribbean, the share in 1650 was 25 percent, and by 1770 it was 91 percent. Fogel and Engerman, *Time*, 22.

22   Albert Bushnell Hart, *Slavery and Abolition, 1831–1841* (New York: Harper

and Brothers, 1906), 67–69. Wade Hampton III, the famous Confederate cavalry general and popularly known as the wealthiest man in the South, was said to have owned more than 20,000 acres of land and 3,000 slaves.

23   Adam Hochschild, *Bury the Chains: Prophets and Rebels in the Fight to Free an Empire's Slaves* (Boston: Houghton Mifflin, 2005), 5.

24   Manisha Sinha, *The Slave's Cause: A History of Abolition* (New Haven: Yale University Press. 2016), 10–11.

25   Available online in Project Gutenberg, *The Works of Aphra Behn*, Vol. 5.

26   *De l'Esprit des Lois* (1777 edition) online at https://archive.org/details/ spiritoflaws0lmontuoft (accessed October 17, 2020). For an excellent survey of Wesley's arguments, see David N. Field, "John Wesley as a public theologian: the case of thoughts upon slavery," *Scriptura* 114 (Stellenbosch, 2015). Wesley's booklet is available online in HathiTrust Books; also found in Wesley, *Works*, 11 (Grand Rapids; Baker Book House, 1979). For an eighteenth-century British perspective on the system in America, see Alexander Hewatt, *An Historical Account of the Rise and Progress of the Colonies of South Carolina and Georgia* (London: 1779), I, 120–125. Mary Stoughton Locke, *Anti-Slavery in America from the Introduction of African Slaves to the Prohibition of the Slave Trade (1619–1808)* (Boston: Ginn and Company, 1901; rpt. New York: Johnson Reprint Corporation, 1968), 9–19.

27   The two most notable of these accounts are Ottobah Cuguano, *Thoughts and Sentiments on the Evil and Wicked Traffic of the Slavery and Commerce of the Human Species* (London: 1787) and Olaudah Equiano, *The Interesting Narrative of the Life of Olaudah Equiano, or Gustavus Vassa, the African* (London: 1789).

28   *Narrative of the Life of Frederick Douglass, An American Slave, Written by Himself* (Dublin: Webb and Chapman, 1845), 74–75. Many editions.

29   Douglass, *Narrative*, 12–15.

30   Hart, *Slavery and Abolition*, 135.

31   See generally Davis, *Inhuman Bondage*, 205–230. The figure of 250 was found by Herbert Aptheker, *American Negro Slave Revolts* (New York, 1943), although many of his reports were unsubstantiated and in some (many?) cases were perhaps nonexistent "plots" created by imaginative white Northerners.

32   Douglass, *Narrative*, 102–106.

33   Fogel and Engerman, *Time on the Cross*, 38–43.

34   Hart, *Slavery and Abolition*, 94; Douglass, *Narrative*, 32–33. Cf. William Goodell, *The American Slave Code, in theory and practice* (New York: American and Foreign Anti-Slavery Society, 1853), 319, citing a Georgia statute providing a fine of $500 for teaching a Negro to read.

35   Hart, *Slavery and Abolition*, 109.

36   Douglass, *Narrative*, 5–6.

37   Hart, *Slavery and Abolition*, 120–122.

38   Hart, *Slavery and Abolition*, 110.

39   Douglass, *Narrative*, 22–24.

40   Hart, *Slavery and Abolition*, 120.

41   Goodell, *American Slave Code*, 24–25.

42   Wilcox, 42. Hart, *Slavery and Abolition*, 128–129. See also Goodell, *American Slave Code*, 85–86. At a time when an able field hand sold for $800,

one beautiful mulatto young woman was sold for $7,500.

43   Daina Ramey Berry, *The Price for Their Pound of Flesh: The Value of the Enslaved, from Womb to Grave, in the Building of a Nation* (Boston: Beacon Press, 2017), esp. 42–43, 68.

44   John Belton O'Neall, ed. *The Negro Law of South Carolina* (Columbia: 1848), 8. Available online at HathiTrust (accessed November 18, 2020).

45   Frederick Law Olmsted, *A Journey in the Back Country* (New York: Mason Brothers, 1861), 55.

46   Hart, *Slavery and Abolition,* 122.

47   Fogel and Engerman, *Time on the Cross,* 44–52. Nonetheless, see the accounts by ex-slaves collected by the WPA Writer's Project and reprinted in Robert Edgar Conrad, ed., *In the Hands of Strangers: Readings on Foreign and Domestic Slave Trading and the Crisis of the Union* (University Park, PA: Pennsylvania State University Press, 2001), 231–245, 259–272. See also the discussion in Kenneth M. Stampp, *The Peculiar Institution: Slavery in the Ante-Bellum South* (New York: Vintage Books, 1956), 245–251. On the related subject of "miscegenation," see Stampp, 350. In response to the controversy aroused by *Time on the Cross,* Fogel in 1989 published *Without Consent or Contract: the Rise and Fall of American Slavery* (New York: Norton, 1989), in which he documents how an economically successful system was eventually brought down on essentially moral and non-economic grounds. For *Time on the Cross,* Fogel and Engermann received the Bancroft Prize in American History.

48   Fogel and Engerman, *Time on the Cross,* 78–86, esp. 79; 54. Cf. below, on treatment of slave families.

49   Fogel and Engerman, *Time on the Cross,* 109–115. Beth Blonigan, "A Re-Examination of the Slave Diet" (unpublished thesis, B.A., College of St Benedict/St John's University, 2004), *passim.* See Herbert C. Covey and Dwight Eisenach, *What the Slaves Ate: Recollections of African American Foods and Foodways from Slave Narratives* (Santa Barbara, CA: Greenwood Press, 2009).

50   Fogel and Engerman, *Time on the Cross,* 115–116.

51   Fogel and Engerman, *Time on the Cross,* 117–126. However, see Robert Fogel, *Without Consent or Contract: The Rise and Fall of American Slavery* (New York: Norton, 1989), 153.

52   Fogel and Engerman, *Time on the Cross,* 125–126.

53   Fogel and Engerman, *Time on the Cross,* 127.

54   Fogel and Engerman, *Time on the Cross,* 127–128. The authors point to the dual legal structure of medieval Europe: the law of the manor and the law of the crown. The situation in the slave states was analogous, essentially a patriarchal relationship between the owners (nobility) and slaves (serfs, peasants). For more on the abolitionists' myths of the Black family, see *Time,* pp. 126–144. See also Goodell, *American Slave Code,* 105–121.

55   Andrew Billingsley, *Climbing Jacob's Ladder: The Enduring Legacy of African-American Families* (New York: Simon & Schuster, 1992), 102–103.

56   Department of the Navy, Navy Historical Center, "Flogging in the U.S. Navy," at http://www.history.navy.mil/library/online/flogging.htm. During the Napoleonic Wars, soldiers in the British Army could be sentenced to 1,200 lashes—more than enough to kill or disable a man. Such massive floggings were

usually administered at a rate of ten or twenty per week until the total was reached.
57   Fogel and Engerman, *Time on the Cross,* 144–157.

Chapter 4, This Outrage on the Rights of Men

1   Samuel Brown Wylie, *Memoir of Alexander McLeod, D.D.* (New York: Charles Scribner, 1855), 504–505.
2   James Ford Rhodes, *History of the United States from the Compromise of 1850 to the McKinley–Bryan Campaign of 1896,* 7 vols. (New York: Macmillan, 1920), I, 62–63. He adds in a footnote, "The anti-slavery agitation is probably the last great reform that the world is likely to see based upon the Bible and carried out with a millennial fervor."—*Life of Garrison,* vol. i. p. xiii. Quoted in D. Ray Wilcox, *The Reformed Presbyterian Church and the Antislavery Movement* (thesis, M.A., Northern Colorado University, 1948), 46.
3   Early Lee Fox, *The American Colonization Society 1817–1840* (Baltimore: Johns Hopkins Press, 1919), 14.
4   *Acts and proceedings of the General Assembly of the Presbyterian Church, in the United States of America, A.D. 1794* (Philadelphia: Printed by R. Aitken & Son, no. 22 Market Street, 1794, Early American imprints). Series I, Evans (1639–1800); no. 27547. A further denunciation was adopted by the Assembly in 1818; see Hinton Rowan Helper, *The Impending Crisis of the South: How to Meet It* (New York: Burdick Brothers, 1857), 260. In neither case was any measure adopted to enforce the ruling on members.
5   Helper, *Impending Crisis,* 269.
6   Helper, *Impending Crisis,* 270. In 1790, the Society of Friends petitioned the U.S. Congress to abolish slavery, but some members retained their slaves. While the resolution of the Philadelphia Conference of Quakers has been often cited, the Quakers are congregationalist and thus unable to enforce their rulings on their churches; and in any case a ruling would apply only to the regional Conference.
7   To John F. Mercer, September 9, 1786, in Helper, *Impending Crisis,* 193. (Emphasis in original.)
8   University of Virginia, *The Washington Papers,* at mountvernon.org/george-washinton/slavery (accessed February 10, 2020). On the law of dower in Virginia, see 1 Vir. Rev. Code 435, cited in George McDowell Stroud, *A Sketch of the Laws Relating to Slavery in the Several States...,* 2nd ed. (Philadelphia: Henry Longstreth, 1856), 231.
9   Helper, *Impending Crisis,* 195–199. One of Jefferson's correspondents, Richard Price of London, had written a pamphlet in 1785 in which he argued that America's revolt against the British power meant that Americans must give up slavery, "for it is self-evident that if there are any men whom they have a right to enslave, there may be those who have had a right to hold them in slavery." Quoted by David Waldstreicher in introducing a Jefferson letter in his edition of *Notes on the State of Virginia* (New York: Palgrave Macmillan, 2002), 70.
10   *Notes on the State of Virginia,* in Thomas Jefferson, *Writings* (New York: The Library of America, 1984), 289 (Query XVIII). In the course of his adult life, Jefferson owned more than 600 slaves.

11   *Notes on Virginia* (Library of America ed.), 264–270 (Query XIV). One wonders about the perspective of Jefferson's mulatto mistress, Sally Hemings.

12   Notes on the Constitutional Convention, 25 August 1787, online at https://founders.archives.gov/documents/Madison/01-10-02-0106 (accessed February 10, 2020).

13   Wilcox, 50. That he used the singular form "mulatto" perhaps implied that the groom, Newport Walker, was not mulatto, but whether he was Black or white is speculation.

14   William Melancthon Glasgow, *History of the Reformed Presbyterian Church in America* (Baltimore: Hill and Harvey, 1888), 77.

15   *Reformation Principles Exhibited by the Reformed Presbyterian Church in the United States of America* (New York: 1807), 123; Glasgow, *History*, 78, 562.

16   In Reformed Presbyterian polity, a man who proposes to become a minister is first examined by the Session (board of elders) of his congregation; if recommended by them, he applies to the presbytery to "be taken under care [of the presbytery]." Upon examination, if the presbytery approves, he may attend seminary to study for the ministry. Being "under care" simply means that the person is recognized as a legitimate candidate for ministerial training, and is accountable to the presbytery for his progress. In modern times this normally means that the presbytery will pay for the candidate's academic expenses.

17   A "call" is an official invitation from a congregation for a particular minister to be their pastor.

18   *Reformation Principles Exhibited by the Reformed Presbyterian Church in the United States of America* (New York: 1807), 123. The minutes of the meeting have been lost. At that time, in the Reformed Presbyterian Church as well as in most other denominations, receiving communion was equated with membership in the congregation or denomination.

19   John McKivigan, *The War Against Proslavery Religion: Abolitionism and the Northern Churches, 1830–1865* (Ithaca: Cornell University Press, 1984), 28, 44.

20   McKivigan, *War Against Proslavery Religion*, 28.

21   Papers of Rev. Thomas Donnelly, published in *Our Banner* 3 (1876), September, October, November, and 4 (1877), January.

22   *Our Banner* 3 (1876), 356.

23   *Our Banner* 3 (1876), 357–358.

24   *Our Banner* 3 (1876), 435.

25   Minutes of March 12, 1801, in *Our Banner* 4 (1877), 29–30. Part of Martin's defense was reported to be, "Ye a' see I'm opposed to slavery, for I ha'e sold mine." D. S. Faris, "Reminiscences of the R.P. Church in South Carolina," *Our Banner* 2 (1875), 347.

26   *Our Banner* 3 (1876), 392. Doubts about the "current legal form" were understandable. In South Carolina, prior to 1800, "anything that showed that the owner had parted with his property" was enough to establish the slave's freedom. Under an Act of 1800, the owner and the slave were required to appear before a panel of a Justice and five freeholders of the village, and vouch for the character of the slave and his/her capability to earn an honest livelihood. Later, under an Act of 1820, manumission required a specific Act of the Legislature. In 1841, the law was again changed to prohibit anyone, including owners, taking a

slave out of the state for the purpose of emancipation. John Belton O'Neall, *The Negro Law of South Carolina* (Columbia: 1848), 10–12. Cf. William Goodell, *The American Slave Code* (New York: American and Foreign Anti-Slavery Society, 1853), 341.

27   *Our Banner* 4 (1877), 30. "Ruling elders," in Presbyterian polity, are lay-members elected by a congregation to be their "governing board." A congregation normally has two or more such elders, in addition to a pastor or "teaching elder." Only a teaching elder may conduct marriages and administer baptism and the Eucharist.

28   Samuel Brown Wylie, *Memoir of Alexander McLeod, D.D.* (New York: Charles Scribner, 1855), 54–55. The calculation of monetary values across time is not an exact science, but makes for interesting general comparison. In terms of *relative earnings*, 3,000 guineas (£3,150) in 1801 is >£3.5 million in 2020 (>US$4.5 million). Alternatively, at the *rate of exchange* in 1801, £1 = \$4.38, this would have amounted to \$13,797 (in 1801 dollars); at today's rate of approximately £1 = ±\$1.30, the equivalent would be ca. U.S. \$4.6 million in 2020 dollars. The two methods arrive at nearly the same result. On the other hand, using the CPI, the current (2018) real price value is a much more reasonable \$315,000. In any case, it is clear that for five small congregations this was a very significant sacrifice.

29   *Our Banner* 2 (September 1875), 348.

30   *Minutes of the Reformed Presbytery*, 1801–1806, 1.

31   *Minute Book of Coldenham Session*, 1801–1823, 16–17. Quoted in Wilcox, 56.

32   *Minute Book of Coldenham Session*, 1801–1823, 18–19. Quoted in Wilcox, 56.

33   *Reformation Principles Exhibited* (1807), 108; (1835), 119; (1853), 108. All editions after 1833 have the title *Reformed Presbyterian Testimony*.

34   *Reformed Presbyterian Testimony* (1864), 236.

35   *Reformed Presbyterian Testimony* (1864), 239–240.

36   William B. Sprague, *Annals of the American Associate, Associate Reformed, and Reformed Presbyterian Pulpit* (New York: Robert Carter and Brothers, 1869), 27.

37   *Our Banner* 3, 130, 348.

38   Glasgow, 500. Located in Pendleton, South Carolina, it was established by the state assembly in 1811 and re-incorporated in 1826.

39   Faris papers; transcribed in Henry Lester Smith, "The Underground Railroad in Monroe County," *Indiana Magazine of History* 13/3 (1917), 292. Usually, a slave was sold "down the river" only if they were unproductive, dishonest, or rebellious, character defects that Faris does not mention.

40   Glasgow, *History*, 500; D. S. Faris, *Life, Work, and Character of Rev. James Faris* (West Barnet, VT: D. C. Faris, 1883), 17. At the time of writing his thesis, Wilcox had in hand the original bill of sale for Isaac. Dr. Samuel Brown Wylie was also Professor of Greek and Latin at the University of Pennsylvania for a number of years. From 1810–1817 and 1823–1827, Wylie was the sole professor in the Reformed Presbyterian Theological Seminary.

41   Note that the issue was fornication, not miscegenation. The mixing of races was not an issue in this case.

42   Letter, James Faris to his wife Nancy, July 30, 1825, TS copy made by Miss Elizabeth Faris; also in D. S. Faris, *Life, Work, and Character*, 17.

43   Wilcox, 62. In the Faris Papers, which in 1948 were in the possession of Mr. Finley Faris of Greeley, Colorado. They were inherited by his grandson, Dennis Dunn, and were lost in a disastrous farm fire at Milliken, Colorado, in approximately 1981. Personal communication, Dennis Dunn to R. M. Copeland, July 2009.

44   D. S. Faris, *Life, Works, and Character*, 18.

45   Elizabeth F. Carson, "An Inordinate Sense of History: James Renwick Willson 1780–1853" (thesis, M.A., The College of William and Mary, 1987), *passim*. See also Glasgow, *History*, 723–724. His namesake, James Renwick, was a Cameronian minister who was martyred in 1688. Underlining the importance of historical memory to group cohesion, many children in Reformed Presbyterian families have been named after Renwick as well as other heroes and martyrs (such as Donald Cargill and Samuel Rutherford).

46   James R. Willson, *The Subjection of Kings and Nations to Messiah* (New York: E. Conrad, 1820), 42.

47   *Subjection*, 32.

48   Marissa D. King and Heather A. Haveman, "Antislavery in America: The Press, the Pulpit, and the Rise of Antislavery Societies," *Administrative Science Quarterly* 53 (2008), 498.

49   *Evangelical Witness* 1 (1822–1823), 310.

50   *Evangelical Witness* 2 (1823), 131. Statistics are attributed to "a paper by George Hervey, Esq., published in the Edinburgh Philosophical Journal" (132).

51   George M. Frederickson, "The Coming of the Lord: The Northern Protestant clergy and the Civil War Crisis," in Randall M. Miller et al., *Religion and the American Civil War* (New York: Oxford University Press, 1998), 114–115. Postmillennialism is the belief that the second coming of Christ will occur *after* the millennium.

52   Quoted in Frederickson, 115, 116.

53   *Evangelical Witness* 2 (1823), 133–134.

54   Ibid., 134.

55   Ibid., 135–136. The term "servile war" was in common use to denote a war by a servant class.

56   *Our Banner* 11 (1884), 41.

57   *Evangelical Witness* 2 (April 1824), 410–411.

58   Ibid., 412–417. From 1828 to 1836 the Reformed Presbyterian Synod sought "an alternative remedy," the American Colonization Society, under the impression that it was an antislavery effort; see chapter 5 below.

59   (Philadelphia: Published by Request, 1838), *passim*.

Chapter 5, We Have, in Fact, Always Been an Abolition Society

1   *Our Banner* 11 (1884), 37–41.

2   David M. Carson, *A History of the Reformed Presbyterian Church in America to 1871* (diss., Ph.D., University of Pennsylvania, 1964), 184–186.

3   "The Two Witnesses," *Reformed Presbyterian* 3 (1839), 12, 13. The Reformed Presbyterian Church has never taken an official position on the views of the millennium, but until the twentieth century, most ministers and members were postmillennialists.

4   *Minutes of Synod*, 1849, in *Reformed Presbyterian* 13 (1849), 150.

5   "Report of the Presbytery of Illinois on Anti-Slavery Societies," *Reformed Presbyterian* 4 (1841), 368.

6   *Reformed Presbyterian* 1 (1837), 316. Throughout the era, Reformed Presbyterians joined in other major reform movements as well: temperance, Sabbath observance, and opposition to oath-bound secret societies, for example. Carson, 187 ff.

7   Douglas R. Egerton, *Gabriel's Rebellion: The Virginia Conspiracies of 1800 and 1802.* (Chapel Hill, NC: University of North Carolina Press, 1993), 21–22. Gabriel is sometimes, though incorrectly, given the surname Prosser, which appears to be the name of his enslavers.

8   Early Lee Fox, *The American Colonization Society 1817–1840* (Baltimore: The Johns Hopkins Press, 1919), 15: "...slavery was looked upon by the leaders of thought in the South and in the North as one of the great national problems that pressed for a solution....The men who are to be considered its founders [the American Colonization Society] recognized in both the free negro and the slave a momentous problem, and the aim of Colonizationists was to find a satisfactory solution of it.

9   Quoted in Fox, *American Colonization Society*, 47.

10   In Fox, *American Colonization Society*, 48. Emphasis original.

11   Jefferson, *Notes on Virginia*, in *Writings* (New York: Library of America, 1984), 270 (Query XIV). His fear of racial mixing (miscegenation) is ironic in light of his fathering several mixed-race children.

12   Thomas Hodgin, M.D., *An Inquiry into the Merits of the American Colonization Society, and a Reply to the Charges Brought Against It* (London: J. & A. Arch, 1833), 4–5.

13   Wendell P. and Frank J. Garrison, *William Lloyd Garrison 1805–1879: The Story of his Life told by his Children* (4 vols., New York, 1885–1889), I, 147.

14   *First Report of the New-York Colonization Society* (New York: J. Seymour, 1823), unpag. Online at http://digital.library.pitt.edu/cgi-bin/t/text-idx? (accessed August 25, 2009).

15   *Evangelical Witness* 1, 425; D. S. Faris, *Life, Work, and Character of Rev. James Faris* (West Barnet, VT, 1883), 17.

16   Henrietta Buckmaster (pseudonym of Henrietta Henkle), *Let My People Go: The Story of the Underground Railroad and the Growth of the Abolition Movement* (New York: Harper & Bros., 1941), 33. See also David Walker, *Appeal...to the Coloured Citizens of the World* (Boston: 1830), 64–65. Available online at https://docsouth.unc.edu/nc/walker (accessed February 12, 2020).

17   William Jay, *Inquiry into the Character and Tendency of the American Colonization, and American Anti-Slavery Societies* (1838), quoted in Robert Edgar Conrad, *In the Hands of Strangers* (University Park, PA: Pennsylvania State University Press, 2001), 338–344.

18   *Minutes of the Synod*, 1836, 16.

19   Ibid., 16–17.

20   Ibid., 18.

21   (Boston: Garrison and Knapp, 1832). Available online at Project Gutenberg, Manybooks, Google Books, etc.

22   Henry Mayer, *All on Fire: William Lloyd Garrison and the Abolition of Slavery* (New York: St. Martin's Griffin, 1998), 142. That ACS statement does not pass the laugh test. How would the ACS explain the conclusion of the Declaration of Independence, "we mutually pledge to each other our lives, our fortunes, and our sacred honor"?

23   Walker, *Appeal*, 69, 71, 79, 82.

24   Mayer, *All on Fire*, 444–445.

25   McKivigan, *War Against Antislavery Religion*, 44.

26   Marissa D. King and Heather A. Haveman, "Antislavery in America: The Press, the Pulpit, and the Rise of Antislavery Societies," *Administrative Science Quarterly* 53 (2008), 507.

27   He was the son of Rev. James Renwick Willson (see pages 50–55).

28   *Our Banner* 11 (1884), 18–19. After the Civil War, the Reformed Presbyterian Church adopted a new Covenant in 1871, in which Willson's view seems to be vindicated by the commitment, "Considering it a principal duty of our profession to cultivate a holy brotherhood, we will strive to maintain Christian friendship with pious men of every name, and to feel and act as one with all in every land who pursue this grand end." On Sloane, see *Life and Work*, 74.

29   *Fifth Annual Report of the Executive Committee of the American Anti-Slavery Society...* (New York: Dorr, 1838), 131, 144.

30   *Sixth Annual Report of the Executive Committee of the Anti-Slavery Society...* (New York: American Anti-Slavery Society, 1839), 33.

31   *Address of the State Anti-Slavery Society to the Ministers of the Gospel in the State of Pennsylvania* (Philadelphia: Merrihew and Gunn, 1838), 12.

32   *Minutes of the Synod*, 1838, 302–303.

33   Glasgow, *History*, 106–108.

34   *Our Banner* 11 (1884), 39.

35   Alexander McLeod Milligan, in *Our Banner* 11 (1884), 39. The "New Lights," through several mergers, were in 1982 incorporated into the Presbyterian Church in America (PCA). For an exposition of the views of the New Lights, see Wylie, *Memoir of Alexander McLeod*, 458–470, and especially 471–481 on slavery.

36   *The Crooked Path to Abolition: Abraham Lincoln and the Antislavery Constitution* (New York: W. W. Norton, 2021).

37   *Reformed Presbyterian Testimony* (1806), 239.

38   *The American Conflict* (Washington, DC: National Tribune, 1902), I: 117.

39   Unpublished; photostat copy in the author's possession. Thompson's son, attorney James R. Thompson of Newburgh, said that he remembered his father telling him that Dr. Sloane replied to the letter. In 1883, Dr. A. M. Milligan said that Greeley had commended the Covenanters for their part in the antislavery movement. Greeley himself did not initially support Lincoln for president, but Edward Bates of St. Louis—a slaveholder. *Recollections* (New York: J. B. Ford, 1868), 389. Bates was later Lincoln's Attorney General.

40   In C. Peter Ripley, *The Black Abolitionist Papers, Vol. III: the United States, 1830–1846* (Chapel Hill: University of North Carolina Press, 1991), 144.

41   *Our Banner* 11 (1884), 40.

42   Hart, *Impending Crisis*, 246–249. The mayor, police, and fire companies

refused to prevent the arson or to put out the fire; their efforts were devoted solely to saving adjoining buildings. The city's official report blamed the fire and riots on the abolitionists, saying they had provoked the violence.

43   Wendell P. and Frank J. Garrison, *William Lloyd Garrison*, I: 435, III: 482.

44   N. R. Johnston, *Looking Back from the Sunset Land* (Oakland, CA: n.pub., 1898), 602.

45   *Our Banner* 11, 37–40. A chaise was a two-wheeled carriage drawn by a single horse.

46   *Life and Work of J. R. W. Sloane*, 83; 90; 88.

47   *Our Banner* 11 (1884), 41; *Centennial of the New Alexandria Reformed Presbyterian Church, October 11, 1916* (n.p.), 12.

48   W. P. and F. J. Garrison, *William Lloyd Garrison*, III: 287.

Chapter 6, The Constitution Is the Magna Carta of Slavery

1   William Sloane, ed., *Life and Work of the Rev. J. R. W. Sloane, D.D.* (New York: A.C. Armstrong & Son, 1888), 143–144. "Declaration of Principles and Constitution of the Church Anti-Slavery Society, adopted March 2, 1859," broadside, *The Church Anti-Slavery Society, Second Anniversary, Tuesday, May 28,* [1861], in the collections of the Massachusetts Historical Society. Online at http://www.masshist.org/database/viewer.php?item_id=1663&img_step=1&mode=large#page1 (accessed August 26, 2014).

2   1852 Free Soil Party Platform, available at http://www.angelfire.com/indie/ourcampaigns/1852.html (accessed September 2, 2014). In 1848 the party called itself the Free Soil Party; in their 1852 platform they refer to themselves as Free Democracy and the Free Democratic Party. On Hodge, see George C. Rable, *God's Almost Chosen Peoples: A Religious History of the American Civil War* (Chapel Hill: University of North Carolina Press, 2010), 16. The same was true of Moses Stuart: there are moral evils associated with slavery, he said, but they do not render slavery in itself sinful. Mark Noll, *The Civil War as a Theological Crisis* (Chapel Hill: University of North Carolina Press, 2006), 38–39.

3   Noll, "The Bible and Slavery," in Randall M. Miller et al., eds. *Religion and the American Civil War* (New York: Oxford University Press, 1998), 66.

4   See David Brion Davis, "Slavery and Sin: The Cultural Background," in Martin Duberman, ed. *The Antislavery Vanguard: New Essays on the Abolitionists* (Princeton: Princeton University Press, 1965), 3–31, for a discussion of the morality of slavery from Greek antiquity through ancient Judaism and the early Christian church. English translations of the biblical words `ebed (`avath), doulos, and *servus* (Hebrew, Greek, and Latin respectively) enabled proslavery readers to conflate "servant," "bond-servant," and "slave," in order to obscure the argument.

5   Jedidiah Morse, *The American Geography* (Elizabeth Town: Shepard Kollock, 1789), 65.

6   "The State and Slavery," in *Life and Work of J. R. W. Sloane* (New York: A.C. Armstrong, 1888), 160. Although undated, the address refers to the debacle of the Democrat convention at Charleston in late April 1860.

7   In a famous but apocryphal story, when Mrs. Stowe was introduced to

President Lincoln, he said, "So you're the little woman who started this big war."
On its day of publication it sold 3,000 copies. In that year it sold 300,000 copies
in the U.S. and 1,000,000 in Britain. In 1855, it was described as "the most
popular novel of our day." Ernest Everon, "Some Thoughts Anent Dickens and
Novel Writing," *The Ladies' Companion and Monthly Magazine* 7/2 (1855): 259.
8   Diary, June 12, 1852. Willson papers.
9   *Life and Work of J. R. W. Sloane,* 207–209.
10   Morse, quoted in McLeod, *Negro Slavery Unjustifiable,* 44 fn.
11   *The Impending Crisis of the South* (New York: Burdick Bros., 1857), 80, 51.
12   *Impending Crisis,* 13.
13   Contrarians, during the past century and more, have attempted to show
that slavery was indeed economically productive; efficient by reason of economies
of scale. The measurements of efficiency and productivity continue to be
controversial, more than half a century after Fogel and Engerman's *Time on the
Cross* (Boston: Little, Brown, 1974). See the discussion above (p. 31).
14   For more detailed information on this compromise, see Garry Wills, *"Negro
President": Jefferson and the Slave Power* (Boston: Houghton Mifflin, 2003), esp.
50–61.
15   In practice, they insisted on the admission of an equal number of free and
slave states: Maine and Missouri, Indiana and Mississippi, etc.
16   The six were South Carolina, Georgia, Alabama, Mississippi, Louisiana, and
Kentucky. Leonard L. Richards, *The Slave Power* (Baton Rouge: Louisiana State
University Press, 2000), 49.
17   For fuller discussion of this term and how it worked, see Leonard L.
Richards's excellent *The Slave Power: The Free North and Southern Domination,
1780–1860* (Baton Rouge: Louisiana State University Press, 2000).
18   Timothy Patrick McCarthy, in "A Culture of Dissent: American
Abolitionism and the Ordeal of Equality" (diss., Columbia University, 2006),
at 14–15, discusses the importance of religion to abolitionism. See especially his
footnote 27 for reference to a number of relevant studies. Mark Noll discusses
the hermeneutical problems in "The Bible and Slavery," in Randall M. Miller et
al., *Religion and the American Civil War* (New York: Oxford University Press,
1998), 43–73. Noll does not consider the Reformed Presbyterian position,
presumably because it was marginalized in the national discussion.
19   XIX.15. Saint Augustine, *The City of God,* tr. Marcus Dods (New York:
Modern Library, 1993), 693–694.
20   Alexander McLeod, *Negro Slavery Unjustifiable* (New York: Printed by T.
& J. Swords, 1802.) At least eleven printings by 1863.
21   See Pamela Newkirk, *Spectacle: the astonishing life of Ota Benga* (New York:
Amistad Press, an imprint of Harper Collins, 2015) and Phillips Verner Bradford
and Harvey Blume, *Ota Benga: the Pygmy in the Zoo* (New York: St Martin's Press,
1992). Benga was also exhibited at the World's Fair in St Louis in 1904.
22   Morton's views were disseminated in Josiah C. Nott and George R.
Glidden's *Types of Mankind: Ethnological Researches* (Philadelphia: Lippincott,
Grambo & Co., 1854). Morton qualified the taxonomy of species to include
three types: *remote* (which never produce hybrids), *allied* (which produce, with
each other, infertile offspring), and *proximate* (which produce, with each other,

fertile offspring). Nott & Glidden, 81. His third category explains why Black people can intermarry with "superior species." Note that McLeod condemns a view that had been in circulation for a quarter century after Edward Long but well before Morton, Nott, and Glidden.

23   Cf. Noll in Miller et al., 72, fn 68, citing two studies of this argument and its fate.

24   In 1810, the African American theologian Daniel Coker made the same argument; see Noll, *Theological Crisis*, 70. I have not discovered whether any writer before McLeod's 1802 treatise raised this point. To kidnap a person and reduce him or her to slavery was punishable by death under both the Code of Hammurabi and the law of Moses.

25   McLeod, 4.

26   *Minutes of Synod* 1836, 16–17.

27   *Reformed Presbyterian* 2/1 (March 1838), 8–13 and 2/2 (April 1838), 39–47. Moses Roney was the editor.

28   See, *inter alia*, the website www.theocracywatch.org, which "monitors the rise of the religious right in the Republican Party."

29   See, e.g., John Coffey, *Politics, Religion and the British Revolutions: The Mind of Samuel Rutherford* (Cambridge: Cambridge University Press, 1997), 155 ff.

30   Dewey D. Wallace, Jr., in Mircea Eliade, ed., *The Encyclopedia of Religion* (New York: Macmillan, 1987), *s.v.* "Theocracy."

31   The Stuart monarchs and others who assert the right of the government to control the internal affairs of the church are known as Erastians, after Swiss theologian Thomas Erastus (1524–1583).

32   See, *inter alia*, "Three Propositions Respecting the Mediatorial Dominion of Christ, as they were agreed upon by The Reformed Presbytery in 1749, and more fully explained in a Postscript published by the Presbytery in 1754." These were acts of the Scottish Reformed Presbytery. Available online at http://www.truecovenanter.com (accessed September 9, 2009).

33   *Constitution of the Reformed Presbyterian Church of North America* (Pittsburgh: 2010), A–70 (Chapter 23. "Of the Civil Magistrate"). The Reformed Presbyterian Church of Ireland maintains the classic view that all legitimate civil rulers must be Christians.

34   See the discussion by Mark Noll in Miller, 61–66.

35   "Reminiscences of the Church in South Carolina," *Our Banner* 3 (1876), 130. Before his 12th birthday the family moved to Sparta, Illinois.

36   *Our Banner* 3 (1876), 130.

37   "Negro Slavery," *Evangelical Witness* 2 (1824), 414.

38   *Covenanter* 7 (1851), 128.

39   *Covenanter* 2 (1847), 307–308.

40   Willson Papers, Library of the Reformed Presbyterian Theological Seminary, Pittsburgh, Box 24, file 4. Dated December 17, 1839.

41   There was no Third New York congregation until 1848; Brooklyn congregation was organized in 1857.

42   Willson papers, Box 23, file 54.

43   For more about Williams and his experience there, see Robert M. Copeland, "The Reformed Presbyterian Theological Seminary in Cincinnati 1845–1849,

Bulletin of the Cincinnati Historical Society 31/3 (Fall 1973), 158–159; Nathan R. Johnston, *Looking Back from the Sunset Land* (Oakland, California, 1898), 70–71. Black students were welcomed at Oberlin College from 1835, and in Pennsylvania the Institute for Colored Youth (now Cheyney State University) was established in 1837.

44   W. M. Glasgow, *History of the Reformed Presbyterian Church in America* (Baltimore: Hill and Harvey, 1888), 672–675.

45   Sloane, *Life and Work*, 77–80 and 79 fn. The footnote on p. 79 quotes the New York *Tribune*'s account of the meeting. Emphasis original.

46   *Life and Work*, 122. Three years later, in a more temperate criticism, he called them "these lovers of a milk-and-water gospel, these rose-water philanthropists who would cure all the evils of society by homeopathic doses of this high dilution of love and charity." He compares them to ostriches: pursued by abolitionists, they hide their heads in the philosophical sand and refuse to see that slaveholding is sin. Ibid., 137, 144.

47   *Life and Work*, 123–124. Abraham Lincoln was also contemptuous of clergy who defended slavery on biblical grounds; see Rable, *God's Almost Chosen People*, 187. Mark A. Noll also remarks that Presbyterians in Britain and Canada had "only contempt for efforts [by James Henley Thornwell and others] to defend Southern slavery on the basis of the Bible." Noll, "The Bible and Slavery," 52.

48   *Life and Work*, 125.

49   *Life and Work*, 125, 126.

50   *Life and Work*, 132–155, at 139–140. Also published in *The Reformed Presbyterian* 24/9 (September 1860), 261–268 and 24/10 (October 1860), 293–299. Tremont Temple was a strongly Abolitionist Baptist church with a racially integrated membership. The Boston crowds often disapproved. For example, on December 3, 1860, abolitionists attempted to hold a meeting there to commemorate the execution of John Brown, but a mob of "Unionists" took over the meeting and forcibly ejected the Black participants and the abolitionists from the building. *Harper's Weekly, a Journal of Civilization* IV, no. 207 (December 15, 1860), 787, with engraving on p. 788. Regarding Sloane's comment about the Chinese, Indians, or Japanese, James M. Pendleton of Kentucky had made a similar point in 1849: If slavery promoted the "holiness and happiness" of slaves, would it not be well if white people were to be enslaved to promote their holiness and happiness? Noll, *Theological Crisis*, 54–55.

51   *Life and Work*, 146–147.

52   *Life and Work*, 148.

53   *Life and Work*, 152, 164, and elsewhere.

54   *Life and Work*, 170–174. Early in the speech, he makes reference to the Democrats' convention in Charleston (p. 158), which suggests a date in 1860 after May 3 (the adjournment of the Charleston convention) and *perhaps* before May 18 (Lincoln's nomination at the Republican convention).

55   *Life and Work*, 176–227. Also published separately as a pamphlet (New York: William Erving, 1861), 40 pp.; available online at http://www.archive.org. Henry Jackson Van Dyke (1822–1891) was pastor of First Presbyterian Church, Brooklyn, and the father of the poet and writer Henry Van Dyke.

56   *Life and Work*, 181–200. The precise nature of the relationship between

Onesimus and Philemon in Paul's writing is unclear and was a subject of debate in the antebellum period. Jesus's sermon quoting Isaiah 61:1–2 (Luke 4:16 ff.) dealt with the prophecies of himself and his work. Sloane's use of that passage should perhaps be understood as a rhetorical or ironic flourish; if it was intended as serious exegesis, it seems somewhat elliptical. Further see John W. Robbins, *Slavery and Christianity: Paul's Letter to Philemon* (Unicoi, Tennessee: The Trinity Foundation, [2007]).

57   *Life and Work,* 209.

58   Paul Worth, *Henry Jackson Van Dyke* (New York: Anson D. F. Randolph and Co., 1892), 9. Available online from Google Books.

59   "Sermon by Rev. J. R. W. Sloane, Third Reformed Presbyterian Church," *New York Times,* December 1, 1861, page 2; available online at http://query. nytimes.com/gst/abstract.html? (accessed August 21, 2009).

60   Frederickson, 120.

61   *Life and Work,* 240, 241.

62   *Life and Work,* 237.

63   *Life and Work,* 245, 251.

Chapter 7, The Duty to Refuse Compliance

1   N. R. Johnston, *Looking Back,* 119–129; Wilbur H. Siebert, *Underground Railroad,* 161; William Still, *Underground Rail Road,* 31. A novel was written about this event, Kate E. R. Pickard's *The Kidnapped and the Ransomed* (1856); rpt. as History, Series I Number I (n.pl.: Negro Publication Society of America, Inc., 1941). Since the book was published in 1856, Pickard necessarily had to omit some facts bearing on people then living whose safety would have been jeopardized.

2   Letter from Mrs. John K. Peoples to D. R. Wilcox, March 10, 1948. Wilcox, 113 fn 2. Mrs. Peoples was the granddaughter of David Stormont, and wife of John Peoples, M.D., a missionary in Mersine, Turkey, in the early twentieth century.

3   *Proceedings and Debates of the House of Representatives of the United States at the Second Session of the Second Congress, Begun at the City of Philadelphia, November 5, 1792,* "Annals of Congress, 2nd Congress, 2nd Session (November 5, 1792, to March 2, 1793)," 1414–1415.

4   STAT AT LARGE 462 (September 18, 1850). Daniel Webster's draft of the Act had provided that alleged escapees were entitled to a jury trial and could testify on their own behalf. 31st Congress, 2nd Session, S. 255. These provisions did not survive the legislative process.

5   "Civil Disobedience," *Writings of Henry David Thoreau* (Boston: 1906), IV: 362–363.

6   William Still, *The Underground Rail Road* (Philadelphia: Porter & Coates, 1872). Still (1821–1902) was born in New Jersey to former slaves, and was active as an abolitionist in the Philadelphia area. The fate of his brother Peter and family has been noted at the beginning of this chapter.

7   Wilbur H. Siebert, *The Underground Railroad from Slavery to Freedom* (New York: The Macmillan Company, 1898). Siebert (1866–1961) taught History at the Ohio State University from the 1890s until his retirement in 1935.

8   Larry Gara, *The Liberty Line: The Legend of the Underground Railroad* (Lexington: University of Kentucky Press, 1961); rpt. with new preface, Lexington: University Press of Kentucky, 1996.

9   Henrietta Buckmaster (Henkle), *Let My People Go*, 42–25.

10   Siebert, *Underground Railroad*, xxi–xxii.

11   Ibid., 47–54.

12   Ibid., 58. Letter quoted in Wilcox, 105.

13   Still, *Underground Rail Road*, 81, and Siebert, *Underground Railroad*, 63–67.

14   J. F. H. Claiborne, in *The Life and Correspondence of John A. Quitman*, II, 28, claimed that the South had lost 100,000 slaves and a value of $30 million due to lax enforcement of the Fugitive Slave Law. How much "property" was actually lost is not known with any accuracy. Most Southern estimates of the effect of abolitionists were wildly exaggerated, particularly before the war, when Southern senators were trying to persuade Congress to enforce the law.

15   Siebert, *Underground Railroad*, 92; 90; 325.

16   Siebert, *Underground Railroad*, 115; 32.

17   In Presbyterian governance, a "stated supply" is a minister who is assigned by the presbytery to minister to a vacant congregation and to serve as moderator of the session on a short-term basis, while a pastor is one who has been called by the congregation and installed by the presbytery, and usually serves as moderator of the session by right rather than by special appointment.

18   *Looking Back from the Sunset Land*, 115–120.

19   Letter, Dr. Samuel E. Greer to D. Ray Wilcox, February 24, 1948; in Wilcox, 110 fn 2. Greer, pastor of First Philadelphia from 1922 to 1950, said that he remembered the oldest members of the congregation telling of this experience. Dr. T. P. Stevenson, pastor of the congregation from 1863 to 1912, was also said to be deeply involved in helping fugitives.

20   *The Centenary of a Covenanter Society, 1822–1922, Being a History of the Brookland Congregation (1922)*, 41–43; quoted in Wilcox, 110 fn 3.

21   *Centenary of a Covenanter Society*, 43. Mary Walkinshaw (1836–1925) was the daughter of Rev. Hugh Walkinshaw, pastor of Brookland from 1835–43, and his wife Lydia Jean Sproull (daughter of Robert Sproull). She married Rev. Robert Reed, pastor of Brookland from 1854–1882. The grandfather mentioned in the account would be Robert Sproull.

22   Susan Linville and Elizabeth Dirisio, *In Hot Pursuit: The Hidden History of the Underground Railroad in Lawrence County, Pennsylvania* (New Castle, PA: Pokeberry Press, 2016). See pp. 66–67, 73–75, 81–83, 102–104, 128–129. Like many houses in western Pennsylvania, the Magee home was built on a steep slope, so that the basement exit was at ground level.

23   Siebert, *Underground Railroad*, 115. Franklin College in New Athens (1818–1919) was another, and was interdenominational and abolitionist.

24   The village of Utica was established in 1810. See generally Roelof R. Brinkerhoff, *A Sesquicentennial History of Utica, Licking County, Ohio, 1810–1960* (Utica, Ohio: Utica Herald, 1960; rpt. 1992).

25   The engineering needed for a tunnel of this scope makes the veracity of the story somewhat questionable. It persists in local lore, however.

26   *The Utica Herald,* April 7, 1938. McFarland's home, on the northeast corner of Spring and Central Streets, no longer exists. D. Ray Wilcox was the pastor here from 1931–1937, and lived in a room in the Kirkpatrick home, which apparently stood approximately where the Utica Elementary School now stands. The tunnel was recalled by Mr. Otto Thiel, age 94, at Utica on August 16, 2009. The grist mill, rebuilt, is a popular ice cream emporium and picnic area. The article in the *Utica Herald* was written by Perry Adams, principal of the grade school in Utica.

27   Glasgow, *History,* 448; letter from Mrs. Mary E. Boyd Reynolds, daughter of J. C. Boyd, to D. R. Wilcox, February 13, 1948, in Wilcox, 112. She described activities of her father and his parishioners at Utica and Sandusky River. At the latter, William Reynolds slept with a corncutter (corn knife) beside his bed. She mentioned families at Utica who helped: Adams, Dunlap, Kirkpatrick, and Watson. The Sandusky congregation was named for the Little Sandusky River, a minor tributary of the Sandusky River, and is not to be confused with the city of Sandusky, Erie Co., on the shore of Lake Erie.

28   *Bellefontaine Examiner* (Bellefontaine, Ohio, 2018), 11. Online at www.examiner.org/images/WebEdition/2018_LoCoBicentennialSection.pdf (accessed Jan 30, 2019). I have not been able to verify the church membership of Torrance and Aiken, but both names are familiar in Reformed Presbyterian circles.

29   Siebert, *Underground Railroad,* 13. Letter from William M. Sloane to W. Siebert, dated Paris, November 19, 1896.

30   W. M. Glasgow, ed., *The Geneva Book* (Philadelphia: Westbrook, 1908), 67. Wilcox, 112.

31   Siebert, *Underground Railroad,* 14; letter from J. S. T. Milligan to Siebert, December 5, 1896.

32   Glasgow, *The Geneva Book,* 68.

33   Communication to Rev. John McMillan, 1948. The account of singing Psalm 119 was communicated to Wilcox by Eleanor Coleman Edgar, date unknown. It has now become folklore in the denomination and has been located in many different congregations, so that it is impossible to know where or in what family it actually occurred. We have placed it here because it very likely happened *someplace,* and this is where Wilcox placed it in a handwritten marginal note. Source of Speer's list: Edna George, "Geneva Hall and the Underground Railroad: Historical Letter," *The Geneva Alumnus* 27/2 (January 1951), 5, including photographs of the document. It is also copied and transcribed in Lorle Porter, *A People Set Apart* (Zanesville, OH: New Concord Press, 1998), 270–271, with modern photos of Speer's house, 272–273.

34   In 1844 an upheaval within the Board at Miami resulted in the election of Dr. Erasmus Darwin McMaster, son of Dr. Gilbert McMaster of the Reformed Presbyterian Church of Duanesburgh, New York (New Light), and a firm abolitionist who suffered the consequences of that position in the politics of the Presbyterian Church. See Glasgow, *History,* 614–616.

35   Quoted in Porter, 256.

36   Diary, unpublished; Faris Family Papers, in Wilcox, 115.

37   Henry Lester Smith,"The Underground Railroad in Monroe County,"

Indiana Magazine of History, 13/3 (September 1917), 289–290.

38　D. S. Faris, *Life, Work and Character of Rev. James Faris* (West Barnet, Vermont: D. C. Faris, 1883), 18.

39　Diary, unpublished, Faris Family Papers; in Wilcox, 117.

40　Paul Donald Faris, *House Built on the Rock: Faris genealogy* (Pahrump, Nevada: mimeo., 1973), 19.

41　Siebert, *Underground Railroad,*, 14–15.

42　Letter, James A. Todd to Miss Iva McMillan of Greeley, Colorado, March 1, 1928. Wilcox, 117. James Todd was the son of A. C. Todd.

43　The story, based on documents preserved by the Hayes and Borders families, is told in Carol Pirtle, *Betwixt Two Suns: a true tale of the Underground Railroad in Illinois* (Carbondale: Southern Illinois University Press, 2000), *passim*. In 2020 Hayes's memory was honored by being inducted into the Randolph Society, a county historical Who's Who. See at RandolphSociety.org (accessed March 10, 2020).

Chapter 8, Ichabod

1　In the Faris Papers, quoted in Wilcox, 127–128.

2　Hugh Thomas, *The Slave Trade* (New York: Simon & Schuster, 1997), 545, 661–662; Thomas A. Bailey, *A Diplomatic History of the American People* (New York: F.S. Crofts & Co., 1947), 222–223.

3　*The Reformed Presbyterian* I (1837), 189–191.

4　Dodd, *Expansion and Conflict* (Boston: Houghton Mifflin, 1915), 137. Dodd (1869–1940) was a native of North Carolina and taught at the University of Chicago, 1908–1933.

5　Eugene D. Genovese, "Religion in the Collapse of the American Union," in Miller et al., *Religion in the American Civil War* (New York: Oxford University Press, 1998), 74–88. As Genovese notes (p. 74), the definition of "sin" was decisive.

6　See the resolution adopted by the Massachusetts Antislavery Society in 1840, in W. P. and F. J. Garrison, *William Lloyd Garrison, 1805–1879* (New York: The Century Co., 1885–1889), II: 338.

7　*Minutes of the Synod* 1849, 159–160.

8　*The Covenanter* II (1847), 192. Later, both Old School and New School split into Northern and Southern churches; in 1865, the two Northern branches reunited, and in 1870 the two Southern branches followed suit. Not until 1983 were the Northern and Southern branches reunited. Stevens, who sat on the Indiana Supreme Court from 1831–1836, was the 1845 candidate for governor from the Liberty Party.

9　For their impact on the antislavery movement, see John R. McKivigan, *The War Against Proslavery Religion: Abolitionism and the Northern Churches, 1830–1865* (Ithaca, NY: Cornell University Press, 1984), 101–105. The group merged back into the New School General Assembly after the war.

10　*Reformed Presbyterian* 13 (June–July 1849), 152.

11　*Reformed Presbyterian* 13 (June–July 1849), 152.

12　William E. Dodd, *Expansion and Conflict* (Boston: Houghton Mifflin, 1915), 178–179.

13   *The Covenanter* 5 (April 1850), 290–292. Emphasis added. *Appendix to the Congressional Globe,* 31 Cong., 1 Sess. (Washington: John C. Rives, 1850), 262–265, March 11, 1850.
14   *The Covenanter* 5 (April 1850), 292, quoted in Wilcox, 126.
15   Wilcox, 127.
16   In the Faris Papers. Wilcox, 127–128.
17   In the Faris Papers. Wilcox, 128.
18   *Minutes of Synod* 1851, 164–165.
19   *Monitor and Missionary Chronicle* (Belfast: December 1850), 748, quoted in Wilcox, 129. See also the excellent discussion in Daniel Ritchie, "Radical Orthodoxy: Irish Covenanters and American Slavery, circa 1830–1865," *Church History* 82/4 (December 2013), 812–847.
20   Dodd, *Expansion and Conflict,* 182–184.
21   Dodd, *Expansion and Conflict,* 189–198.
22   Dodd, *Expansion and Conflict,* 231–240.
23   Dodd, *Expansion and Conflict,* 231–240.
24   *The Covenanter* 9, 276.
25   United States Congress. House. *Report of the Special Committee Appointed to Investigate the Troubles in Kansas* (Washington: 1856), 13, 22–23. Online at http://www.archive.org/details/reportofspecialc00unitrich. (accessed August 4, 2009).
26   Horace Greeley, *The American Conflict: A History* (Washington, DC: the National Tribune, 1902), I: 236.
27   See especially Jay Monaghan, *Civil War on the Western Border: 1854–1865* (New York: Bonanza, 1955) and Donald L. Gilmore, *Civil War on the Missouri–Kansas Border* (Gretna, Louisiana: Pelican Publishing Company, 2006).
28   This was not the only bleeding in Congress; see Joanne B. Freeman, *The Field of Blood: Violence in Congress on the Road to Civil War* (New York: Farrar, Straus & Giroux, 2018).
29   Interview, R. M. Copeland, with Mr. Harvey McGee of Olathe, May 30, 1975. Recording in possession of the author. McGee was the son of pioneers at Olathe and a lifelong member of the Reformed Presbyterian Church there.
30   John Stauffer, *The Black Hearts of Men: Radical Abolitionists and the Transformation of Race* (Cambridge, MA: Harvard University Press, 2002), 8–14, 20–22, 27. On the precursors of this party, cf. pp. 22–35.
31   *Scott v. Sandford,* 60 U.S. 393 (1857). The court misspelled the name of the respondent, Sanford, and Sandford it is in law.
32   *Scott v. Sandford,* at 407, 408.
33   *Scott v. Sandford,* at 427.
34   This interpretation of the *Dred Scott* case is argued in Bernard Schwarts, *A History of the Supreme Court* (New York: Oxford University Press, 1993), 105–125. Further, see Don E. Fehrenbacher, *The Dred Scott Case: Its Significance in American Law and Politics* (Oxford: Oxford University Press, 1978).
35   William L. Roberts, *The Reformed Presbyterian Catechism* (New York: n.pub., 1853), 153–173.
36   *The Covenanter* 12 (1858), 278–279.
37   Abraham Lincoln, *Speeches and Writings, 1832–1858* (New York: Library of

America, 1980), 426. Speech at Springfield, Illinois, June 16, 1858. (Hereinafter "House Divided.")

38   Lincoln, "House Divided," 431–434.

39   Lee was an Army officer, but in the crisis of the arsenal seizure he happened to be the nearest U.S. field-grade officer so was given command of the operation. His report to the Adjutant General of the Army is online at http://www.law. umkc.edu/faculty/projects/FTRIALS/johnbrown/leereport.html   (accessed July 10, 2009).

40   F. B. Sanborn, ed., *The Life and Letters of John Brown, Liberator of Kansas, and Martyr of Virginia* (Boston: Roberts Brothers, 1885), 583–584.

41   *Centennial of the New Alexandria Reformed Presbyterian Church, October 11, 1916* (n.pl.: n.pb., 1916), 49–51. In 1861, Milligan named his newborn son Ossawattomie Brown Milligan.

42   *Centennial,* 51–52; also in Sanborn, *Life and Letters,* 610; and photostat copy in McCartney Library, Geneva College.

Chapter 9, An Inalienable Right

1   Andrew Todd Kennedy, *A Stump for My Pillow: Civil War 1861–1864,* ed. Robert Metcalfe, M.D. (Nashville, TN: unpublished, 1989), 108–110, 117–130. From its description, the wound must have been from a musket ball rather than the more destructive Minié ball. Both types were in use by both armies during the war.

2   *National Republican Platform, adopted at the National Republican Convention, held in Chicago, May 17, 1860* (Chicago: Printed by the Press & Tribune Office), single-sided broadsheet, online at http://cprr.org/Museum/ Ephemera/Republican_Platform_1860.html (accessed July 13, 2009).

3   William E. Dodd, *Expansion and Conflict* (Boston: Houghton Mifflin, 1915), 262.

4   J. W. Shaw, *The Reformed Presbyterian* 24, 318.

5   *The Reformed Presbyterian* 24 (October 1860), 317–318; 331.

6   To see how ordinary soldiers—those who actually fought the war—felt about the issues, see James M. McPherson, *For Cause and Comrades: Why Men Fought in the Civil War* (New York: Oxford University Press, 1997) generally; esp. chapter 9.

7   *The Reformed Presbyterian* 24 (1860), 37–43. For a balanced perspective on *jus ad bellum* and the Civil War, see the excellent chapter by Gregory R. Jones, "The Fractured Union and the Justification for War," in the volume edited by Mark David Hall and J. Daryl Charles, *America and the Just War Tradition* (Notre Dame: University of Notre Dame Press, 2019), 114–132.

8   *Minutes of the Synod* 1861, 210. On Christ's "Mediatorial authority," see the section "Covenanter Theory of the State," in chapter 5 above.

9   D. S. Faris, "The Covenanter Church in the Civil War and Now," *The Christian Nation 5,* No. 1411 (October 4, 1911), 6–7. They took the army oath in August 1861. Todd was censured by both the Illinois Presbytery and the Synod of 1861 for leaving his congregation without permission. Because Missouri was a Border State, it had units on both sides in the war; the Confederate 10th was designated the 10th Regiment Missouri Infantry.

10　*Centennial of a Covenanter Society, 1822–1922,* 46–47. On October 19, 1864, Sheridan galloped a furious twenty miles from Winchester, Va., rallied the dispirited Union army, and turned the tide at the Battle of Cedar Creek. His ride was immortalized in a popular poem, "Sheridan's Ride," by Thomas Buchanan Read.

11　Glasgow, *The Geneva Book* (Philadelphia, 1908), 142–143.

12　General Samuel Wylie Crawford, originally an army surgeon, became a line officer and saw action at Fort Sumter, Cedar Mountain, Antietam, Petersburg, and was present at Appomattox. At Gettysburg, he commanded the Fifth Corps, Third Division, and was at Little Round Top. He was one of two Union officers to witness both the beginning and end of the war.

13　"The Covenanter Church in the Civil War," *The Christian Nation* 4 (October 4, 1911), 6–7.

14　*Looking Back from the Sunset Land* (Oakland, CA: n.pub., 1898), 266–267.

15　*Reformed Presbyterian* 25 (1861), 333–335; 363–365.

16　Letter, A. Lincoln to H. Greeley, May 14, 1861, quoted in McPherson, 56.

17　Eggleston, *History of the Confederate War*, New York: Sturgis & Walton, 1910), II: 4; cf. I: 37. Available online at Project Gutenberg, eBook [#45609] and [#46175] (accessed April 28, 2020). Quoted in *The Christian Nation* 4 (1911), 8. David Herbert Donald, *Lincoln Reconsidered: Essays on the Civil War Era*, third edition (New York: Vintage Books, 2001), 45.

18　McPherson, *What They Fought For*, chapter 2, esp. 30–33.

19　Quoted in Richard Striner, *Father Abraham: Lincoln's Relentless Struggle to End Slavery* (Oxford: Oxford University Press, 2006), 62.

20　McPherson, 67.

21　*Father Abraham,* 2.

22　*The Covenanter* (Ireland), December 1860, 21–23.

23　Printed in *The Reformed Presbyterian and Covenanter* 1 (January 1863), 16–17. The president met with a number of clergy delegations throughout the war.

24　Bingham (1815–1900) served eight non-consecutive terms in the House, was a judge in the trial of Lincoln's assassins and a prosecutor in the impeachment trial of Andrew Johnson, the principal author of the 14th Amendment, and the first United States Ambassador to Japan (1873–1885). His remark was quoted in Milligan's report, *RP&C* I (February 1863), 50–51.

25　*RP&C* I (1863), 16–18, 48–52, reprinted from the Pittsburgh *Gazette,* December 12, 1862.

26　John T. Woolley and Gerhard Peters, *The American Presidency Project* [online]. Santa Barbara, CA: University of California (hosted), Gerhard Peters (database). Available online at http://www.presidency.ucsb.edu/ws/index.php?pid=69891 (accessed July 20, 2009). It is interesting—even ironic—that the Constitution of the Confederacy (in contrast to that of the United States) specifically "invok[es] the favor and guidance of Almighty God" and that Jefferson Davis issued a total of ten proclamations of fast days for the Confederacy, while Lincoln issued only three for the Union.

27　*Minutes of Synod* 1863, *RP&C* I (1863), 201.

28　*Life and Work of J. R. W. Sloane, D.D.* (New York: A. C. Armstrong, 1888), 101 fn.

29   "Reminiscence of President Lincoln," *RP&C* III (1865), 347.

30   David M. Carson, *History,* 226 fn. Gideon Welles, *The Diary of Gideon Welles,* 3 vol. (Boston: Houghton Mifflin, 1911), II, 190.

31   George C. Rable, *God's Almost Chosen People: A Religious History of the American Civil War* (Chapel Hill: University of North Carolina Press, 2010), 193–194.

32   Carson, *History,* 214; Jesse B. Barber, *History of the Work of the Presbyterian Church Among the Negroes in the United States of America* (New York: Board of National Missions, Presbyterian Church in the U.S.A., 1936), 28. It is not clear whether his first work was in Beaufort or Port Royal.

33   *Minutes of Synod* 1862, 215; *Covenanter* 17 (1862), 281–286.

34   *RP&C* 1 (February 1863), 52; 2 (1864), 255 and 359–361.

35   W. M. Glasgow, *History,* 772–773.

36   *RP&C* 2, 175–177 and 338.

37   *Reformed Presbyterian Witness,* Scotland, November 1, 1865, 307.

38   Carson, *History,* 218. Quakers encountered the same problem, with their austere worship style being quite unfamiliar to Black people.

39   Carson, 220; "Our Mission," *RP&C* 5 (1867), 89–90.

40   Glasgow, *The Geneva Book,* 80–81. James L. McCartney was the father of Clarence Edward McCartney, the well-known conservative pastor of Arch Street Presbyterian Church, Philadelphia and later of First Presbyterian Church, Pittsburgh, and Moderator of the General Assembly of 1924.

41   Glasgow, *The Geneva Book,* 82. Up to the present, Black students have always been prominent at Geneva College, especially in athletics, debate, and scholarship.

42   *Minutes of Synod* 1884, 233; 1910, 81; 1930, 74; 1932, 73; 1933, 81; 1934, 92; 1936, 64; 1937, 169.

43   Further see Nancy L. Stormont, *An Experiment in Negro Education, Being the Story of a Mission School* (thesis, M.A., School of Education, New York University, 1929).

Bibliography

PRIMARY SOURCES

Minutes

Minutes of the Coldenham Session, 1801–1823. MS.

Minutes of the General Meeting of the Princeton (Ind.) congregation, 1841–1859. MS.

Minutes of the Committee of the Reformed Presbytery, 1800. *Our Banner*, September 15, 1876.

Minutes of the Reformed Presbytery, 1801–1806. Pittsburgh: Bakewell and Marthens, 1874.

Minutes of the General Synod of the Reformed Presbyterian Church, Session 18, met in the city of Pittsburgh, October 1836. Albany: Henry D. Stone, 1836.

Minutes of the General Synod, Session 19. Newburgh, New York: J. D. Spalding, 1836.

Minutes of the General Synod, Session 20. Newburgh: J. D. Spalding, 1840.

Minutes of the Synod of the Reformed Presbyterian Church of North America, Sessions 24–118, 1847–1947. Prior to 1896, these were published in the church periodicals *The Reformed Presbyterian*, *The Covenanter*, and *The Reformed Presbyterian and Covenanter*. Thereafter, they appeared as separate volumes.

Other Unpublished Sources

Brown, Rev. Claude, Letter to D. Ray Wilcox. April 7, 1948, re: Selma, Ala.

Cuthbertson, John, *Diary, 1751–1791*. MS, Barbour Library, Pittsburgh Theological Seminary. TS copy, Library of the Reformed Presbyterian Theological Seminary, Pittsburgh.

Faris Papers. A collection of letters, essays, scrapbook, diary, and other papers beginning in 1816 by Rev. James Faris and continuing for over a century, collected by Rev. D. S. Faris of Sparta, Illinois. In 1949, these were in the possession of Finley Faris of Greeley, Colorado, and consulted extensively by D. Ray Wilcox. At Faris's death, they passed to his son Dennis. In approximately 1981, they were lost in a disastrous fire at Dennis Faris's farm at Milliken, Colorado. (Personal communication, Dennis Faris to Robert M. Copeland, July 2009.)

Greeley, Horace, Holograph letter. September 2, 1860, to Rev. James R. Thompson of Newburgh, New York.

Greer, Rev. Samuel E., Letter to D. Ray Wilcox. February 24, 1948, re: First Philadelphia RPC.

Kennedy, Andrew Todd, "A Stump for My Pillow: Civil War 1861–1864." Ed. Robert Metcalfe, M.D. Nashville, TN: unpublished, 1989. 178. Taken from the daily journals and family letters of Andrew Todd Kennedy, edited by his grandson.

McMillan, Rev. John, Letter to D. Ray Wilcox. March 4, 1948, re: New Concord, OH.

McGee, Harvey, Interviewed by Robert M. Copeland. Olathe, Kansas, May 30, 1975. Cassette tape, Robert M. Copeland.

Moore, Ida B. and Ella McGee, Essays on the history of the Olathe, Kan., congregation.

Peoples, Mrs. John K., Letter to D. Ray Wilcox. March 10, 1948, re: Princeton, Ind., congregation.

Reynolds, Mrs. W. W., Letter to D. Ray Wilcox. February 13, 1948, re: Utica, Ohio.

Shanklin, Easson, Letter. Undated, re: Southfield, Mich., congregation.

Thiel, Otto, Interviewed by Robert M. Copeland. Utica, Ohio, Presbyterian Church, August 16, 2009.

Todd, James A., Letter to Miss Iva McMillan. March 1, 1928, re: his father, Rev. Andrew C. Todd and the Underground Railroad in southern Illinois.

Willson Papers. A collection of sermons, diaries, letters, and other papers from James Renwick Willson and other members of the Willson family. Archives of the Reformed Presbyterian Church, in the library of the Reformed Presbyterian Theological Seminary, Pittsburgh.

Periodicals

Albany Quarterly, James R. Willson and S. M. Willson, eds. Newburgh, New York: 1833.

Harper's Weekly, a Journal of Civilization, IV, no. 207, December 15, 1860.

The Christian Nation, IV, October 4, 1911.

The Covenanter, James M. Willson, ed. Philadelphia, August 1845–July 1857. Moses Roney, ed., 1837–1855; Thomas Sproull, ed., 1855–62.

The Covenanter, Thomas Houston and J. Dick, eds. Belfast, Ireland, 1830–1840. Reformed Presbyterian Church of Ireland.

The Evangelical Witness, James R. Willson, ed. Newburgh, New York, 1822–1824.

The Geneva Alumnus, 27, no. 2, January 1951.

The Monitor and Missionary Chronicle, Belfast, Ireland IV (1850) and III, no. 33, (New Series), 1855. Reformed Presbyterian Church of Ireland.

The New York Times, December 1, 1861.

The Reformed Presbyterian, Moses Roney, ed. (until 1855), Thomas Sproull (to 1863), when merged to form *The Reformed Presbyterian and Covenanter.*

The Reformed Presbyterian and Covenanter, Thomas Sproull and J. M. Willson, eds. until 1863; Thomas Sproull, ed., thereafter, joined by his son John W. Sproull in 1868. I–XVIII, January 1863 to January 1880.

The Reformed Presbyterian Witness, Glasgow, Scotland, 1864–1867.

The Utica Herald, Utica, Ohio, April 7, 1938.

The Washington Post, September 3, 2006.

Our Banner, J. C. K. Milligan and D. Gregg, eds., 1874–86; J. H. Boggs 1874–80; N. R. Johnston to 1892. Philadelphia, 1874–1887.

Pennsylvania Gazette, Philadelphia, 1728–1800. Benjamin Franklin, ed. from 1729. Online at www.accessible-archives.com.

Proceedings and Debates of the House of Representatives of the United States at the Second Session of the Second Congress, Begun at the City of Philadelphia, November 5, 1792.

Books, Articles, and Pamphlets

Anonymous, *A Cloud of Witnesses, For the Royal Prerogatives of Jesus Christ; or, The Last Speeches and Testimonies of Those Who Have Suffered for the Truth in Scotland Since the Year 1680. With an Appendix: Containing the Queensferry Paper; etc.* 1714. 15th ed., enl. & corr. Pittsburgh: Eichbaum & Johnston, 1824. Edinburgh: Oliphant, Anderson, & Ferrier, 1871. Many other editions.

Acts and proceedings of the General Assembly of the Presbyterian Church, in the United States of America, A.D. 1794. Philadelphia: R. Aitken & Son, 1794.

Augustine of Hippo, *The City of God.* tr., Marcus Dods. New York: Modern Library, 1993.

Birney, James G., *The American Churches, the bulwarks of American slavery.* 1840. 2 ed. Newburyport, MA: Charles Whipple, 1842.

Conrad, Robert Edgar, *In the Hands of Strangers: Readings on Foreign and Domestic Slave Trading and the Crisis of the Union.* University Park, PA: Pennsylvania State University Press, 2001.

Cuguano, Ottobah, *Thoughts and Sentiments on the Evil and Wicked Traffic of the Slavery and Commerce of the Human Species.* London: 1787.

Department of the Navy, Naval Historical Center, "Flogging in the U.S. Navy." Online at http://www.history.navy.mil/online/flogging. htm.

Douglass, Frederick, *Narrative of the Life of Frederick Douglass, An American Slave, Written by Himself.* Dublin: Webb & Chapman, 1845. Many editions.

Eggleston, George C., *History of the Confederate War, Its Causes and Its Conduct.* New York: Sturgis & Walton, 1910.

Eldridge, Shalor Winchell, *Recollections of Early Days in Kansas.* Publications of the Kansas State Historical Society, vol. 2. Topeka: Kansas State Printing Plant, 1920.

Equiano, Olaudah, *The Interesting Narrative of the Life of Olaudah Equiano: or, Gustavus Vassa, the African.* London, 1789. Many editions. Modern Library Classics (2004). Edited and with Notes by Shelly Eversley, Introduction by Robert Reid-Pharr.

Faris, D. S. (David Smith), *Life, Work, and Character of the Rev. James Faris.* West Barnet, VT: D. C. Faris, 1883.

Fields, S. Helen, *Register of Marriages and Baptisms Performed by Rev. John Cuthbertson, 1751–1791.* Lancaster, PA: Lancaster Press, 1934. Rpt., Bowie, MD: Heritage Books, 2001.

Fifth Annual Report of the Executive Committee of the American Anti-Slavery Society. New York: Dorr, 1838.

Fiftieth Anniversary of the Reorganization of the First Reformed Presbyterian Church, Philadelphia, Pa. Philadelphia: *The Christian Statesman,* 1884. A reprint of the Semi-Centennial Number of *Our Banner,* January 1884.

First Report of the New-York Colonization Society. New York: J. Seymour, 1823.

Garrison, William Lloyd, *Thoughts on African Colonization: or an impartial exhibition of the doctrines, principles and purposes of the American Colonization Society, together with the resolutions, addresses and remonstrances of the free people of colour.* Boston: Garrison & Knapp, 1832.

Garrison, W. P. and F. J., *William Lloyd Garrison, 1805–1879, The Story of His Life Told By His Children.* 4 vols. New York: The Century Co., 1885–1889.

George, Edna, "Geneva Hall and the Underground Railroad: Historical Letter." *The Geneva Alumnus* 27, no. 2 (January 1951).

Goodell, William, *The American Slave Code in Theory and Practice.* New York: American and Foreign Anti-Slavery Society, 1853. Rpt., Charleston, SC: BiblioLife, n.d.

Greeley, Horace, *Recollections of a Busy Life.* New York: J. B. Ford & Co., 1868.

Hart, A. B., ed., *American History Told by Contemporaries*. 4 vols. New York: Macmillan, 1929.

Helper, Hinton Rowan, *The Impending Crisis of the South: How to Meet It*. New York: A. B. Burdick, 1857. Rpt., CreateSpace, 2012.

Hodgin, Thomas, M. D., *An Inquiry into the Merits of the American Colonization Society, and a Reply to the Charges Brought Against It*. London: J. & A. Arch, 1833.

Howie, John, of Lochgoin, *The Scots Worthies*. 1775. Edinburgh: Oliphant, Anderson, & Ferrier, 1902. Many editions.

Jefferson, Thomas, *Notes on the State of Virginia*. 1787. In *Writings*, ed., Merrill D. Peterson. Library of America C17. New York: Library of America, 1984.

Johnston, Nathan Robinson, *Looking Back from the Sunset Land: or, People Worth Knowing*. Oakland, CA: n.pb., 1896.

Knox, John, *The History of the Reformation of the Church of Scotland, Containing the Manner, and by what Persons, the Light of Christ's Gospel has been Manifested unto this Realm*. 2 vols. Paisley: John Neilson for David Gardner, 1791. Many editions.

Lincoln, Abraham, *Speeches and Writings, 1832–1858*. New York: Library of America, 1980.

McCord, David J., ed., *The Statutes at Large of South Carolina, Vol. 7. Containing the Acts Relating to Charleston, Courts, Slaves, and Rivers*. Charleston: A. S. Johnston, 1840.

Madison, James, *The Debates in the Federal Convention of 1787, Reported by James Madison, a delegate from the state of Virginia*. Gaillard Hund and James Brown Scott, eds. Oxford: Oxford University Press, 1920.

McLeod, Alexander, *Negro Slavery Unjustifiable, A Discourse*. New York: 1802. 10th ed., New York: Alexander McLeod, 1860.

Morse, Jedediah, *The American Geography*. Elizabeth Town: Shepard Kollock, 1789. Rpt., New York: Arno Press, 1970.

National Republican Platform adopted at the National Republican Convention, held in Chicago, May 17, 1860. Chicago: Printed by the Press and Tribune Office. Single-sided broadsheet, at http://cprr.org/Museum/Ephemera/Republican_Platform_1860.html.

Nelson, Truman, ed., *Documents of Upheaval: Selections from William Lloyd Garrison's The Liberator, 1831–1865*. New York: Hill & Wang, 1966.

Olmsted, Frederick Law, *A Journey in the Back Country*. New York: Mason Brothers, 1861.

O'Neall, John Belton, ed., *The Negro Law of South Carolina, collected and digested by John Belton O'Neall, one of the judges of the courts of law and errors of the said state*. Columbia: Printed by John G. Bowman, 1848. Available on Google Books.

Pennsylvania Anti-Slavery Society, *Address of the State Anti-Slavery Society to the Ministers of the Gospel in the State of Pennsylvania.* Philadelphia: Merrihew & Gunn, 1838.

Redpath, James, *The Roving Editor, or Talks with Slaves in the Southern States.* 1859. John R. McKivigan, ed. University Park: The Pennsylvania State University Press, 1996.

Reformation Principles Exhibited by the Reformed Presbyterian Church. New York: Hopkins & Seymour, 1807.

Reformation Principles Exhibited, Being the Declaration and Testimony of the Reformed Presbyterian Church in North America. 3rd ed. Published by the General Synod, 1843. Other editions 1852, 1871. This is the edition of the "New Light" Covenanters who left the denomination in 1833.

Reformed Presbyterian Testimony. Editions of 1824, 1859, 1875, 1911, etc.

Reformed Presbyterian Church of North America, *Constitution of the Reformed Presbyterian Church of North America.* Pittsburgh: Crown and Covenant Publications, 2010.

Reformed Presbytery, "Three Propositions Respecting the Mediatorial Dominion of Christ, as they were agreed upon by The Reformed Presbytery in 1749, and more fully explained in a Postscript published by the memorial in 1754." At http://www.truecovenanter.com.

Renewal of the Covenants, National and Solemn League; A Confession of Sins; An Engagement to Duties; and a Testimony; As they were carried on at Middle Octorara in Pennsylvania, November 11, 1743. Philadelphia: B. Franklin, 1748. Rpt., 1748. Beaver Falls, PA: W. M. Glasgow, 1895. 1748 edition in library of the Presbyterian Historical Society, Philadelphia.

Ripley, C. Peter, *The Black Abolitionist Papers, Vol. III: the United States, 1830–1846.* Chapel Hill: University of North Carolina Press, 1991.

Roberts, William L., *The Reformed Presbyterian Catechism.* New York: n.pb., 1853.

Sanborn, F. B., ed. *The Life and Letters of John Brown, Liberator of Kansas, and Martyr of Virginia.* Boston: Roberts Bros., 1885.

Shields, Alexander, *A short Memorial of the Suffering and Grievances past and present of the Presbyterians in Scotland, particularly of those called by nick-name Cameronians.* Edinburgh, 1690.

Sixth Annual Report of the Executive Committee of the Anti-Slavery Society. New York: American Anti-Slavery Society, 1839.

Sloane, William M., ed., *Life and Work of J. R. W. Sloane, D. D.* New York: A. A. Armstrong & Son, 1888.

Sprague, William B., *Annals of the American Associate, Associate Reformed, and Reformed Presbyterian Pulpit. Or Commemorative Notices of Distinguished Clergymen of These Denominations in the United States.* New York: Robert Carter & Bros., 1869.

Stewart, Reid, ed., *The Minutes of the Correspondent, May 1780 to February 1809 (Being the Oldest Minutes of any Presbyterian group west of the Allegheny Mountains)*. Apollo, PA: Presbyterian Historical Society of the Upper Ohio Valley, 1994.

Still, William, *The Underground Railroad, A Record of Facts, Authentic Narratives, Letters, Narrating the Hardships, Hair-breadth Escapes, and Death Struggles of the Slaves in their Efforts for Freedom, by Themselves and others, or Witnessed by the Author; Together with Sketches of some of the Largest Stockholders, and Most Liberal Aiders and Advisors, of the Road*. Philadelphia: Porter & Coates, 1872.

Stowe, Harriet Beecher, *Uncle Tom's Cabin, or, life among the lowly*. Boston: John P. Jewett, 1852. Many editions.

Stroud, George McDowell, *A Sketch of the Laws Relating to Slavery in the Several States*. 2nd ed. Philadelphia: Henry Longstreth, 1856.

Supreme Court of the United States, *Dred Scott, Plaintiff in Error, v. John F. A. Sandford*, 60 U.S. 393; 19 How. 393; 15 L.Ed. 691. 1857. Consulted at http://www.law.cornell.edu/supct/html/historics/USSC_CR_0060_0393_ZO.html

Swisshelm, Jane Grey, *Half a Century*. Chicago: Janssen, McClurg, 1880. Paul Dennis Sporer, ed. Chester, NY: Anza Publishing Co., 2005.

Taney, Roger B., *Scott v. Sandford*. Opinion of the Court. See above, Supreme Court of the United States.

Taylor, William Harrison and Peter C. Messer, eds. *Faith and Slavery in the Presbyterian Diaspora*. Bethlehem, PA: Lehigh University Press, 2016. See esp. Roulson, William J. "The Reformed Presbyterian Church and Antislavery in Nineteenth-Century America," pp. 149–174.

Thomas, Alfred A., ed., *Correspondence of Thomas Ebenezer Thomas, Mainly Relating to the Anti-Slavery Conflict in Ohio, Especially in the Presbyterian Church. 1834–1874*. n.pl.: Published by Alfred Thomas's son, 1909. Clarified and Copyrighted [sic] 1997 by Arthur W. McGraw. n.pl., n.pb.

Thoreau, Henry David, "Civil Disobedience." *The Writings of Henry David Thoreau* (Walden Edition). 20 vols. Boston: Houghton Mifflin Co., 1906. IV: 356–387.

United States Congress, House of Representatives, *Report of the Special Committee Appointed to Investigate the Troubles in Kansas*. Washington: Cornelius Wendell, Printer, 1856.

Washington, George, The Washington Papers, at mountvernon.org/george-washington/slavery.

Weld, Theodore D., *American Slavery As It Is: Testimony of a Thousand Witnesses*. New York: American Anti-Slavery Society, 1839.

Welles, Gideon, *The Diary of Gideon Welles*. 3 vols. Boston: Houghton Mifflin, 1911.

Wheeler, Jacob B., *A Practical Treatise on the Law of Slavery, being a compilation of all the Decisions Made on That Subject in the Several Courts of the United States, and State Courts.* New York and New Orleans: n.p., 1837.

Willson, James R., *An Address on West India Emancipation. Delivered on the First of August, 1838, before the Union Anti-Slavery Society of Philadelphia.* Philadelphia: Published by Request, 1838.

Willson, James R., *The Subjection of Kings and Nations to Messiah. A Sermon, Preached on Monday, December 6, 1819, Immediately After the Dispensation of the Lord's Supper, in the Reformed Presbyterian Church, in the City of New York.* New York: E. Conrad, 1820.

Wodrow, Robert, *The History of the Sufferings of the Church of Scotland from the Restoration to the Revolution.* (1721–1722). 4 vol., Glasgow: Blackie & Son, 1836.

Wylie, Samuel Brown, *Memoir of Alexander McLeod, D.D.* New York: Charles Scribner, 1855.

SECONDARY SOURCES

Adams, Ephraim D., *The Power of Ideals in American History.* New Haven: Yale University Press, 1913.

Bailey, Thomas A., *A Diplomatic History of the American People.* New York: F. S. Crofts & Co., 1947.

Baldwin, Alice M., "Sowers of Sedition." *The William and Mary Quarterly,* V, no. 1 (January 1948).

Bales, Kevin, *Disposable People.* Berkeley: University of California Press, 1999.

Barber, Jesse B., *History of the Work of the Presbyterian Church Among the Negroes in the United States of America.* New York: Board of National Missions, Presbyterian Church in the U.S.A., 1936.

Barnes, Brian L., "Antislavery Schism: Abolitionists, Colonizationists, and the Debate Over Radical Reform, 1830–1860." Diss., Ph.D., University of Washington, 2008.

Beard, Charles A. and Mary R. Beard, *The Making of American Civilization.* New York: Macmillan, 1937.

Beringer, Richard E., et al., *The Elements of Confederate Defeat: Nationalism, War Aims, and Religion.* Athens, Georgia: University of Georgia Press, 1988.

Berry, Daina Ramey, *The Price for Their Pound of Flesh: The Value of the Enslaved, from Womb to Grave in the Building of a Nation.* Boston: Beacon Press, 2017.

Billingsley, Andrew, *Climbing Jacob's Ladder: The Enduring Legacy of African-American Families.* New York: Simon & Schuster, 1992.

Blonigan, Beth, "A Re-Examination of the Slave Diet." Unpublished thesis,

B.A., College of St. Benedict/St. John's University, 2004.

Brinkerhoff, Roelof R., *A Sesquicentennial History of Utica, Licking County, Ohio, 1810–1960.* Utica, Ohio: Utica Herald, 1960. Rpt., 1992.

Buckmaster, Henrietta, Pseud. of Henrietta Henkle (q.v.).

Carson, David Melville, "A History of the Reformed Presbyterian Church in America to 1871." Diss., Ph.D., University of Pennsylvania, 1964.

Carson, Elizabeth F., "An Inordinate Sense of History: James Renwick Willson 1780–1853." Thesis, M.A., The College of William and Mary in Virginia, 1987.

Centenary of a Covenanter Society, 1822–1922. N.pl., n.pb., n.d. 67 pp. Centennial of the Brookland RPC. in Westmoreland Co., Pa., with a brief history.

Centennial of the New Alexandria Reformed Presbyterian Church, October 11, 1916. N.pl., n.pb., n.d. 69 pp. Contains a history of the congregation from 1816 to 1868 by J. C. Elder, and from 1868 to 1916 by J. Oliver Beatty.

Coffey, John, *Politics, Religion and the British Revolutions: The Mind of Samuel Rutherford.* Cambridge: Cambridge University Press, 1997.

Conrad, Robert Edgar, *In the Hands of Strangers.* University Park: Pennsylvania State University Press, 2001.

Copeland, Robert M., "The Reformed Presbyterian Theological Seminary in Cincinnati 1845–1849." *Bulletin of the Cincinnati Historical Society,* 31, no. 3 (Fall 1973), 151–163.

Covey, Herbert C. and Dwight Eisenach, *What the Slaves Ate: Recollections of African American Foods and Foodways from Slave Narratives.* Santa Barbara, CA: Greenwood Press, 2009.

David, Paul A. et al., *Reckoning with Slavery: Critical Essays in the Quantitative History of American Negro Slavery.* New York: Oxford University Press, 1976.

Davis, David Brion. *Inhuman Bondage: the Rise and Fall of Slavery in the New World.* Oxford: Oxford University Press, 2006.

Davis, David Brion. "Slavery and Sin: the cultural background." In *The Antislavery Vanguard: New Essays on the Abolitionists.* Martin Duberman, ed. Princeton: Princeton University Press, 1965.

DeRamus, Betty, *Forbidden Fruit: Love Stories from the Underground Railroad.* New York: Atria Books, 2005.

Diffie, Bailey W., *Latin American Civilization, Colonial Period.* Harrisburg, PA: Stackpole Sons, 1945.

Dillon, Merton L., *The Abolitionists: the Growth of a Dissenting Minority.* DeKalb, IL: Northern Illinois University Press, 1974.

Dodd, William E., *Expansion and Conflict.* Boston: Houghton Mifflin, 1915.

Donald, David Herbert, *Lincoln Reconsidered: Essays on the Civil War Era. 1947.* New York: Vintage, 2001.

Douglas, J. D. (James D.), *Light in the North*. Grand Rapids, MI: Eerdmans, 1964.

Dow, George Francis, *Slave Ships and Slaving*. n.pl.: Marine Research Society, 1927.

Dumond, Dwight Lowell, *Antislavery Origins of the Civil War in the United States*. Ann Arbor: University of Michigan Press, 1939. Rpt. Westport, CT: Greenwood, 1980.

Early, Jubal Anderson, *Heritage of the South: A History of the Introduction of Slavery; Its Establishment from Colonial Times, and Final Effect upon the Politics of the United States*. Lynchburg, VA: Brown-Morrison Co., 1915.

Egerton, Douglas R., *Gabriel's Rebellion: the Virginia conspiracies of 1800 and 1802*. Chapel Hill: University of North Carolina Press, 1993.

Eliade, Mircea, ed., *The Encyclopedia of Religion*. New York: Macmillan, 1987.

Faris, Paul Donald, *House Built on the Rock: Faris Genealogy*. Pahrump, NV: mimeo., 1973.

Fehrenbacher, Don E., *The Dred Scott Case: Its Significance in American Law and Politics*. Oxford: Oxford University Press, 1978.

Fogel, Robert, *Without Consent or Contract: The Rise and Fall of American Slavery*. New York: Norton, 1989.

Fogel, Robert William, and Stanley L. Engerman, *Time on the Cross: The Economics of American Negro Slavery*. Boston: Little, Brown, 1974.

Fox, Early Lee, *The American Colonization Society 1817–1840*. Baltimore: The Johns Hopkins Press, 1919.

Fredrickson, George M., "The Coming of the Lord: the Northern Protestant clergy and the Civil War crisis." In *Religion and the American Civil War*, Randall M. Miller et al., eds. New York: Oxford University Press, 1998.

Frederickson, George M., *The Inner Civil War: Northern Intellectuals and the Crisis of the Union*. New York: Harper Torchbooks, 1968.

Freeman, Joanne B., *The Field of Blood: Violence in Congress on the Road to Civil War*. New York: Farrar, Straus & Giroux, 2018.

Gara, Larry. "The Fugitive Slave Law in the Eastern Ohio Valley." *Ohio History* 72, no. 2 (April 1963), 116–128, 170–171.

Gara, Larry, *The Liberty Line: the Legend of the Underground Railroad*. 1961. Lexington: University Press of Kentucky, 1996.

Genovese, Eugene D., "Religion in the Collapse of the American Union." In *Religion and the American Civil War*. Randall M. Miller et al., eds. New York: Oxford University Press, 1998.

Glasgow, William Melancthon, ed., *The Geneva Book, Comprising a History of Geneva College and a Biographical Catalogue of the Alumni and Many Students*. Philadelphia: Westbrook Publishing Co., 1908.

Glasgow, William Melancthon, *History of the Reformed Presbyterian Church in America: With Sketches of all Her Ministry, Congregations, Missions, Institutions, Publications, etc., and Embellished with Over Fifty Portraits and Engravings.* Baltimore: Hill and Harvey, 1888. Rpt. 2008. A corrected edition is available in PDF format online at http://reformedpresbyterian.org.

Goldstone, Lawrence, *Dark Bargain: Slavery, Profits, and the Struggle for the Constitution.* New York: Walker & Co., 2005.

Greeley, Horace, *The American Conflict: A History of the Great Rebellion.* 2 vols. Hartford: O. D. Case & Co., 1864–1866. Washington, DC: The National Tribune, 1902.

Guasco, Michael, *Slaves and Englishmen: Human Bondage in the Early Modern Atlantic World.* Philadelphia: University of Pennsylvania Press, 2014.

Gutman, Herbert G., *Slavery and the Numbers Game: A Critique of Time on the Cross.* Urbana: University of Illinois Press, 1975.

Hall, Mark David and J. Daryl Charles, eds. *America and the Just War Tradition: a History of U.S. Conflicts.* Notre Dame, Indiana: University of Notre Dame Press, 2019.

Harrold, Stanley, *American Abolitionists.* Seminar studies in history. Harlow, Essex: Pearson Education Ltd., 2001.

Hart, Albert Bushnell, *Slavery and Abolition, 1831–1841.* The American Nation Series. New York: Harper & Brothers, 1906.

Heinrich, Adam R., "Some Comments on the Archaeology of Slave Diets and the Importance of Taphonomy to Historical Faunal Analyses." *Journal of African Diaspora Archaeology and Heritage*, I, no. 1, 2012.

Henkle, Henrietta, (Pseud.: Henrietta Buckmaster.) *Let My People Go: the Story of the Underground Railroand and the Growth of the Abolition Movement.* (1941; rev. 1959). Southern Classics Series, No. 17. Columbia: University of South Carolina Press, 1992.

Hetherington, W. M., *History of the Church of Scotland, from the Introduction of Christianity to the Period of the Disruption in 1843.* 4th American from the 3rd Edinburgh ed. New York: Robert Carter, 1848.

Hewatt, Alexander, *An Historical Account of the Rise and Progress of the Colonies of South Carolina and Georgia.* 2 vols. London, 1779.

Heywood, Linda M. and John K. Thornton, *Central Africans, Atlantic Creoles, and the Foundation of the Americas, 1585–1660.* Cambridge, UK: Cambridge University Press, 2007.

Hinks, Peter P., *To Awaken My Afflicted Brethren: David Walker and the Problem of Antebellum Slave Resistance.* University Park, PA: The Pennsylvania State University Press, 1997.

Hochschild, Adam, *Bury the Chains: Prophets and Rebels in the Fight to Free an Empire's Slaves*. Boston: Houghton Mifflin, 2005.

Hofstadter, Richard, *America at 1750*. New York: Alfred A. Knopf, 1970.

Hunter, James Davison, *To Change the World: The Irony, Tragedy, and Possibility of Christianity in the Late Modern World*. Oxford: Oxford University Press, 2010.

Jackson, Clare, *Restoration Scotland, 1660–1690: Royalist Politics, Religion and Ideas*. Woodbridge: Boydell, 2003.

Johnston, John Black, *The Prayer Meeting: its History, as identified with the life and power of Godliness, and the revival of religion*. Philadelphia, 1870.

King, Marissa D. and Heather A. Haveman, "Antislavery in America: The Press, the Pulpit, and the rise of Antislavery Societies." *Administrative Science Quarterly* 53 (2008), 492–528.

Klett, Guy B., *Presbyterians in Colonial Pennsylvania*. Philadelphia: University of Pennsylvania Press, 1937.

Klingaman, William K., *Abraham Lincoln and the Road to Emancipation, 1861–1865*. New York: Viking, 2001.

Las Casas, Bartolomé de, *The Only Way*. Ed. Helen Rand Parish, tr. Francis Patrick Sullivan, S.J. New York: Paulist Press, 1992.

Lathan, Robert, *History of the Associate Reformed Synod of the South, To Which is Prefaced a History of the Associate Presbyterian and Reformed Presbyterian Churches*. Harrisburg, PA: Robert Lathan, 1882. Facs. rpt., Due West, SC, 1982.

Lauber, Almon Wheeler, "Indian Slavery in Colonial Times within the Present Limits of the United States." Diss., Ph.D., Columbia University, 1913, in *Studies in History, Economics and Public Law, Edited by the Faculty of Political Science of Columbia University*, 54, no. 3, 1914. Available online at Google Books.

Lindsay, Thomas, *A History of the Reformation*. New York: Charles Scribner's Sons. 1814.

Locke, Mary Stoughton, *Anti-Slavery in America from the Introduction of African Slaves to the Prohibition of the Slave Trade (1619–1808)*. Boston: Ginn and Company, 1901. Rpt., New York: Johnson Reprint Corporation, 1968.

Lowance, Mason I. Jr., ed., *A House Divided: The Antebellum Slavery Debates in America, 1776–1865*. Princeton: Princeton University Press, 2003.

McBurney, Charles, *Reformed Presbyterian Ministers, 1950–1993*. Pittsburgh: Crown and Covenant, 1994.

McCarthy, Timothy P., "A Culture of Dissent: American Abolitionism and the Ordeal of Equality." Diss., Ph.D., Columbia University, 2006.

McKivigan, John, *The War Against Proslavery Religion: Abolitionism and the Northern Churches, 1830–1865*. Ithaca, NY: Cornell University Press, 1984.

McPherson, James M., *The Struggle for Equality: Abolitionists and the Negro in the Civil War and Reconstruction.* Princeton: Princeton University Press, 1964.

Macy, Jesse. *The Anti-Slavery Crusade: A Chronicle of the Gathering Storm.* New Haven: Yale University Press, 1919. Rpt., CreateSpace, 2014.

Mayer, Henry, *All on Fire: William Lloyd Garrison and the Abolition of Slavery.* New York: St. Martin's Griffin, 1998.

Miller, Randall M., Harry S. Stout, and Charles Reagan Wilson, eds., *Religion and the American Civil War.* New York: Oxford University Press, 1998.

Moberg Robinson, Emily, "Immigrant Covenanters: Religious and Political Identity, from Scotland to America." Diss., Ph.D., University of California at Santa Cruz, 2004.

Monaghan, Jay, *Civil War on the Western Border 1854–1865.* New York: Bonanza Books, 1955.

Montesquieu, Charles Louis de Secondat, baron de La Brède et de Montesquieu, *De l'Esprit des Lois.* Genève: Barillot et fils, 4 vol., 1748. Edition Garnier, 1777. Online at wikisource.org (accessed July 3, 2020).

Moore, Joseph S., *Founding Sins: How a Group of Antislavery Radicals Fought to Put Christ Into the Constitution.* New York: Oxford University Press, 2016.

Morgan, Philip D., "The Ownership of Property by Slaves in the Mid-Nineteenth-Century Low Country." *Journal of Southern History* 49, no. 3 (1983).

Morrill, John, ed., *The Scottish National Covenant in its British Context.* Edinburgh: Edinburgh University Press, 1990.

Noll, Mark A., "The Bible and Slavery." In Randall M. Miller et al., eds., *Religion and the American Civil War.* New York: Oxford University Press, 1998.

Noll, Mark A., *The Civil War as a Theological Crisis.* Chapel Hill: University of North Carolina Press, 2006.

Oakes, James, *The Crooked Path to Abolition: Abraham Lincoln and the Antislavery Constitution.* New York: W. W. Norton, 2021.

Perry, Lewis and Michael Fellman, eds., *Antislavery Reconsidered: New Perspectives on the Abolitionists.* Baton Rouge: Louisiana State University Press, 1979.

Pickard, Kate E. R., *The Kidnapped and the Ransomed.* 1856. Rpt., As History, Series I Number I n.pl.: Negro Publication Society of America, Inc., 1941.

Pirtle, Carol, *Betwixt Two Suns: A True Tale of the Underground Railroad in Illinois.* Carbondale: Southern Illinois University Press, 2000.

Poole, William Frederick, "Anti-Slavery Opinions Before the Year 1800:

Read before the Cincinnati Literary Club, November 16, 1872." Cincinnati: Robert Clarke & Co., 1873.

Porter, Lorle, *A People Set Apart: Scotch-Irish in Eastern Ohio.* Zanesville, Ohio: New Concord Press, 1998.

Rable, George C., *God's Almost Chosen Peoples: A Religious History of the American Civil War.* Chapel Hill: University of North Carolina Press, 2010.

Rein, Lisa, "Mystery of Va.'s First Slaves is Unlocked 400 Years Later." *The Washington Post,* September 3, 2006.

Rhodes, James Ford, *History of the United States from the Compromise of 1850 to the McKinley–Bryan Campaign of 1896.* 7 vols. New York: Macmillan, 1920. Library Rpt., 2007.

Richards, Leonard L., *The Slave Power: the Free North and Southern Domination, 1780–1860.* Baton Rouge: Louisiana State University Press, 2000.

Riegel, Robert E., *America Moves West.* New York: Henry Holt, 1930.

Roth, Randolph A., "The First Abolitionists: The Reverend James Milligan and the Reformed Presbyterians of Vermont." *The New England Quarterly,* 55, no. 4 (Dec. 1982), 540–563.

Roulston, William J., "The Reformed Presbyterian Church and Antislavery in Nineteenth-Century America." In William Harrison Taylor and Peter C. Meisser, eds. *Faith and Slavery in the Presbyterian Diaspora.* Lanham: Rowman and Littlefield, 2016.

Rutherford, Samuel, *Lex, Rex: The Law and the Prince. A Dispute for the Just Prerogative of King and People.* London: John Adams, 1644.

Schwartz, Bernard, *A History of the Supreme Court.* New York: Oxford University Press, 1993.

Siebert, Wilbur H., *The Underground Railroad from Slavery to Freedom.* New York: Henry Holt, 1898.

Sinha, Manisha, *The Slaves's Cause: A History of Abolition.* New Haven: Yale University Press, 2016.

Smith, Alvin W., *Covenanter Ministers 1930–1963 of the Reformed Presbyterian Church of North America.* Mars, PA: Alvin W. Smith, 1964.

Smith, David Grant, "On the Edge of Freedom: The Fugitive Slave Issue in South Central Pennsylvania, 1820–1870." Diss., Ph.D., The Pennsylvania State University, 2006.

Smith, Henry Lester, "The Underground Railroad in Monroe County." *Indiana Magazine of History* 13, no. 3 (1917).

Smith, Timothy L., *Revivalism and Social Reform: American Protestantism on the Eve of the Civil War.* Nashville: Abingdon Press, 1957. Rpt., Gloucester, MA: Peter Smith, 1976.

Stampp, Kenneth M., *The Peculiar Institution: Slavery in the Ante-Bellum South.* New York: Vintage Books, 1956.

Stauffer, John, *The Black Hearts of Men: Radical Abolitionists and the Transformation of Race.* Cambridge, MA: Harvard University Press, 2002.

Stevens, William D., "Enslaved Labor in the Gang and Task Systems: A case study in comparative bioarchaeology of commingled remains." Diss., Ph.D., University of South Carolina, 2016.

Stormont, Nancy L., "An Experiment in Negro Education, Being the History of a Mission School." Thesis, M.A., School of Education, New York University, 1929.

Stout, Harry S., *Upon the Altar of the Nation: a moral history of the Civil War.* New York: Viking Press, 2006. Penguin Books, 2007.

Striner, Richard, *Father Abraham: Lincoln's Relentless Struggle to End Slavery.* Oxford: Oxford University Press, 2006.

Switala, William J., *Underground Railroad in Pennsylvania.* Mechanicsburg, PA: Stackpole Books, 2001.

Temple, Oliver P., *The Covenanter, The Cavalier, and The Puritan.* Cincinnati: Robert Clarke Co., 1897.

Thomas, Hugh, *The Slave Trade: The Story of the Atlantic Slave Trade: 1440–1870.* New York: Simon & Schuster, 1997.

Thompson, Owen F., *Sketches of the Ministers of the Reformed Presbyterian Church of North America, from 1888 to 1930.* Blanchard, IA: Owen F. Thompson, 1930.

Turner, Frederick J., *The Frontier in American History.* New York: Henry Holt, 1921.

Van Dyke, Henry, and Paul Van Dyke, *Henry Jackson Van Dyke.* New York: Anson D. F. Randolph and Co., 1892.

Van Tyne, C. H. (Claude Halstead), "Influence of the Clergy and of Religious and Sectarian Forces on the American Revolution." *American Historical Review* XIX (October 1913).

Vos, Johannes G., *The Scottish Covenanters: Their Origins, History, and Distinctive Doctrines.* Tsi-tsi Har, Manchuria: the author, 1940. Rpt., Pittsburgh: Board of Education and Publication of the Reformed Presbyterian Church of North America, 1980. Rpt., Edinburgh: Blue Banner Productions, 1998.

Walton, Gary M., ed., "A Symposium on Time on the Cross." *Explorations in Economic History* 12 (1973).

Warren, Wendy, *New England Bound: Slavery and Colonization in Early America.* New York: Liveright Corporation, 2016.

Weber, Max, *The Sociology of Religion.* Introduction, Talcott Parsons. Foreword, Ann Swidler. 4th ed., rev., Johannes Winckelmann. English tr., Ephraim Fischoff. Boston: Beacon Press, 1993. First publ. in Germany, 1922, as "Religionssoziologie," from *Wirtschaft und Gesellschaft* Id.

Wilcox, David Ray, *The Reformed Presbyterian Church of North America and the Anti-Slavery Movement.* Thesis, M.A., Greeley: University of Northern Colorado, 1948.

Wills, Garry, *"Negro President": Jefferson and the Slave Power.* Boston: Houghton Mifflin, 2003.

Wooley, John T., and Gerhard Peters, *The American Presidency Project* [online]. Santa Barbara, CA: University of California (hosted); Gerhard Peters (database). Available at http://www.presidency. ucsb/ws/index.php?pid=69891.

Index

Boston Unitarians 8
Boston Weekly Journal 169
Boyd, James 120
Boyd, John Calvin 116
Breckinridge, John C. 153
Britain 17, 26, 80, 129, 139, 158, 162, 202, 204
Brown, Claude 174
Brown, John 58, 71, 94, 143, 148, 204, 210, 218
Brown, William 166
Burwell Hospital 174

C

Calhoun, John C. 48, 133, 138
Canada 61, 103–104, 108, 110, 126, 148, 189, 204
Cannon, Robert B. 112
Caribbean 23, 191, 192
Carithers, John 125
Casas, Jesuit Bartolomé de las 25
Cheever, George B. 71, 94
Chesnut, James 19
Church of England 15
Civil War 2–4, 6–7, 10, 24, 42, 47, 69, 72, 74, 86, 104, 108–109, 112, 139, 151–
    152, 154, 156, 174–175, 187–188, 198, 200–202, 208–210, 214, 221–222,
    225–226
Clair, Arthur St 127
Clark, James 125–126
Clay, Cassius M. 40
Clay, Henry 40, 61, 108, 133, 152
Coffin, Levi 103, 108–109, 111
Collins, Charles 129
Colonization Society 60–64, 87, 93, 96, 195, 198–199, 216, 222
Columbus, Christopher 22
Compromise of 1850 58, 108, 133, 137, 140, 195, 226
Confederate/Confederacy 4, 19, 101–102, 151, 155–158, 161, 167, 191, 193, 211,
    212, 216, 220
Congregational Church 4
Conklin, Seth 103, 109, 127
Constitution, U.S. 6, 17–19, 40, 46, 54, 60, 67–69, 72–73, 87, 95, 101–102, 104,
    125, 129, 133, 136, 144–147, 152, 155, 158, 166, 200–201, 203, 211, 218,
    223, 225
Cook, Billy 143
Lord, Cornwallis 16
Craighead, Alexander 14–15

About the Authors

Robert M. Copeland has immersed himself in Reformed Presbyterian history and genealogy for over sixty years, while also pursuing a career as a musician and music historian. Among other works, he is the author of Spare No Exertions: The Reformed Presbyterian Theological Seminary Through 175 Years and Louis Bourgeois' Le Droict Chemin de Musique, and a biography of the composer Isaac Baker Woodbury. Dr. Copeland grew up in Nebraska, and his ancestors have been in the Reformed Presbyterian Church since the time of the American Revolution. He is retired after forty-one years of teaching, mostly at Geneva College, and has been a ruling elder in the Reformed Presbyterian Church since 1973. He is married to his college sweetheart, Louise, and they have three children and nine grandchildren.

D. Ray Wilcox, pastor, teacher, and college dean, believed that Christian faith should be biblically grounded and demonstrated through action to help the poor and powerless. He was first attracted to the Reformed Presbyterians because he found in them this kind of Christian love. Wilcox graduated from the Reformed Presbyterian Theological Seminary in Pittsburgh, Pa. and served pastorates in Ohio, Kansas, Ontario, and Illinois—including three that had been deeply involved in the Underground Railroad. He visited congregations whose members had been active in the antislavery cause and corresponded with those whose close family had participated. Collecting and preserving a heritage that would otherwise have been lost, his scholarship brings the benefits of over seventy years of more recent study of the antislavery movement and a small but vocal denomination.

Copeland builds on a body of research that Wilcox submitted as his graduate thesis at the University of Northern Colorado in 1948.

MORE FROM CROWN & COVENANT PUBLICATIONS:

History of the Reformed Presbyterian Church of North America 1871–1920: Living by Its Covenant of 1871 by William Edgar

Learn how this persecuted remnant of the Church of Scotland held to Second Reformation orthodoxy in the New World; how the RP Church denounced the American Constitution for its protection of race-based slavery and for its godlessness; and more.

History of the Reformed Presbyterian Church of North America 1920–1980: Decade by Decade by William Edgar

Learn how the RPCNA discarded its "Covenanter" nickname; how they turned to centralized authority and multiplying programs for youth, attempting to stem numerical decline; how war ended missions in Middle East and opened a door to Japan; how the Christian Amendment Movement and Reformation Translation Fellowship began; and more.

The White Chief of Cache Creek by Faith Martin and Charles McBurney

In 1889, William Work Carithers left his comfortable home in western Pennsylvania to become a missionary to the Indians of southwestern Oklahoma. He wanted to bring Christianity to American Indians and at the same time he wanted to help them gain skills necessary to survive in the white culture that was about to envelop them.

Redemption, Reconciliation, and Reformation by Alexander McLoed, edited by Gordon Keddie

Alexander McLeod (1774–1833) was a celebrated writer and well-known abolitionist leader in his time, but the body of his work has been inaccessible to the modern reader—until now.

Jeanette Li: A Girl Born Facing Outside translated by Rose Huston

Jeanette Li was ever ready to proclaim the gospel, despite suffering at the hand of Communist China. This autobiography deftly illustrates God's supreme love, protection, and provision amid affliction.